The Realism of William Dean Howells, 1889-1920

# THE REALISM OF
# WILLIAM DEAN HOWELLS
## 1889-1920

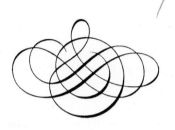

### GEORGE N. BENNETT

1973
VANDERBILT
UNIVERSITY PRESS
*Nashville*

**Library of Congress Cataloguing-in-Publication Data**

Bennett, George N
  The realism of William Dean Howells, 1889–1920.

  Includes bibliographical references.
    1. Howells, William Dean, 1837–1920.
  I. Title.
  PS2034.B4   1973     813'.4     72–1345
  ISBN 0–8265–1180–5

The author and publisher make grateful acknowledgment to William White Howells, executor of the estate of William Dean Howells, for permission to quote from the works of the novelist listed below:

*The Leatherwood God* by William Dean Howells. Copyright 1916 by the Century Company.

*The Vacation of the Kelwyns* by William Dean Howells. Copyright 1920 by Harper and Brothers.

*Life in Letters of William Dean Howells*, edited by Mildred Howells. Copyright 1928 by Doubleday, Doran and Company, Inc.

Printed in the United States of America by
Kingsport Press, Inc., Kingsport, Tennessee

*For*
JoAnn and Michael

# CONTENTS

vii

# PREFACE

It is already too long a time since Edwin Cady (in the *New England Quarterly* [September 1959]) pointed to the need for the critical exploration and elucidation of each of the novels of William Dean Howells (1837–1920), and it is hoped that this book constitutes a valid contribution to that end. To the less initiated reader of Howells, however, the limitation of this study to the novels of 1889–1920 may need a word of explanation. I have chosen—was, in fact, forced by the limitations of space—to begin with *Annie Kilburn,* the first of the economic novels. But even the uninstructed reader will note that the discussions of the economic novels—with the exception of the section on *The World of Chance,* which offered special opportunities to explore Howells's abandonment of this kind of fiction—are briefer and more general than some of the following analyses of novels conventionally regarded as less important. Rather than to provide comprehensive evaluations of the economic novels— which, of all of Howells's work, have received the most attention and the most acclaim from modern critics—my intent was to use them to indicate the basis of certain judgments about Howells's artistic development and to establish certain lines of inquiry that could be profitably followed in investigating the fiction that succeeded them. That first subject—the study of Howells's progress from comedies of manners to social novels to the critical realism of *A Hazard of New Fortunes*—has been studied by a whole generation of critics whose names appear frequently in the documentation of this book. And since I, too, had made a statement about this period in my earlier book, *William Dean Howells* (Norman, Oklahoma: University of

Oklahoma Press, 1959), it seemed possible to try to work from a general context to the detailed examination of the later fiction.

The ready availability of varied biographical studies of Howells has made it unnecessary to provide, as I did in my first book, biographical backgrounds for the critical analyses. I have, however, tried, by drawing freely on Howells's comments on fiction and other matters in the "Editor's Study" and "Editor's Easy Chair," in his letters and elsewhere, to document my understanding of the intellectual, moral, and spiritual context from which his fiction issued. That understanding has made me an admirer of the positive decency and the willed amenity of Howells's life, but I hope, too, that it has curbed any tendency to be merely inventive or extravagant in my claims for the excellence of his later fiction.

The inadequacies of this study are, of course, wholly mine. They cannot affect my gratitude for the support given to me during its writing by John and Marie Aden, whose friendship is of the truest kind that responds to need rather than desert. I should also like to express my appreciation to Vanderbilt University for a leave of absence which enabled me to write an earlier version. Finally, I am grateful to Professor W. W. Howells for permission to quote from sources under copyright held by the estate of William Dean Howells.

The Realism of William Dean Howells, 1889-1920

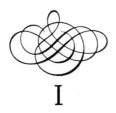

# I

## INTRODUCTION:
## CONTEXTUAL NOTATIONS

THERE is nothing new in calling William Dean Howells a psycho-logical novelist, but several clarifications can result from a renewed emphasis on this fact. The term had special significance for Howells himself. In 1902, asked as an eminent novelist to pronounce on the perennial question of whether the novel would survive, he answered, "It is probable that the psychological novel will be the most enduring as it has been the most constant phase of fiction."[1] The term recurs throughout his critical and theoretical comments on fiction. A few months later, for example, he declared that, though it was being given new application, the term did not really describe a new element but, in fact, named "what is best known in fiction, and is not less evident in Tolstoy, in Gorky, in Ibsen, in Björnson, in Hauptmann, and in Mr. Henry James, than in Maeterlinck."[2]

To be helpful, the term must be understood to have had for Howells a breadth of reference well beyond the conventional under-standing of an emphasis on the mental states of his characters. It is because Howells's sense of its inclusiveness leads to a consideration,

1. "Will the Novel Disappear?" *North American Review,* CLXXV (Sep-tember 1902), 293.
2. "Editor's Easy Chair," *Harper's Monthly,* CVII (June 1903), 149.

in his own work, not merely of motivation, but of interrelated questions of conscience and morality and faith, questions of novelistic form and method and purpose, and the question of whether to adopt the tragic or comic view as his controlling attitude toward human affairs that it is a useful point of departure. Such an approach suggests too that it may not be entirely accurate to see Howells's progress as a novelist as adequately defined by a growing social awareness culminating in the explicit economic criticism of the novels of the early nineties and lapsing thereafter into tepid repetition and critical timidity. If that progress is measured by the standard of the psychological novel, some of the artistic difficulties of the economic novels are more readily perceived, and some of the later novels can be retrieved from neglect or dismissal.

No single term, of course, is adequate to sum up the complexities of a major writer's theory and practice of the novel, but a special advantage of the designation *psychological novel* to the study of Howells lies in what it eliminates: "Novels of adventure, novels of character, novels of fashionable life, novels of crime and novels of its detection, novels of art and novels of business, novels of incident and novels of analysis."[3] The standard which Howells now asserted was that every novel "lives or dies by so much or so little psychology as it has in it."[4] Although this is a reflective judgment, made after the economic novels were well in the past, it is not a repudiation of his own past theory and practice, which included his early admiration for Turgenev and his own developed preference for the dramatic method. In the light of Howells's persistent emphasis on the central importance of the psychological element in fiction, it is useful to remember that this was from the first a method with a purpose, which was to get his "characters away from their belongings" and let them "act upon one another."[5]

The methodology was valuable to the extent that it was functional, and undoubtedly something of the confidence resulting from

3. *North American Review*, CLXXV (September 1902), 293.
4. *Ibid.*
5. William Dean Howells, *Life in Letters of William Dean Howells*, edited by Mildred Howells, 2 vols. (Garden City, New York: Doubleday, Doran and Company, Inc., 1928), I, 233 (hereafter cited as *Letters*).

having just written *A Modern Instance* went into his assurance in pronouncing on that function when he outraged the British by declaring James a finer artist than Dickens and Thackeray. Even his reservations about James made for the same point. The method was valuable as it minimized the concern with mere story and concentrated on "character-painting," on providing the writer a means of going about his main business of giving his reader "a due conception of his characters and the situation in which they find themselves." If James had a fault, it was in violating the dramatic method to offer "analysis of motive" and to comment "upon the springs of action in the persons of the drama, both before and after the facts." In so far as this was an error in the service of the "philosophic desire" to gratify the reader's proper interest in "what the novelist thinks about persons and situations"[6] it was, however, venial.

Almost every subsequent comment by Howells on James contains some reference to the unimportance of mere story to the novel. And running as a unifying thread throughout the criticism and reviews in the "Editor's Study" and the "Editor's Easy Chair" is the assumption that realism is most valuable because it reveals character and that it is required to do nothing that does not contribute in some way to that purpose. It does not, for example, demand that the plot be brought to a conventional outcome unless that process may contribute to the revelation of character. A clear instance of the kind of significance that fiction ought to develop and beyond which it should not attempt to go was James's *The Tragic Muse*:

Here was a thing called a novel, written with extraordinary charm; interesting by the vigor and vivacity with which phases and situations and persons were handled in it; inviting . . . [the reader] to the intimacy of characters divined with creative insight; making him witness of motives and emotions and experiences of the finest import; and then suddenly requiring him to be man enough to cope with the question itself; not solving it for him by a marriage or a murder, and not spoon-victualling him with a moral minced small and then thinned with milk and water, and familiarly flavored with sentimentality or religiosity.[7]

6. "Henry James, Jr.," *Century*, XXV (November 1882), 26–29.
7. "Editor's Study," *Harper's Monthly*, LXXXI (September 1890), 640.

Howells began, then, by defending his practice of the dramatic method and afterwards praised that method where he found it. But that his real concern was with the realism which that method produced is strongly evidenced in the consistency, extending through and beyond the period of the economic novels, with which he held to "psychology" as the central test. In 1906, for example, he measured the greatness of Ibsen by the degree to which he fulfilled the "highest office of art" through "the representation of character, and the study of personality."[8] In this case, the method of the art was not at issue, and what makes the remark valuable to an understanding of Howells is the specific way it cuts through other tests, such as the social or economic, which have been applied to Howells's work.

To become the kind of novelist he wanted to be, however, Howells had to do more than master a method. Since he insisted that he would "feel degraded merely to amuse people," that his fiction, without being didactic, should "unmistakably teach a lenient, generous, and liberal life," he needed a basis for making judgments about the nature of such a life. At the time he made these remarks, he confessed that he was "very often puzzled to know . . . the truth,"[9] and through a long and productive life thereafter he never claimed to have seized possession of it. But he knew that, if his fiction were to serve an ethical purpose through asking questions which would at least put conventional assumptions to the test, he must have some reasoned convictions and attitudes of his own. This meant that he must apprentice himself, not merely to his craft, but to life itself: he must learn both to write and to know himself. If experience did not provide neatly formulated answers to what he called in 1872 "the whole intolerable mystery of things,"[10] it could at least establish the nature of his own doubts and uncertainties. It could provide him with a knowledge of his own character, enable him to trace his own motives to the impulses of his heart and being.

8. "Henrik Ibsen," *North American Review,* CLXXXIII (July 1906), 5.

9. William Dean Howells, "The Letters of Howells to Higginson," edited by George S. Hellman, *Twenty-Seventh Annual Report of the Bibliophile Society* (Boston: The Bibliophile Society, 1929), p. 38 (hereafter cited as Hellman). This letter is dated September 17, 1879.

10. *Letters,* I, 173.

Such self-knowledge was the *sine qua non* of "realistic fiction" as opposed to the "brilliant and very perfect romance" or poem which might be produced by a young writer who had not yet passed through the educative process of experience and self-examination. To write realistic fiction, Howells said in *Literature and Life* (1902), a writer

> needs experience and observation, not so much of others as of himself, and he will need to know motive and character with such thoroughness and accuracy as he can acquire only through his own heart. A man remains in a measure strange to himself as long as he lives, and the very sources of novelty in his work will be within himself; he can continue to give it freshness in no other way than by knowing himself better and better.

This retrospective self-assessment, which included the remark that "until he is well on towards forty . . . [the writer] will hardly have assimilated the materials of a great novel, although he may have amassed them,"[11] links method with purpose. For Howells, realistic fiction could not become "great" merely through psychology, through a knowledge of "motive and character"; that knowledge must, by being shaped into a literary form which is something more than a story or a plot, embody an ethical effect. The process involves at least an awareness of—if not answers to—questions of how human behavior is related to larger questions of the individual's accountability not only to himself but to a higher intelligence and of the individual's significance in a universal moral order. Thus when Howells tried to account for his own development as a realist by recalling the varied literary passions which contributed both negatively and positively to the formulation of his theory, it was natural for him to offer praise in terms which linked religion and art. Recalling his reaction to Goldoni when he himself was not yet a "fictionist," Howells emphasized his discovery of the truthfulness which he "loved . . . above all other things." He then characterized the effect of such literature:

11. *Literature and Life* (New York: Harper and Brothers, 1902), pp. 29–30.

He had the power of taking me out of my life, and putting me into the lives of others, whom I felt to be human beings as much as myself. To make one live in others, this is the highest effect of religion as well as art, and possibly it will be the highest bliss we shall ever know . . . and I may as well confess here that I do not regard the artistic ecstasy as in any sort noble. . . . If you cannot look beyond the end you aim at, and seek the good which is not your own, all your sacrifice is to yourself and not of yourself, and you might as well be going into business.[12]

The insistence on self-knowledge, the defining of the justifying power of fiction as its ability to produce, not vicarious excitement, but the sense of shared experience and knowledge, and the defining of its ethical function as that of making men "know one another better, that they may all be humbled and strengthened with a sense of their fraternity"[13]—these and other pronouncements which Howells made, not just at one point in his career, but consistently throughout it—all converge toward an implicit assumption. The fulcrum on which the realist balances his art is not an ethical proposition, not a judgment of society, neither a criticism of nor plan for the correction of the economic system, but the study of individuals. To understand this is to understand Howells's uses of such terminology as *psychological novel* to distinguish the kind of fiction which would outlast all other more narrowly conceived and popular accounts of adventure, crime, business, and the like, or his redefinition of "what we used to call the novel of manners" as "realistic fiction."[14] Just as there was a developing connection between Howells's thinking about the broad religious question of man's place in the universe and the shape and substance of his maturing fiction, so what he came to mean by the "psychological novel" or "psychological romance" had its origins in his thinking about the related question of man's place in the world, his functioning in this life with other men.

The psychological novel for Howells, then, was not primarily a

12. *My Literary Passions* (New York: Harper and Brothers, 1895), pp. 208, 211–212.

13. William Dean Howells, *Criticism and Fiction and Other Essays*, edited by Clara Marburg Kirk and Rudolf Kirk (New York: New York University Press, 1959), p. 87 (hereafter cited as *Criticism and Fiction* [1959]).

14. *Literature and Life*, p. 29.

*revelation* of the complicated mental states of its characters in the sense that a novel by James, for example, or Joyce, may be so denominated. Rather it was a study of what Howells called the "miracles of the inner world"[15]—the conflicts between unconscious desire and conscious motive, selfish wish and necessary duty, pride and shame, vanity and humility, fear and hope, sexuality and spirituality, avarice and benevolence, appetite and self-control which issue into action evidencing some kind of balance or imbalance.

The effect of this kind of psychological probing is not merely to reveal states of mind, not merely to achieve an understanding of human motivation and, in individual cases, evaluate its "justice," but to determine (and here we are back to the ethical effects of art) its "wisdom": "It will no longer suffice that we have had the best motives in this or that; we must have the wisest motive, we must examine the springs of action, the grounds of conviction." Again, however, this is an artistic and not a didactic function, as it is with Ibsen, who "does not wish to teach so much as he wishes to move."[16]

An understanding of the cluster of meanings which Howells assigned to such terms as *psychological* and *character* leads to clarifications of several aspects of his career and his fiction. It provides a retrospective gloss to his apologetic comments in the opening of *Their Wedding Journey* (1872), where he disqualifies himself from rehearsing the prior love story of Basil and Isabel March because he distrusts his "fitness for a sustained or involved narration." But among other things he feels qualified to offer is an occasional "sketch of character."[17] What is revealing here to Howells's future as a novelist is the awareness that such "sketches" are not the requisite *characterizations,* for mere complication does not "sustain" a narrative, and true involvement can only be studied through motivation.[18] That kind of fiction would simply have to wait for the

15. "Editor's Easy Chair," *Harper's Monthly,* CXXIV (March 1912), 636.

16. *North American Review,* CLXXXIII (July 1906), 4–5.

17. *Their Wedding Journey,* edited by John K. Reeves (Bloomington, Indiana: Indiana University Press, 1968), p. 3.

18. Howells was probably thinking in such terms about *A Chance Acquaintance* (1873) when he replied to James's criticism by saying about Kitty

maturing and assimilative process to do its work. Howells's repeated emphasis, then, on the novelist's responsibility to character and situation rather than story, his liking for the "intensity" of *A Modern Instance*,[19] which undoubtedly owed something to his sense of success in this kind of psychological fiction, his assertion in his seventy-fifth year that "the facts of finance and industry and invention" are valuable to fiction only as they can be dealt with "as the expressions of character"[20]—these comments all issue from a coherent and continuous literary consciousness and practice.

A further note on Howells's sense of "a due conception" of character and situation and the relationship of character to incident and narrative is appropriate to this discussion. The connection is important because it is the basis for Howells's countless animadversions against "effectism, or the itch of awaking at all cost in the reader vivid and violent emotions,"[21] often through "moving accidents" and "violent events." Such methods and results are false because "character resides in habit," and for the novelist to depend upon these devices to reveal fundamental truth is "as stupid as for the painter to expect an alarm of fire or burglary to startle his sitter into a valuable revelation of his qualities."[22] Equally important, character cannot be defined by a list of "attributes" of the kind the old romancers offered when the reader was no longer entirely "satisfied with what the heroes and heroines did and suffered" because "character is rooted in personality."[23] The explanation for this ap-

---

Ellison, "I like her because she seems to me a character"; about Arbuton, he could only say, "The man, I own is a simulacrum" (*Letters*, I, 174).

19. Henry J. Harper, *The House of Harper* (New York: Harper and Brothers, 1912), p. 323.

20. "Editor's Easy Chair," *Harper's Monthly*, CXXIV (March 1912), 636.

21. "Editor's Easy Chair," *Harper's Monthly*, LXXIX (November 1889), 964.

22. *Heroines of Fiction*, 2 vols. (New York: Harper and Brothers, 1901), I, 40–41 (hereafter cited as *Heroines*).

23. *Ibid.*, I, 65. Howell's many comments on Dickens illustrate well his conception of false "types," which "are outwardly of our every-day acquaintance, but inwardly moved by a single propensity and existing to justify in some fantastic excess the attribution of their controlling quality" (*Heroines*,

parently arbitrary substitution of the word *personality* for *habit* within the space of a few pages can be pieced together from still another remark from *Heroines of Fiction* and from evidence in Howells's own fiction. In discussing one of the writers he most admired (for her ethics rather than her art), George Eliot, Howells spoke of the ability to deal with complex characterizations as a measure of an author's maturity:

Acquaintance with life brings an increasing sense of the prevalence of mixed motives in the actions of men, and a keener perception of the fact that personality resides rather in the motives than the actions of men. An action is black or white; a motive is commonly the blend of several if not all the colors. This law of life the ripening talent gladly makes the law of its art.[24]

The primary point of all this—a point which will lead to Howells's conception of man and his idea of man's responsibility to his fellows—is that characterization cannot be accomplished simply by an enumeration of fixed qualities and a weighing of moral quantities or by the expedient of describing the individual's actions and reactions in one or more overtly dramatic incidents. Character, for Howells, is not simply a given condition, a stasis of convictions and attitudes and capabilities which intermittently find expression as the appropriate occasion releases them. What Howells's terminology is unsystematically expressing is that character is the result of process, and that process is accessible to individual control. It begins in motive, i.e., will (which produces personality); and a succession of motivated actions *becomes* character when that succession is fixed in habit. But even habit is a precarious fixity and must be constantly strengthened by conscious practice and by conscious guarding against the destructive potentialities of mere "temperament," or impulse. In *The Coast of Bohemia* (1893), the heroine is forced by her own impulsive actions to a self-scrutiny which produces some disturbing insights:

---

I, 162). Such comments offer an explanation, too, of the differentiation Howells made between "the novel of character" and the psychological novel.
    24. *Heroines*, II, 62.

Cornelia was . . . puzzled and perplexed with herself, and dismayed with the slightness of her hold upon impulses of hers which she thought she had overcome and bound forever. She made the discovery, which she was yet far too young to formulate, that she had a temperament to deal with that could at any time shake to ruins the character she had so carefully built upon it, and had so wholly mistaken for herself.[25]

"Character," then, is not the self in any absolute sense, but what one builds out of the materials of the self, and its delineation in fiction is achieved by a subtle and patient art and not by the manipulation of cataclysmic events. It does not require a cataclysm to produce revelation. More important, revelation, however produced, is merely the starting point, the moment for observing character in flux. This was not a view of character Howells came to through his analyses of famous fictional heroines or through his own late fiction. It is enunciated, for example, in *Dr. Breen's Practice* (1881) and movingly exemplified in the immediately following portrayals of Marcia and Bartley Hubbard. In the earlier novel, in the course of dealing with what was already becoming a familiar love story, he paused to analyze at some length the general failure of self-understanding:

We all treat ourselves upon a theory. We proceed each of us upon the theory that he is very brave, or generous, or gentle, or liberal, or truthful, or loyal, or just. We may have the defects of our virtues, but nothing is more certain than that we have our virtues, till there comes a fatal juncture, not at all like the juncture in which we had often imagined ourselves triumphing against temptation. It passes, and the hero finds, to his dismay and horror, that he has run away; the generous man has been niggard; the gentleman has behaved like a ruffian, and the liberal like a bigot; the champion of truth has foolishly and vainly lied; the steadfast friend has betrayed his neighbor, the just person has oppressed him. This is the fruitful moment, apparently so sterile, in which character may spring and flower anew; but the mood of abject humility in which the theorist of his own character is plunged and struggles for his lost self-respect is full of deceit for others. It cannot last: it may end in disowning

25. William Dean Howells, *The Coast of Bohemia* (New York: Harper and Brothers, 1893), p. 279.

and retrieving the error, or it may end in justifying it, and building it
into the reconstructed character, as something upon the whole unexpectedly fine; but it must end, for after all it is only a mood.[26]

Howells was so sure that all of his mature novels were "psychological romances"—i.e., realistic fictions—in this general sense that
he could fill them with the moving accidents he inveighed against
in his criticism, usually having a character comment on their lack of
verisimilitude and their inappropriateness to strict realism. But he
was never being *merely* careless or arch. He always used such occasions to make the point that they were *not* of special value as
revelation, that they were mere accidents or absurd coincidences[27]
which were equally meaningless in life itself. If Howells had wished
to cite justification for this practice, he might well have referred to
the example of "the greatest of . . . gifted women," Jane Austen.
What he chose to say about her, however, is more directly indicative
of his positive aims: "in the expression of personality . . . and the
subordination of incident to character" she was the greatest of
English novelists.[28]

To study *character* in the sense of Howells's terminology, then,
is necessarily to represent human relationships and decisions which,
however trivial they seem to a superficial view, involve ethical effects.
For if those relationships and decisions are depicted with sufficient
realistic art, the reader will be forced to an examination of the
grounds of his own response to them—not provided with pronouncements upon them—and one result of that reaction should be a
recognition (or increased awareness) of the value of a "lenient,
generous, and liberal life."

Unstated as yet, however, is an assumption on Howells's part
which establishes the connection between character and morality (or
the lack of it). Character is a product of will—temperament is im-

26. William Dean Howells, *Dr. Breen's Practice* (Boston: James R. Osgood and Company, 1881), pp. 187–188.

27. For example, for an amassing of the coincidences which govern the
plot of *The Story of a Play* and for the kind of comment which misses the
point of Howell's intention, see Oscar W. Firkins, *William Dean Howells: A
Study* (Cambridge: Harvard University Press, 1924), pp. 177–178.

28. *Heroines*, I, 38.

pulse, personality an expression of the willed character controlling the temperament—and, therefore, subject to the judgment of conscience. Howells would not accept a merely relativistic standard of conscience or morality, a testing by the operative mores of present society (or, as will be seen, by some fanatically strained or egoistically reasoned principle). What he finally insisted upon was a religious view. Conscience, he was to claim, came with Christianity, and though "Beauty may have its own excuse for being . . . right has no excuse save through the conscience that lives in man from his assurance of a life hereafter." It was useless, therefore, "to feign that . . . [morality] does not, sensibly or insensibly, refer itself to a belief in some life after this."[29] If it were not so, there could be no abstract concept of right and wrong, since in the lapse of time the individual's particular choices of conduct would not matter. This was the same point he had made some years earlier, at the very time he was confronting the contradictions in his concurrent indignation with economic conditions and his despairing sense that they could be effectively changed only by the application of an immediate altruism. In reviewing a book called *Ethical Religion* and taking exception to the author's understanding of the meaning of the life of Christ, Howells argued:

When . . . [the author] says, "Morality is this going out of one's self and living in, living for, something larger," he is presenting, in other words, Tolstoï's declaration that there is no such thing as personal happiness, no bliss but forgetting ourselves and remembering others, no life but in its loss for goodness' sake. But Tolstoï is repeating this truth with reference to its origin in Christ and its effect in eternity; and so we find greater support in it than when that same ideal of conduct seems to restrict itself to time and space.[30]

This was an expression of a faith which gives no hint of the actual doubts which beset Howells concerning immortality and the rule of Providence, doubts especially strong in his formative years as

29. "Editor's Easy Chair," *Harper's Monthly*, CX (April 1905), 804–805.
30. "Editor's Study," *Harper's Monthly*, LXXIX (August 1889), 479.

a novelist. But the very fact that Howells was very much involved in the religious conflicts of his age—a fact which has long since been thoroughly demonstrated[31]—provides an important perspective on the formation of his literary attitudes. Religious questions were so deeply involved in the total process of his intellectual and moral development that they are inextricably a part of the conception of the novel, both its function and its method, which he eventually arrived at. He always remembered the seventies and the eighties as a time of "prevailing agnosticism,"[32] and his letters to his father and others in the early seventies, when his realistic career was still more potential than actual, show him trying to accommodate the new ideas of evolutionary science to the Swedenborgian views of immortality, the conflicting claims of faith and reason, and the problem of a moral life.[33] Through a long lifetime he confronted in his life and art alike what he often called the riddle of the painful earth. He never solved the riddle but could only learn through sceptical optimism to tolerate the mystery. His fiction, therefore, consciously refused the prophetic or the hortatory voice, though always claiming for itself ethical and moral relevance.

This scepticism about final answers in combination with the determination to make his fiction both ethically and aesthetically effective can be seen in the late seventies in his reply to T. W. Higginson's friendly criticism: "I am very often puzzled to know what is the truth, and that may account for the 'stopping-short' which you notice. It is, however, also a matter of artistic preference."[34] Many years after that, he was still holding to a hopeful suspension of pronouncement. He noted that fiction, now "calling itself psychological, as realism called itself scientific," was returning to the same

31. See Graham Belcher Blackstock, "Howells's Opinions on the Religious Conflicts of His Age as Exhibited in Magazine Articles," in *Howells: A Century of Criticism,* edited by Kenneth E. Eble (Dallas: Southern Methodist University Press, 1962), p. 204. The essay originally appeared in *American Literature,* XV (November 1943), 262–278, and is a valuable discussion of Howells's lifelong struggle for religious certainty.

32. "Eighty Years and After," *Harper's Monthly,* CXL (December 1919), 21.

33. See, for example, *Letters,* I, 165–166.

34. Hellman, p. 38.

old questions which he and the kindred spirits he had been praising
for years in the "Editor's Study" and elsewhere had always asked:

We have, indeed, in our best fiction, gone back to mysticism, if indeed
we were not always there in our best fiction, and the riddle of the painful
earth is again engaging us with the old fascination. The old insoluble
problems of life and death, of good and evil, present themselves to us with
a novel promise of comfort, inviting us to repose in their insolubility with
the patience which each must use, and with the faith that this patience
shall be rewarded in each.[35]

The extent to which such concerns permeated Howells's fiction,
both in specific thematic developments in the individual novels and
as the *ambiance* of his realism, deserves recognition and assessment.
A canvass of themes from the fiction, early and late, indicates, if not
the centrality, at least the continuity, of Howells's attention to such
matters as immortality, the moral government of the universe, the
character of evil, the nature of the Christian life, the nature and
consequences of fanaticism, and the recurring manifestations of the
Puritan conscience. Equally suggestive is a canvass of the occasions
on which Howells used a minister either as the protagonist or as an
important secondary character to provide a religious—or, more precisely, an ethical—viewpoint: the Reverend Messrs. Sewell, Peck,
Breckon, Nevil, Gregory, Ewbert, and Glendenning are all of
major importance; and there are still other ecclesiastical and lay personages who suggest this concern: Don Ippolito, Mr. Waters, Dr.
Enderby, Shaker elders, temperamental religieuses like Alice Pasmer
and Miss Vance, and religious sceptics like Squire Gaylord and Matthew Braile.

The point of these remarks is not to claim that Howells was
primarily a religious writer—indeed, his own approach to the kinds
of question named was always philosophical rather than specifically
religious—but to support an emphasis. From the time of the earliest
novels, many varied aspects of "real life" occupied Howells, and the
religious questions became inextricably mixed with consideration of
broad and deep social and economic inequities in the nineties. But

35. "Editor's Easy Chair," *Harper's Monthly*, CVII (June 1903), 149.

the religious question came first, in association with limited private and social questions, and its coming in the particular form of *The Undiscovered Country* (1880) produced his first major novel.[36] Equally important, it outlasted the attempts to deal artistically with such specific economic problems as the relation between capital and labor, defalcation as a symptom of systemic rather than individual sickness, the morally corrupting effects of wealth, and the accidental bases of commercial success. It is thus of fundamental importance to an evaluation of both the totality and the particularity of Howells's achievement as a novelist: to the perception of strong and valid lines of interconnection between the late and early novels, to an understanding of the "posteconomic" phase as a period of continued moral commitment and artistic integrity, and to an assessment of such novels as *Ragged Lady* (1899), *The Kentons* (1902), and *Miss Bellard's Inspiration* (1905) as freshly imaginative and powerful exhibits in a realist's gallery rather than reshadings from a depleted palette.

An awareness of this interrelated concern with "the problems of religion and of man's relation to the cosmos" [37] and man's moral psychology merely points the way. It is valuable, however, because the judgments which inform the realism Howells practiced in *all* his novels—not merely in the "critical realism" of the economic novels, or in the "realistic tragedy"[38] of some of the novels, but in the entire body of his fiction—originate in this context. These are judgments which have to do, as we have said, with the relationship be-

---

36. See Kermit Vanderbilt, *The Achievement of William Dean Howells* (Princeton: Princeton University Press, 1968), pp. 11–48, for a discussion which solidly establishes the importance of *The Undiscovered Country* as a study of "the cultural dislocations of American life" in the 1870s, adopting "the traditional mode of pastoral" (p. 14) and achieving "unity through the religious conflict" (p. 24). For my own analysis of the importance of the religious theme, see George N. Bennett, *William Dean Howells* (Norman, Oklahoma: University of Oklahoma Press, 1959), pp. 97–104.

37. Eble, *A Century of Criticism,* p. 204.

38. The terminology is taken, respectively, from Everett Carter, *Howells and the Age of Realism* (Philadelphia: J. B. Lippincott Company, 1954), p. 171, and Edwin H. Cady, *The Realist at War* (Syracuse: Syracuse University Press, 1958), p. 102.

tween personality and character and the individual responsibility to shape character; with the relationship between character and conditions, will and determinism; with the relationship between conscience and virtue; with the relationship between private and public responsibility—the correlatives could be indefinitely elaborated. There was, in other words, significant interaction between Howells's view of man's place in the universe—basically, from *The Undiscovered Country* on, a sceptical hopefulness or a suspended doubt concerning a moral government and immortality—and man's moral function in the world.

The logic of Howells's faith—or, perhaps, more accurately, the faith of Howells's logic—was, then, part of the very substance of his fiction. It provided the enclosing context of the actions of his characters and gave significance even to the apparent commonplaces in which Howells often involved them. It was the nature of Howells's experience not to be led to a doubt of God Himself, not to hurl a Melvillean challenge at the Godhead in the name of the sacred personality of man, but to be led to a doubt of man's ability to understand the nature of God's arrangements for man. Howells's questioning concerned whether God provided for immortality and for a moral government which ultimately balanced the sufferings and catastrophes and inequities which were a large part of his earthly condition. Late in life, speaking as the "unreal editor" of the "Editor's Easy Chair," Howells could only remark his consistent will to believe: " 'I think optimism is as wise and true as pessimism, or is at least as well founded; and since the one can no more establish itself as a final truth than the other, it is better to have optimism.' "[39]

The remark is made in a context which makes it an especially revealing clue to Howells's fiction. The essay is one of several by Howells on the nature of the Christmas celebration. In this case, the subject has been prompted by the broad socio-economic proposal that "the way back to the age of gold lies through justice, which will substitute cooperation for competition."[40] The discussion leads to such familiar formulations as that Christ's message is "the brotherhood,

39. *Imaginary Interviews* (New York: Harper and Brothers, 1910), p. 5.
40. *Ibid.*

the freedom, the equality of men"[41] and that the lesson of Christmas giving should be that "there is really no such thing as selfish, as personal happiness." These interpretations are so familiar, in fact, that the unreal editor's companion in conversation—the literal Easy Chair, temporarily rescued from the warehouse—simply replies, " 'Tolstoy.' "[42] The optimism is not blind, however, and there is no mistaking the Christian message for the Christmas condition. The unreal editor, therefore, asks not for an impossible spiritual transformation and immediate social revolution, but for "alleviations": " 'I love justice, but charity is far better than nothing; and it would be abominable not to do all we can because we cannot do everything. Let us have the expedients, the ameliorations, even the compromises, *en attendant* the millennium.' "[43]

The major elements of the broad context in which Howells presented his fiction are present at least by implication in this ostensibly whimsical essay. There is, first of all, the will to hopefulness, with the immediate admission that it is merely a willed attitude, since the "final truth" is not susceptible of rational proofs. That fact centers his concern on the here and now. Although it is assumed that man's motives and actions *must* have reference to his immortality and to an ordered plan of existence, that is a responsibility and not an answer. That assumption makes doubly difficult the more immediate question of the arrangements man makes for himself and of his conduct among them, because it affirms a God who has given man a conscience and a will and thereby gives him the power of choice. The unreal editor first says that men are not "the architects of their own personalities" and is immediately warned that such a view will lead him to a reductive assessment of men as nothing more than "creatures of . . . environment." He counters by saying that though they are "not the architects of their own personalities . . . they are masters of themselves."[44] This was a view which

41. *Ibid.*, p. 5.
42. *Ibid.*, p. 10.
43. *Ibid.*, p. 5.
44. *Ibid.*, p. 6. Howells is not always consistent in his use of terminology. I understand the term *personality* in this context to mean "temperament" in a sense that will be discussed later.

Howells had already advanced, at the very time he was shaken by his new understanding of the power of the economic environment: "The will of the weak man is *not* free; but the will of the strong man, the man who has *got the habit* of preferring sense to nonsense and 'virtue' to 'vice,' is a *freed* will."[45]

The moral purpose that Howells always tried to serve in his fiction was to be accomplished through a series of studies of how men, masters of themselves, actually lived, through an evaluation of how well men actually mastered themselves. Howells would provide characters vitally concerned with the question of immortality—Dr. Boynton in *The Undiscovered Country* and Clarence Ewbert in "A Difficult Case" come particularly to mind—and speculations about a moral government of the universe would become a leitmotif, but the fact that these could only be rhetorical questions turned the major thrust of his fiction toward this world and its problems.

A roughly analogous process can be discerned in Howells's social thinking and its expression in fiction. Comfortable in an inclusive faith in American democracy and the social and economic opportunities it afforded everyone, he could concern himself with variations of manners, with contrasts between American innocence and European decadence, or with dissections of individual character. A growing doubt about the perfection of the so-called democratic system would lead him to broader and deeper studies in which presumably personal situations were related to serious social and religious dislocations in the fabric of American life. A complex of factors would produce a disavowal of the whole economic system by which America lived. But the examination which produced that apostasy also resulted in a view much like that in which the ultimate religious questions simply had to be suspended: not a doubt of the facts, an uncertainty as to whether the system was good or bad, but an admission of an inability to see what could be done about the total system by the individual. Man is master of himself and thus, in a theoretical sense, of the system: men could vote the system out of existence. In actuality, however, men were not masters of the circumstances in which they lived and could only become so by learning to

45. "Editor's Study," *Harper's Monthly*, LXXXIII (July 1891), 315.

act as one man. The reality, therefore, was that, in any foreseeable future, the system was self-perpetuating, was stronger than men, and was a condition that would simply have to be accepted—again, with willed optimism, with the hope that eventually man could find a way to salvation from it.

It was this latter proviso that stopped Howells short of naturalism, that made him deny that men are merely the "creatures of environment," and which made him willing to accept such "ameliorations" and "even compromises" as could be found. It is also arguable that, just as he did not devote the major attention of his fiction to the broad religious questions because they were unanswerable, so he turned away from direct economic considerations when he could not reach a reasoned program of action but could only put his faith in some ultimate corrective process. Both impasses turned him back to those concerns on which some kind of ethical perspective could effectively be brought to bear, since man was a responsible moral being, since he was possessed of conscience and reason and will, and therefore capable of making judgments. The question for Howells's realism, therefore, became one of taking into account the way things are, and what man is, and what he should do. That, at least, is the effect of Howells's realism; the question he actually addressed himself to is, what *does* man do? And, he believed that if he answered the question honestly enough, an answer to the ethical question would be implicit in the account.

# II

# HAZARDS AT ECONOMICS

## Socialistic Fiction

When *The World of Chance,* the last of the economic novels, was behind him, Howells received an inquiry from a friend about a "socialistic novel" he was reported to be writing. He answered that the report was true only in "so far as every conscientious and enlightened fiction is of some such import." He went on to describe his current project in terms that identify it as *The Story of a Play* (1898).[1] This is a novel which criticism has largely ignored. Such comment as it has received has tended to dismiss it as a sometimes amusing but superficial working of Howells's own experiences in the theater. Yet the implications of Howells's statement as they may apply to the relationship between the economic novels and the far greater mass of Howells's other work deserve consideration.

The term *economic novels,* whose critical currency dates to 1932, when Walter Fuller Taylor analyzed a group of four as adaptations of Howells's "objective realism . . . to the treatment of economic problems," has always been something of a misnomer. When

1. William Dean Howells, *Life in Letters of William Dean Howells,* edited by Mildred Howells, 2 vols. (Garden City, New York: Doubleday, Doran and Company, Inc., 1928), II, 40. Mildred Howells identifies the novel in question as *The World of Chance,* which, however, appeared serially from March to November 1892 and in book form on March 29, 1893.

the terminology leads, as it did with Taylor, to the conclusion that what Howells was creating was a "form of the problem novel" which by "a high order of craftsmanship . . . relieves its didacticism and preserves the artistry of good fiction,"[2] it is unfortunate. Howells was never a "problem novelist": not in such early novels as *Dr. Breen's Practice,* nor in later ones such as *Miss Bellard's Inspiration,* both of which deal with women in professional life; and not in the economic novels.

The worth of these novels of the nineties as expressions of a complexity of vision which includes but is not confined to economic conditions has been solidly established since Taylor's pioneering study.[3] That fact makes it possible to suggest, therefore, that in prizing them, the subsequent fiction need not be deplored. If it is true that only *"The Landlord at Lion's Head* and *The Leatherwood God* are of comparable quality,"[4] then it is also true that such a standard would depreciate most of the fiction before *Annie Kilburn.* Even if exceptions were made for *A Modern Instance, Indian Summer,* and *The Rise of Silas Lapham,* the loss of *The Undiscovered Country,*

2. Walter Fuller Taylor, "William Dean Howells and the Economic Novel," in Howells: *A Century of Criticism,* edited by Kenneth E. Eble (Dallas: Southern Methodist University Press, 1962), pp. 183, 192. The article originally appeared in *American Literature,* IV (May 1932), 103–113. So much attention has been paid to the work of this relatively brief period of Howells's career, especially to *A Hazard of New Fortunes,* that it may be a proper restoration of perspective to emphasize that there were only four economic novels: *Annie Kilburn, Hazard, The Quality of Mercy,* and *The World of Chance,* these appearing between 1889 and 1893.

3. See especially George Arms, "Howells' New York Novel: Comedy and Belief," *New England Quarterly,* XXI (September 1948), 313–325, and "Introduction" to *A Hazard of New Fortunes* (1890; reprint edition, New York: E. P. Dutton and Company, Everyman's Library, 1952), pp. vii–xviii; Everett Carter, *Howells and the Age of Realism* (Philadelphia: J. B. Lippincott Co., 1954), pp. 201–224; Edwin H. Cady, *The Realist at War* (Syracuse: Syracuse University Press, 1958), pp. 80–187; Kermit Vanderbilt, *The Achievement of William Dean Howells* (Princeton: Princeton University Press, 1968), pp. 144–191; and Kenneth S. Lynn, "Howells in the Nineties," *Perspective in American History,* IV (1970), 56–61.

4. William M. Gibson, *William Dean Howells* (Minneapolis: University of Minnesota Press, 1967), p. 14.

say, or *April Hopes* would be considerable. On their own merits, then, such novels as *The Story of a Play, Ragged Lady,* or *The Kentons* can be expected to justify critical attention. At any rate, the critical process which has effected the establishment of Howells as a major novelist, primarily through a study of his growth toward the work of the nineties, invites an extension to the late fiction. If detailed analysis proves the inferiority of that fiction, at least the terms will be more exactly specified. If it discovers continued excellence, no other justification is required.

The assumption that Howells meant something serious in saying that he regarded all his fiction as "socialistic" is a good beginning. If Howells felt no absolute or decisive differences in the quality or purposes of his fiction between the period of his "strong emotioning in the direction of the humaner economics"[5] and his attempt in *The Kentons* to help "people know themselves in the delicate beauty of their every day lives, and to find cause for pride in the loveliness of an apparently homely average,"[6] then an attempt to understand the later fiction in *his* terms is warranted. One of the intentions of the discussion of Howells as a psychological novelist was to suggest— and the revaluations of the economic novels as novels of complicity support the view—that the body of Howells's fiction is a more closely knit totality than has been supposed. There is less danger of heresy now in proposing that even the neglected late fiction may be taken as part of a consistently valuable artistic vision, expressing an admirably broad and humanistic theory of realism.

What has been called "the best single definition of critical realism"[7] can, for example, be applied—with varying results—to all of his fiction. That definition is taken from the essay in which Howells formulated his sense of Ibsen's greatness as a realist by pointing to "his power of dispersing the conventional acceptations by which men live on easy terms with themselves, and obliging them to examine the grounds of their social and moral opinions."[8] Applied to the posteconomic fiction, this test shows that though these

5. "Author's Preface," *A Hazard of New Fortunes* (1952), p. xxii.
6. *Letters,* II, 161.
7. Carter, *The Age of Realism,* p. 192.
8. *North American Review,* CLXXXIII (July 1906), 3.

novels do not bring such a wide range of "acceptations" into question, they are, except for such deliberately minor exercises in lightly realistic comedy as *An Open-Eyed Conspiracy* or such lightly fictionalized travel literature as *Their Silver Wedding Journey*, still very much concerned with "the grounds of moral opinion" beneath deceptively commonplace surfaces.

The general level of excellence Howells maintained in the "psychological novels" of the later period—in *The Story of a Play, The Landlord at Lion's Head, The Kentons, The Son of Royal Langbrith, Miss Bellard's Inspiration, The Leatherwood God, The Vacation of the Kelwyns*—makes it possible to assume that "critical realism" may properly be critical of more than the economic system, may find important moral questions "grounded" in facts and relationships which are only generally conditioned by social or economic circumstances. If the later novels are approached with this sense of possibility and not prejudged as fallings-off from the economic novels, certain comparative demurrers about the economic novels themselves are even possible. It may be seen, for example, that their breadth was not achieved without some sacrifice of depth and complexity and some loss of meaningful form.

The 1912 essay in which Howells—surely consulting his own experience—rejected "the facts of finance and industry and invention" which "are wholly dead" except as they "are expressions of character," provides another relevant statement. It points the way to an understanding of Howells's intention in the posteconomic novels, and, though the question of their relative quality will still remain to be decided by particular analyses, it offers a basis of judgment which has not customarily been granted: "If we . . . [are] ever to discover our greatness to others we must withdraw from our bigness to the recesses of that consciousness from which characters as well as camels are evolved. The American, no more than any other man, shall know himself from his environment, but he shall know his environment from himself."[9]

One interpretation of the retrospective significance of this remark

9. William Dean Howells, *Criticism and Fiction and Other Essays*, edited by Clara Marburg Kirk and Rudolph Kirk (New York: New York University Press, 1959), p. 346.

is that the economic novels were a kind of testing ground on which Howells fought the battle for his personal art against the demands of immediate issues on his attention while at the same time carrying forward the psychological novel. Certainly, one of the technical problems of *A Hazard of New Fortunes* was how to combine the several seperate stories into a "complicitous" whole, and the solution of having them all drawn into the orbit of *Every Other Week* was as much dramatic contrivance as persuasive realism or even analogy. Howells found it impossible to maintain his prejudice against "stories in which I have to drop the thread of one person's fate and take up that of another." The technique that he chose was an attempt, in spite of the number of characters involved, to adapt his principle of working to keep "their fates . . . interwoven and . . . constantly in common before the reader,"[10] and it showed the strain.

The forcing of technique to indicate interconnection suggests a similar forcing in Howells's thinking about the relationship between man and his environment. Like Basil March, Howells was compelled by experience and new knowledge to question man's moral responsibility. If the system was so inherently corrupt as to make embezzlement a symptom, an effect, rather than a viral infection poisoning an essentially healthy polity; or if men lived in a purely competitive world in which they must go "pushing and pulling, climbing and crawling, thrusting aside and trampling underfoot,"[11] in which the only law is the law of survival; or if men lived in a world of chance uncontrolled even by some ultimate moral government, then the kind of philosophical and ethical questions to which Howells had previously devoted his fiction were irrelevant, and his purpose to teach by it "a lenient, generous, and liberal life" merely naïve.

But the fact is, though Howells could have March say in a moment of disgust that "conditions *make* character" (p. 486), the only hope he could find that civilization would base itself "anew on a

10. *Letters,* I, 233.

11. *A Hazard of New Fortunes* (1952), p. 486. Hereafter page references to the novels under discussion will be given, after the first reference, in parentheses in the text.

real equality" was the "immediate altruism"[12] of men—which is to say, character. Even the economic novels do not arrive at a completely deterministic view of man, though they clearly represent the deepest point of Howells's pessimism. But it is the interaction of character and conditions that make a Dryfoos rather than a Lapham, a Northwick rather than a Hilary, or, to take less obvious examples, a Kane rather than a David Hughes, a Jenny Denton rather than a Peace Hughes. Even in tracing out the most devastating effects to which conditions could lead—for example, the deaths of Lindau and Conrad—Howells preserved a wide margin of freedom for moral judgment. If a Dryfoos has been corrupted from good citizenship and his family relationships distorted by money, both Lindau and Conrad have been twisted by their varying fanatical devotion to their ideals and to some degree choose their fates.

Howells's turning away from the special subject matter of this brief series of novels may be interpreted, then, as a return to his dominating interest in studying the primary bases in character of moral choice. His early letter to Warner, already cited, had reasoned to an analogous choice, though he had approached it from a different angle, arguing on the authority of Turgenev against the necessity for length and sheer size in the novel: "I find . . . that I don't care for society, and that I do care intensely for people. I suppose therefore my tendency would always be to get any characters away from their belongings, and let four or five people act upon each other."[13] The testimony of his fiction and his expressed convictions seems to be that he found through the writing of the novels that dealt extensively with people's "economic belongings" that both the technique and the purposes of his art could be better served by a narrower focus.

Such a decision did not require the selection of one alternative in an either-or proposition, an exclusion through incapacity of one half of the artistic whole. It could reflect the attitude that "conditions" may be more or less in intensity but "conditions" of some sort are in-

12. *Letters*, I, 417–418.
13. *Ibid.*, p. 233.

escapable, are merely the context within which the moral drama is enacted. Since Howells found little hope of immediate, practical, revolutionary change in conditions—his frequent advocavy of the use of the Australian ballot by workers to vote their rights to improved pay and working conditions into law, for example, was merely a despairing alternative to the bloodshed and other human wrongs of strikes and open warfare between labor and capital[14]—the question that remained was: Given the conditions, what shall a man do? His own well-known answer was to be a theoretical socialist and practical aristocrat and to be comforted by being "right theoretically, and . . . ashamed of one's self practically."[15] Another answer was to continue to write novels of undiminished moral seriousness for whatever aid they could offer in dealing with the riddle of the painful earth, in strengthening embattled mortals "with a sense of their fraternity," and "clearly or obscurely" making "the race better and kinder."[16]

### Christian Socialism: *Annie Kilburn*

Many of the artistic difficulties with which Howells struggled in the economic novels are related to the attempt to accommodate the psychological substance and dramatic mode of his fiction to the demands of his widened vision. There are, therefore, threads of continuity extending from such an early major novel as *A Modern Instance* all the way *through* the economic fiction to the final work. (Another evidence of continuity was his writing of the critically approved "noneconomic" novels *The Shadow of a Dream* and *An Imperative Duty* between *Hazard* and *The Quality of Mercy*.) It has been remarked that admiration for the economic novels need not cause antipathy for the other novels. Conversely, it is not necessary to devalue the economic novels to enhance the remainder of Howells's work, but the possibility of their receiving greater critical favor may be increased if the lines of connection are seen as devel-

14. See, for example, *ibid.,* II, 25–26.
15. *Ibid.,* 1.
16. *Criticism and Fiction* (1959), p. 87.

oping from honest artistic conviction rather than from an exhaustion of social radicalism or literary imagination.

From this perspective, one of the reasons that even Howells's economic novels never really offered many specifics on the subject of economics becomes clearer. Although Howells became increasingly aware of economics as a determinant of American conditions and recognized that the American economic system was a contradiction of the American dream, his foremost concern continued to be with the moral quality of average American life in *all* its aspects. A comment he made in the "Editor's Study" in 1890—the year in which *A Hazard of New Fortunes* appeared—is indicative of this emphasis and of his ultimate reference of all aspects of American life to a religious ideal:

If America means anything at all, it means the sufficiency of the common, the insufficiency of the uncommon. It is the affirmation in political terms of the Christian ideal, which when we affirm it in economical and social terms will make us the perfect state.[17]

The problem was how to bring about the "recognition" of the Christian ideal in "economical" terms, and for that problem Howells had no solution either as a citizen or as an artist. As a citizen he looked to others like Lawrence Gronlund to provide the answers and could only record his disappointment in failing to find them: "He believes it the duty of all to facilitate the peaceful solution of the problems before us, but he does not point out the measures to be actually taken by a people accustomed to express their purposes in suffrage and legislation."[18] As a literary artist, Howells knew that his function was to question, to "move," rather than to "teach." His novels, therefore, do not go beyond a depiction of the symptoms of the economic disease to a diagnosis of the disease itself and a prescription for its cure. Clearly it was an infection disseminated by individual selfishness and greed, but the breeding place was the fertile ground of competitive capitalism. Thus Howells found himself at

17. "Editor's Study," *Harper's Monthly*, LXXXII (February 1890), 479.
18. "Editor's Study," *Harper's Monthly*, LXXVI (April 1888), 803.

an impasse, unable to conceive of justice under present economic conditions but also unable to conceive of a change in those conditions except by an exercise of character which would nullify their effects and thus create an ecology in which a viable antidote was possible.

Meanwhile, however, the realistic writer had a responsibility not fully conveyed by the conventional connotations of that designation and yet stopping short of prescriptive formulations. However serious the economic problems, they were, after all, part of a larger context of experience and meaning. The "Christian ideal" must find expression in political and social terms as well, if the "perfect state" was to be achieved. This was a lesson which the realistic novel might properly teach. It was early in the period of Howells's most intense concern with the kind of question characterizing the economic novels, the period of his profound response to the teachings of Tolstoy, that he offered a statement expressing his own sense of the inadequacy of the term *realist* to define the quality of such writers as Turgenev, Tolstoy, and Dostoevsky (and, presumably, himself). These writers were realists "in ascertaining an entire probability of motive and situation in their work," but some other word was necessary to define both the deeper quality and the moral function of that work:

Perhaps humanist would be the best phrase in which to clothe the idea of their literary office, if it could be limited to mean their simply, almost humbly, fraternal attitude toward the persons and conditions with which they deal, and again extended to include a profound sense of that individual responsibility from which the common responsibility can free no one.[19]

It is perhaps no accident that this statement of a humanistic ideal of fiction appeared at the very time that *Annie Kilburn* (1889), the novel conventionally placed in evidence as marking Howells's entrance into a new novelistic phase, was appearing serially in *Harper's Monthly*. Whether the connection is direct or not, the comment offers a useful context in which to place all four of the economic nov-

19. "Editor's Study," *Harper's Monthly*, LXII (September 1886), 639.

els. Even more importantly, it does much to explain why Howells could go right on in the same period with very different novels without evidencing any sense that he was betraying realistic principles or shirking novelistic responsibility; and to explain why he could shortly give up the economic novel altogether.

The readings of *Annie Kilburn* have generally been keyed to Howells's own remark that the novel is a plea "for *justice,* not *alms*"[20] and have found a specifically polemical intent in it, have taken it as a direct socialistic attack on capitalistic economics. From the moment he began to write it, however, Howells's conception of his subject was broader than this, and he invoked the honored name of Tolstoy in speaking of it. His sense of the difference between this new novel and his previous fiction was expressed by his saying that it would "deal rather with humanity than love." This early, too, he gave evidence that he was working toward a view that economic problems could not be solved or even understood in economic terms alone. The character who would serve to bring into focus the inequitable economic arrangements which caused some and perpetuated other kinds of injustice was to be "a minister who preaches the life rather than the doctrine of Christ." And he ended these comments to his sister with a question: "Have you read Tolstoi's heart-searching books?"[21]

The claim, therefore, that an adequate reading of *Annie Kilburn* requires more than a perception of the novel's concern with social and economic problems is convincing. The argument is that "not poverty nor social and economic injustice . . . is the theme" but "Annie's vision of life's vast interdependency, its unity in multiple difference."[22] Such a reading is consistent with the fact that *Annie Kilburn* is still as much dramatic as it is "panoramic"—i.e., "concerned with the lives of many rather than few characters."[23] The technique of limited omniscience is used to center the story in

20. *Letters,* I, 419.

21. *Ibid.,* 405.

22. William McMurray, *The Literary Realism of William Dean Howells* (Carbondale and Edwardsville, Illinois: Southern Illinois University Press, 1967), pp. 55, 66.

23. Gibson, *William Dean Howells,* p. 32.

Annie's consciousness, and the "lives" of the other characters—Putney, Gerrish, Mrs. Munger, Lyda Wilmington—are mostly sketched in to establish the context of the viewpoints toward social and economic questions which they represent. The essential *experience* is Annie's as she is caught between her intellectual commitment to Peck and her emotional attraction to Dr. Morrell. The effect of her experience is to educate her not merely to the true meaning and practical difficulties of altruism and charity but to a modified conception of self in all its interrelated aspects—religious, social, psychological, intellectual.

It has been pointed out that Howells was so conscious of the audacity of the new ideas he was expressing in *Annie Kilburn* that he felt obliged to "sugar-coat [his] medicinal properties." However, this effect was achieved neither by masking the ideas themselves (they are not only developed in the dramatic dialogue but openly summarized in Peck's final sermon) nor by discounting them as the limited perceptions of a near-sighted, spinsterish do-gooder. In fact, Annie's experience comes closest, of all those represented in the novel, to Howells's own.[24] In keeping the focus on it, Howells was not merely using her to smuggle in his ideas to an audience with different expectations concerning his fiction;[25] he was dramatizing a conflict between the ideal and the practicable, the theoretical and the actual. Any softening of the force of the ideas results not from a failure of clarity in their presentation—there is no ambiguity about Howells's attitude toward the dehumanizing effects of the economic system—but from their being finally held in ironic irresolution, from

24. Dr. Morrell, as a man and an intelligent and objectively sympathetic observer of the social and economic inequities, might be cited as the kind of central character Howells ought to have chosen. However, Dr. Morrell has made his adjustment to conditions through his work, which at least enables him to provide some practical and visible alleviations. Part of Howells's problem was his doubt whether his intensification of awareness and concern resulting from the reading of Tolstoy and from the Haymarket experience could find effective implementation through his fiction; whether, something like Annie Kilburn's Winged Victory, his fiction would become an embarrassingly ineffective expression of right feeling.

25. The interpretation to which I am taking exception here is that of Cady, *The Realist at War*, pp. 82 ff.

Howells's refusal to make them prescriptive and hortatory. That he was yet forced to explain to a friend that the novel was a plea for Christian justice, for an ideal of brotherhood, and not a call for alms suggests that his final openness was concealment enough to misdirect even his initiated readers.

The attempt to preserve the form of the dramatic and psychological novel, whose resources Howells had exploited in differing ways in *A Modern Instance* (1882) and *April Hopes* (1888), while expressing his new comprehension of the deep conflicts produced by economic conditions, resulted in a rather loose union. The use of Annie as the central consciousness and of the Reverend Mr. Julius Peck as the intellectual center of the novel made for a separation between its emotional force and its economic demonstration. It is true that Annie becomes intellectually committed to Peck's view that the only solution to the problems of capitalism lies in the "end of competition," of "strife, of rivalry, of warfare,"[26] by the universal exercise of perfect Christian justice. But that conviction is almost coincident with Peck's death, which removes the rather remote possibility that Annie will put it into action by following the minister to Fall River to work in the mills or help in maintaining a home for him. Even as she had told Dr. Morrell of her plan, she knew it was "folly," and her subsequent feeling was shame that Morrell "had divined the cowardice and meanness in which she had repented it" (p. 318). It is emotionally satisfying, then, and appropriate to the limits of Annie's education in complicity—in social and economic responsibility—that she ends by abandoning the large theoretical questions and by adopting Idella Peck, working in the Peck Social Union, and waiting for a proposal of marriage from Dr. Morrell.

The Reverend Mr. Peck, on the other hand, is never much more than the sum of his ideas. Although they are a wholly consistent—even fanatic—expression of the ideal of Christian brotherhood, Peck himself is as little a brother as a good man can be. There is general agreement with Putney's summation that his effect is to freeze out his fellows with a " 'hard-headed cold-bloodedness. . . . He seems to be a man without an illusion, without an emotion' " (p. 129). It

26. *Annie Kilburn* (New York, Harper and Brothers, 1891), p. 241.

may be argued that the effect of such a characterization is to dramatize the chasm between the ideal and the reality in an America which
is busily engaged in transforming its Hatboro' villages into divided
industrial towns and emerging suburbias. But another effect is to de-
humanize the ideal and to diffuse the emotional impact of the ideas
which Peck embodies. A kind of impersonal grief is felt at his death,
and this reaction extends to the failure of his ideas to do more than
bring Annie to an ironic awareness of the "vicious circle" in which
"she dwells . . . and mostly forgets, and is mostly happy" (p. 327)
or to arouse the brilliant but alcoholic Putney to thwart the threat
to Peck of dismissal from his pastorate.

What has happened in this novel is that Howells's own passion
(the Haymarket experience was in the immediate background of its
writing) was given expression in the "audacity" of Peck's ideas, but
his sense of the futility of trying to live socialistically in capitalistic
conditions was *dramatized* in Annie's story. Like Jane Austen, with
her "fatal gift of observation,"[27] Howells had the gift of balance, of
rationality, a gift fatal to polemics and pronouncements. In *Annie
Kilburn,* he remarked that "one of the dangers of having a very definite point of view is the temptation of abusing it to read the whole
riddle of the painful earth" (p. 328). A few months after its completion, he was remarking in the "Editor's Study" that "one of the
evils of having very firm convictions is that you want to deny all
merit to people who have different ones."[28]

One inference from the novel and these remarks is that Howells
could not imagine a man like Peck as the *center* of his fiction,[29]
could not build his drama from his ideas but only from those average Americans whose concern was less with discovering solutions to
the riddle than with learning how to live with it. This "economic

27. "Introduction" to *Pride and Prejudice* by Jane Austen (1813, reprint
edition, New York: Charles Scribner's Sons, the Modern Student's Library,
1918), p. ix.

28. *Harper's Monthly,* LXXIX (September 1889), 641.

29. It is characteristic that Howells undercuts the crisis of the threatened
dismissal by having Peck resign and then avoids the necessity of tracing out
the consequences of that act by having Peck killed. Howells's concern was
always with dramatizing problems; he never claimed to incorporate solutions.

novel," then, while it obviously accommodates a considerable degree of one kind of "critical realism"—that "which truthfully reports on warped and maladjusted social relationships so that men may study and improve them"[30]—is equally a psychological novel. In its narrative development of "the fascination of man for man, not to say the fascination of man for woman, or the reverse,"[31] it is the kind of psychological novel that Howells defined as representing the fiction of the future. It is new in the ideas it introduces, but the partially unresolved difficulties of introducing those ideas were eventually to lead Howells to a succession of novels which testify that his turning back to concentrated psychological studies was not a failure of nerve, not a reduction of moral purpose or a commercial compromise. It represented, rather, a shrewd assessment of his own talents and an assertion of his right as an artist to choose the areas of American life he would study.

## Economic Education: *A Hazard of New Fortunes*

It is important that this question of the relation of the economic novels to the work that preceded and followed them be fully examined before it is lost in the generalizations of literary history. A recent work, for example, states that the result of the awakening of Howells's social conscience was that "he tried temporarily to change the character of his fiction," and then "returned to his own brand of social comedy, now characteristically infused with a large amount of psychology. . . ."[32] The important questions—the degree of success or the reasons for failure in the attempted change, the content and seriousness of the social comedy, the exact nature or "amount" of the psychology—are ignored in the service of pronouncing on the graph of Howells's career.

Fortunately, the questioning of *A Hazard of New Fortunes* is still proceeding. One charge that has been brought against it—the claim that its "ultimate meaning" is clouded by the inconclusiveness and

30. Carter, *The Age of Realism*, p. 171.
31. *North American Review*, CLXXV (September 1902), 294.
32. Edward Wagenknecht, *William Dean Howells: The Friendly Eye* (New York: Oxford University Press, 1969), pp. 37, 6.

vagueness of its ending—is of special relevance.[33] The view that, in trying to deal with economic conditions, Howells found that he could only circle back to his "profound sense of that individual responsibility from which the common responsibility can free no one"[34] makes for a different judgment. In that context, the novel is not inconclusive, but uncommitted, open.

What is not resolved is the possibility of individual effectiveness in reforming the conditions. The novel is definite enough about such matters as the irresponsibility of the purely aesthetic view of life, about the inartistic character of didactic fiction, and about the ineffectiveness of art as an instrument of specific social reform. The openness of the ending is not a sign of failure to find solutions to the economic problems *Hazard* brings under scrutiny nor of evasiveness resulting from the desire to avoid didacticism. Howells had already made it clear that he looked to such social philosophers as Laurence Gronlund for programs and solutions. The record of his public and private utterances before and after *Hazard* indicates that he never found fully satisfactory solutions and that he always had reservations about the proposals of Marxian and socialistic thinkers.[35] This kind of tentativeness did not simply overtake him at the end of the novel and betray its intentions. As far as the *dramatic* requirements of the novel are concerned, the openness is appropriate. Howells was concerned with characters, with their attitudes and with the interrelationships among them determined by those attitudes and other factors of personality and moral posture. On this score, there is sufficient *resolution* in Basil's deepened understanding, in the deaths of Lindau and Conrad, in the marriage of Fulkerson and Miss Woodburn, the final misery of Beaton, in the *lack* of moral change in

33. Vanderbilt, *The Achievement of William Dean Howells,* p. 179. The charge is part of a complex and provocative analysis of *Hazard* as a novel which absorbs "basic social, economic, and moral problems of capitalism . . . into the issues of esthetic controversy in the late nineteenth century" (p. 146). My discussion, without being able to do summary justice to Vanderbilt's arguments, takes issue with some of them.

34. *Harper's Monthly,* LXII (September 1886), 639.

35. For a useful study of Howells's social thinking, see Robert Hough, *The Quiet Rebel* (Lincoln, Nebraska: University of Nebraska Press, 1959).

Jacob Dryfoos. Basil's inability to make any conclusive interpretation of the meaning of his experience or of the deaths of Lindau and Conrad, the ambiguity of the new relationship of Basil and Fulkerson to *Every Other Week,* the reduction to irrelevance of Basil's determination to resign from the magazine by Lindau's resignation and the concommitant release of Fulkerson from the necessity of deciding between expediency and principle—all these and other developments of the narrative are appropriate dramatic ironies in which the suspension of clear-cut significance is the meaning and the realistic resolution.

On the other hand, there was a real threat to Howells's art posed by his method of showing the complexity of the economic problems by assembling a cast of representative characters embracing the spectrum of economic opinion. From the start of his career, Howells had fallen into a habit of commenting or having a character comment on his more extravagant plot devices—often his use, as noted earlier, of the romanticistic situations he deplored in others—and some such self-consciousness seems to lie behind his having Basil remark,

"I don't believe there's another publication in New York that could bring together, in honor of itself, a fraternity and equality crank like poor old Lindau, and a belated sociological crank like old Woodburn, and a truculent speculator like old Dryfoos, and a humanitarian dreamer like young Dryfoos, and a sentimentalist like me, and a nondescript like Beaton, and a pure advertising essence like Fulkerson" (pp. 359–360).

There has never been a consensus on the degree of success Howells achieved with his variations of this device. Taylor found that Howells preserved realistic objectivity by creating "a series of chorus characters of such nature that their speeches, while thoroughly in character, should express Howells's own views."[36] Alfred Kazin, however, objected that because these characters were used as "witnesses to spiritual disorder, observers of social change," who acted "as a Greek chorus and to furnish the spare but haunting commentary that gives these novels their purpose and texture," they also

36. Eble, *A Century of Criticism,* p. 186.

lost dramatic force. They "did not revolt against the established order; *they testified against it.*" This "stratification of character became so necessary to Howells" in dealing with such subjects that he "rejected formal realism" for the "morality play" of *A Traveler from Altruria*.[37] Vanderbilt has argued that Howells's awareness of the problem, forced on his attention by the writing of *Annie Kilburn,* is reflected in the greater skill of *Hazard* in concealing his "message": "Exegesis and speech-making occur in *Hazard* . . . but Howells seems purposely to have made such moments as brief as possible."[38]

The dilemma—involving both the failure of the novel to prescribe solutions and the artistic danger of creating characters who were mere *raisoneurs*—may be stated in yet another way. The evidence of Howells's developing theory of realism makes it clear that the "failure" may be taken as a *refusal;* and the artistic difficulty is not that the characters give voice to varied opinions (including Howells's own), but that those opinions too often remain abstractions, do not sufficiently affect or are not sufficiently affected by the dramatic action to become vital *motives* and thus part of the developing significance of the story. Some drama develops in the dialectic itself, in the play of the conflicting ideas, but unless those ideas are significant expressions of character and motivations to action, the result is, as Kazin said, a kind of morality play.

The difficulty that Howells encountered here and in all the economic novels was, on a smaller scale, the one he pointed to in claiming that a "national novel," the "Great American Novel," would never be written because its necessary materials—"our giant operations, our tremendous industries, our convulsive finance, our seismic politics, our shameless graft"—could not be made the "stuff of an *imaginative* work."[39] It was in *Hazard* that Howells most nearly succeeded, but even there stresses are discernible. One of them is signalled by the necessity of abandoning his usual practice of maintaining a single viewpoint. Howells's concern for breadth, which was the cause of the change, not only forced him into some awkward

37. Alfred Kazin, *On Native Grounds* (New York: Reynal and Hitchcock, 1942), pp. 40–41.
38. Vanderbilt, *The Achievement of William Dean Howells,* p. 180.
39. *Criticism and Fiction* (1959), p. 347. My italics.

shifts of focus, but it forced him beyond the usual limits of his own rather cavalier use of coincidence and contrivance in bringing his varied cast of characters into a semblance of organic economic relationship through their association with *Every Other Week.*

This relationship is more appearance than reality because *Every Other Week,* the magazine owned by Dryfoos which Basil March, at Fulkerson's urging, goes to New York from Boston to edit, is more a mechanical device of aggregation than a microcosm of the economic system. It is not merely that Dryfoos holds it in rather loose control, his interest being to involve his son in business and not to develop its potential as a profit-maker; it is not that the magazine differs from more representative commercial enterprises in proposing to share its profits with its workers nor that it is in part a literary as well as an economic venture: its symbolic usefulness is limited because it is not really an economic *determinant* in the lives of the people associated with it. In every case, their connection is tentative or partial. (Basil's is the most complete, making his risk of his position in defense of Lindau's right to have opinions heroic and making his one of the successfully *dramatized* stories. Even Basil, however, has the cushion of "two thousand a year" which he and his wife had already considered as giving them enough to "pinch through on" if the New York venture failed [p. 17]. Fulkerson, too, is committed, but one can hardly imagine him without an emergency plan.) The result is that the theoretical statements of the injustices of the economic chance world are considerably stronger than the dramatized effects of its workings, and the urgency of the novel as a protest is thereby diminished.

The novel generates its greatest power at those points where Howells is able to establish dramatically the connection between psychological—i.e., moral—experience and economic circumstance and to explore that experience in depth. This he accomplishes in the story of Basil's conversion from a complacently aesthetic view of experience to an awareness, not only of his own relative helplessness in a dog-eat-dog economic world, but of the suffering and degradation of others. He accomplishes it also in the story of the moral corruption of Jacob Dryfoos by money and the splitting apart of the Dryfoos family as a consequence of their various attempts to adjust to the changed circumstances produced by wealth. The stories of Lindau and Conrad Dryfoos are also powerful in their facts, but they are told much more from the outside; and the fanaticism of Lindau and the ineffectuality of Conrad reduce their potential as instrumentalities of economic and social criticism. Beaton is merely an example of selfish indifference to conditions except as they affect his immediate welfare or comfort; and characters like Mrs. Horn and Colonel Woodburn are given no "stories": they are narrative conveniences and socio-economic attitudes.

For many readers, over a number of generations, this increased breadth in the representation of the complexity of the economic situation through the lives and characters of a various group of people associated with *Every Other Week* has been enough to make *Hazard* Howells's best novel. But it evidenced another, more serious, novelistic strain which would become increasingly manifest in *The Quality of Mercy* and *The World of Chance*. Not only did the arbitrary assembly of spokesmen for a range of economic views work to weaken the dramatic power of the novel; it betrayed Howells's difficulty in showing how the *working* of the economic facts in the lives of average Americans posed a valid moral issue.

Certain limited results are achieved by the device of taking Basil March to New York to serve as editor. His mainly aesthetic point of view is exposed to shocks of a varied economic experience, thus providing a plausible link between social and economic generalization and private experience. His education to new perceptions of the inequities of the economic chance world is suddenly taken from the realm of intellectual and aesthetic responses and made frighteningly real when his own livelihood is threatened. His decision to resign is morally admirable, therefore, but it settles nothing—not merely because it is made irrelevant by Lindau's resignation, but because it applies only to this situation. At the end, Basil is shown as willing to accept *Every Other Week* on favorable terms from Dryfoos and to set about putting it on a more businesslike footing. Nor is there the "lesson" of tragedy in the story of Jacob Dryfoos. He is not morally transformed by his son's death: he recognizes their failure of understanding but does not recognize his own corruption as its cause. He clearly exemplifies an inherent wrong in the system of values to

which he commits himself, but the only deduction made possible by
his actions is that a wiser man would not have made the same commitment. Neither his story nor Basil's—nor, for that matter, the
alternative extremes represented by Conrad and Lindau—provides
any really useful clue as to what the individual should do to act
*against* the system.

It is in this sense that Howells was forced to a view of the economic pressures as simply another of the conditions among which
men must live. Like any other condition, the system can at times
force the individual to a specific moral choice, and he is always faced
with the problem of making his own adjustment (acceptance, accommodation, rejection) to it, but beyond that the question is largely
theoretical. Thus, what makes the meaning of *Hazard* (and all the
economic novels) inconclusive is not that they do not propose in-
stitutional reforms that Howells never had any delusions of being
able to formulate, not that Howells suddenly was wary of the doctrinaire novel that would result if he took an open moral position,
but his recognition that he could offer only the most generalized kind
of answer to the individual moral question.

It is true that Howells "urged a diagnostic, not a therapeutic,
theme in *A Hazard of New Fortunes*."[40] Yet he always meant to do
more than just evoke an emotional reaction: the reader must be
"moved" in the right moral direction. A later comparison between
Ibsen, a realistic touchstone for Howells, and Shaw enforces this
point. Shaw, Howells said, "learned from Ibsen the great trick of
forcing us to see where we stand. But in Ibsen this power sometimes
subdues whatever is antic in us to seeing our duty as well as our footing, and strengthens us for it; while in Mr. Shaw it frees the antic
in us to mockery of the notion of ever finding out the right standing or taking any step to it."[41] It would be absurd to
speak of Howells's ever freeing the antic in us to mere mockery,
especially in a work of his profoundest imagination such as *Hazard*,
but it is not clear how that work enables us to see more than the
familiar Tolstoyan "duty" that "the first thing we are to do for the

40. Cady, *The Realist at War*, p. 106.
41. "Editors Easy Chair," *Harper's Monthly*, CXXVI (May 1913), 958.

other sinners and sufferers is to stop sinning and suffering ourselves."[42] The effect produced by the openness of the ending and the general dialectical strategy is not to free us to mockery but to reduce us to helplessness. If the novel is an "investigation of the state of the American dream . . . conducted by Basil March in the center with Lindau and Jacob Dryfoos as the polar opposites,"[43] the results are inconclusive with respect to the economic pressures and what a man should do to change them. There is no equivocation about the wrongness of Dryfoos's pursuit of money, or about the fanaticism of Lindau. There is, on the other hand, considerable doubt about the practical efficacy of Conrad's goodness and only private satisfaction in Basil's stand for principle.

Howells's final resort, therefore, was to a kind of helpless irony in which the inadequacies of both individual actions and theoretical general solutions are revealed. Thus it is fitting that Basil is relieved from the necessity of putting to the full test his resolve to resign in support of Lindau. This kind of irony is in keeping with Howells's realistic sense that the affairs of life seldom disentangle themselves sufficiently from the involvements of personality and sheer circumstance to stand as clear-cut and exemplary lessons in virtue. But a larger irony is produced by the clear-sightedness which could perceive the goodness in Conrad and Miss Vance, Lindau and Woodburn, Fulkerson and even Dryfoos, while it equally penetrated to a recognition of the consequences of such goodness. The novel makes clear that the defects of their virtue could only contribute to the perpetuation of the system or lead to their destruction, and its tone is finally as much resigned as "critical."

By the time Howells had written two more ambitious economic novels, there was a further clarification of his reasons for giving up this kind of fiction. The amount of creative energy expended in creating the varied panel of characters and in continuing his attempts to depict the workings of economic conditions in their lives— all of which at best brought Howells to a kind of moral impasse in which he could only condemn the facts and continue to speak for

42. "Editor's Study," *Harper's Monthly*, LXXV (July 1887), 316.
43. Cady, *The Realist at War*, p. 111.

individual character against conditions—might very easily and quickly seem disproportionate to the results. Moreover, the experience of writing *The Quality of Mercy* and *The World of Chance* might well have shown him that he was sacrificing the kind of novel that, from *The Undiscovered Country* through *April Hopes,* he had demonstrated that he could write with a sense of both artistic and moral control. These earlier works were novels which, in their concentration on the psychological experience of a few characters, yet managed to encompass a deeply critical awareness of disruptive changes in the national life: the decay of religious belief, the economic shifts involved in urbanization, the social inequities of a theoretical democracy. Now, however, a focus on the pervasiveness of economic conflict and injustice necessarily made for either some psychological shoaling in treating such characters as Conrad Dryfoos, Alma Leighton, Margaret Vance, Colonel and Miss Woodburn, or for a discrimination between economic theses and psychological penetration, as in the case of Angus Beaton.

This is to suggest that the real problem was not that Howells could not adequately meet the artistic text of avoiding the doctrinaire novel. Nor was it that he could not discover a way to make the novel an instrument of specific economic and social reform. On that score it was not only art that was ineffective: so was any form of immediate social or political action, and Howells fell back on the hope of an evolutionary process. His faith in the moral function of art survived, the faith which lay behind not only the economic novels, but the whole body of writing from which he had evolved his theories of the craft and significance of literature. What did not survive was the belief that the representation of economic conditions could in themselves be made to express anything more than the fact of their injustice, which was only one kind of injustice among which people must live. Such conditions are a context of living, but they are not life itself: "Nobody really lives in them, though for the most part we live among them."[44]

The analytical rather than prescriptive treatment of economics

44. "Editor's Easy Chair," *Harper's Monthly,* CXXIV (March 1912), 124.

was a kind of failure, then, not because it evaded the necessity of offering specific choices among the theories which it juxtaposed, but because it was a moral dead-end. The act of critical analysis of the system merely returned the individual to the ultimate problems, whatever the immediate conditions: the problems of "merciful judgment, humble helpfulness, and that brotherly responsibility, that duty of man to man, from which not even the Americans are emancipated."[45] This did not mean that Howells's novels would thereafter be confined to the purely personal and private experience. There were still important "problems of existence"—"economical . . . social . . . domestic . . . civic and moral and religious problems"[46]— involved in the kind of psychological experience which he had continued to write about in the other novels of the economic period and which would continue to engage his attention.

## Economic Accusation: *The Quality of Mercy*

On first impression, *The Quality of Mercy* (1892) seems to reveal Howells resolving the tensions between his "strong emotioning in the direction of the humaner economics" and his equally strong realist's sense that his art could not be used in the service of even humane propaganda. Focusing on a single economic phenomenon —defalcation, whose commonness was symptomatic of the corruption of the whole system—provided a manageable control of the "critical" element of this novel. Centering the story on the defalcator, J. Milton Northwick, allowed at the same time for psychological depth and complexity. That both these factors are operative is evident in the synopsis of the novel which Howells provided for its publisher, S. S. McClure.[47] The representative character of the "subject" is clear, as Howells enumerated, by citing actual contemporary cases, the possibilities of action open to Northwick when the secret of his embezzlement comes out: suicide, prison, or flight. His interest

45. "Editor's Study," *Harper's Monthly,* LXII (September 1886), 639.
46. *Criticism and Fiction* (1959), pp. 337–338.
47. The entire synopsis, from which the following quotations are taken, is printed in Cady, *The Realist at War,* pp. 164–165.

in the larger implications is expressed in his distinction between the
"subject" and the "motive," that is, the theme to be developed "in the
deep interior way" where he would seek his "strongest dramatic effects." And the detailed "story" of Northwick is directed toward the
psychological interest of showing "how without resources in himself,
life must begin to pall upon him" until he is possessed by the "idea
of expiation."

In execution, however, the novel does not entirely satisfy the
expectations raised by the synopsis, nor does it justify the initial impression of difficulties resolved. The critical realism turns out to be as
much accusation as demonstration. The account of the radiating effects of Northwick's crime is connected to economic analysis only in
the obvious sense that it was embezzlement and that it changes the
material circumstances in which his family must live. To a large
degree, it is the effects of *a* criminal act that are dramatized. Moreover, the dramatic force of the penetrating study of Northwick's
psychological and physical deterioration is diminished by being diffused among several subsidiary stories.

If the deep interior meaning Howells was aiming for was a
dramatized indictment of the plutocratic society which inevitably
produced a series of Northwicks—and there are more than a sufficiency of *statements* from Matt Hilary, Brice Maxwell, and Ralph
Putney rejecting Northwick's guilt as irrelevant and attributing the
responsibility to environment, to society—his literary success was at
best partial. The novel provides no clear demonstration of the me-
chanics by which the economic system works to produce embezzlers.
It simply assumes this to be the case and frequently asserts Northwick's lack of significance as an individual criminal. Its dramatic substance, however, is an account of Northwick's egotistical emptiness
and of the psychological and practical effects of his actions on the
lives of a variety of characters.[48] There is a logical causal connection

48. When Howells dealt again with the subject of embezzlement, just a
few years later, in "The Circle in the Water," he did not make society responsible but explored the question of how far the effects of the crime had
to spread outward before they were absorbed and halted by love and forgiveness. The story appeared in *Scribner's,* XVII (March, April 1895), 293–

established for these lines of radiation: Eben Hilary is president of
the business plundered by Northwick; Hilary's daughter Louise is a
friend of Northwick's daughter Sue; his son Matt, a theoretical
socialist, becomes romantically involved with Sue; Louise is attracted
to a reporter, Brice Maxwell, who writes a "philosophized" account of
the criminal affair; Ralph Putney, still the critic of our commercial
civilization and an alcoholic lawyer, is retained by the Northwick
daughters; William Gerrish is available to offer virtuous fulminations
against violations of the commercial ethic, and Mrs. Munger is available to gossip and pry; Dr. Morrell, now the husband of Annie Kilburn, is useful in countering Putney's "sardonic metaphysics"[49] with
disinterested rationalism, and there is a new ministerial view in the
person of Matt's friend, Caryl Wade.

There is no attempt here at a centralizing device such as *Every
Other Week* in *Hazard*. In one sense, this loosening of the structure
and the consequent de-emphasis of the specifically economic involvement of the characters is a more effective illustration of Howells's
notion of the guilt of complicity, the permissiveness which allows
corruption through indifference or silence or ignorance. (Howells directly makes the point that, after their first interest in the sensational-
ism of the crime, the laboring people in Hatboro' were too busy and
too tired to think much about Northwick or about the injustice of his
daughters' continuing to live on his ill-gotten property.) The looseness also points to an intransigence in the materials that Howells was
trying to combine. Even more than in *Hazard*, the split between the
psychological interest—naturally resulting from Howells's tested
method of letting characters interact to work out their own fates—
and the forcing of their stories for economic significance becomes
apparent. It is apparent here in the degree to which the "economics"
—the general meaning of Northwick's defalcation, the representation
of its effects on the community at large—is carried by sheer talk or
by Maxwell's editorializing.

That theorizing takes a "very high philosophical ground" in

303, 428–440, and then in *A Pair of Patient Lovers* (New York: Harper and
Brothers, 1901).

49. *The Quality of Mercy* (New York: Harper and Brothers, 1892),
p. 322.

placing the responsibility for the daily appearance in the news of J. Milton Northwicks on "the structure of society" and "the average morality of our commercial life" (p. 140). The dramatized action, however, shows this cause and effect relationship only generally, as the corporation which Hilary heads moves with impersonal efficiency to claim from Northwick's daughters whatever is legally recoverable and accepts, with corporate moral complacency, property from them and monetary restitution from Hilary which it could not legally exact. Northwick himself was simply "born with . . . the instinct of respectability" (p. 14), an instinct which became an intensified drive in reaction to his father's impracticality and disgrace. Whatever the qualities of business acumen and personal force that served to establish Northwick's position in a commercial culture which valued and used them, the story of their development and confirmation is antecedent to this one.

From his first reaction to Hilary's denunciation of his scoundrelism, his feeling of being "curiously shrunken and shattered" (p. 12), to the "feeble and formless" (p. 413) desire for expiation with which he slips into death, the story of Northwick is a story of emptiness exposed. The fact of his emptiness—of the failure of status and power to provide any resources of character and spirit and love—is a clear condemnation of those materialistic goals as absolutes. It is not, in Northwick's case, an exploration of their false basis and their operation within the society. Incapable of real love, lacking in the power of abstract imagination, indifferent to the life of the mind, Northwick can be used by business interests in a relatively important function, but he is not a convincing projection of the systemic corruptions of capitalism. Though Howells is incisive in showing how the system furnishes a rationale for the Northwicks and the Gerrishes and the board members, his development of the larger motive is less successful.

There are indications in the structural arrangements which Howells worked out for *The Quality of Mercy* that a variety of other stories were making their demands upon his attention. The three-part division, for example, does not make for a concentrated focus on Northwick's defalcation, his mental deterioration, and his death. Northwick figures in person in only the first six of the twenty-four chapters of Part First and the first seven of the twenty-one in Part Second. What happens in these other chapters is, necessarily, connected to what Northwick has done and is doing (or failing to do), but that action now develops in its own terms of social and psychological relationships. Even the fate of North-wick's daughters is determined in such a way as to deprive it of any general significance as the working out of the consequences of their father's illustrative corruption. Adeline dies from the shocks to which she is subjected by her father's troubles, but her distress is sympathetic and includes little understanding of what has caused those troubles. The pride of both sisters is literally humbled by the move to "the porter's lodge at the gate of the avenue" from "the great house" (p. 182), but they are never in real danger of destitution or even of serious want. Howells is careful to point out that even the dresses and the jewels which they had left behind are returned to them through the offices of Louise Hilary, with whom Sue has pridefully severed social connections. Ralph Putney is glad to provide them with legal protection in pursuance of his view that "any fight against a corporation . . . [is] a kind of holy war" (p. 184). Meanwhile, Mr. Hilary is hovering ready to provide any financial assistance they may need, and Matt Hilary has de-clared his love for Sue, thus ensuring her future whenever she is prepared to accept it.

As an economic novel, then, *The Quality of Mercy* turns out to be more of an indictment of the individuals who sustain the system than an exposé of the system which creates the individuals. There are, to be sure, some signs of the latter: whatever possibilities for moral sensitivity and spiritual awareness a J. Milton Northwick may have originally possessed, the system did nothing to promote their development and indeed sanctioned their atrophy. He could never have been an Eben Hilary with ideals "far above those which com-mercial honor permits a man to be content with" (p. 40), and the fact that he rises to a certain degree of power and status within the system by virtue of his very limitations is clear enough comment on that system. Yet the theoretical indictment and the drama never really fuse into an effectively coherent and representative whole.

That Northwick became a business success and then an embezzler is simply information provided by the author. Apart from that, what Howells succeeds in giving is an acute sense of North-wick's complete dependence on his public image, his rapid disintegration into apathy and fantasy, the psychological adjustments made by his family and associates to the disclosure of his true character, and the variously opportunistic, ethical, and merely indifferent reactions of the members of the community at large. The result is a novel in which the parts are better than the whole, the central feeling stronger than the prosecuted case, the individual psychology and the social interaction more convincing than the sociology.

## Economic Impasse: *The World of Chance*

The last of the economic novels, *The World of Chance* (1893), is a convenience to the critic, for it is itself the best evidence of why Howells turned to his editorial columns and to the romance for the expression of his radicalism. Choosing for his protagonist a young novelist from Midland who is instructed in the realities of the economic chance-world both by his experience of assaulting New York City with his manuscript and by his exposure to the theories and behavior of a coterie of radicals he encounters there, Howells specifically introduces the question of the social responsibility and function of art. Yet that choice for the central consciousness of the novel was also a way of refusing the question. Percy Bysshe Shelley Ray is a naively idealistic and romantic young writer who, though he eventually returns to Midland with fewer illusions and greater sophistication, gives little evidence of having achieved significant intellectual or moral growth. Howells's choice of protagonist has the effect of keeping discrete the two orders of experience—i.e., the "initiation" of the country youth into the multifarious life of the great city, and the specific education of a naive believer in America as a land of economic opportunity to the actual inequities and terrible injustices of the economic system. Ray is constantly alive to the possible "literary" uses of his experiences, but since his reactions to them are almost entirely personal, since he has not absorbed their larger meanings, he cannot function to dramatize in a serious way the question of how literature may serve a social purpose.

This separation between individual experience and social meaning also has the effect of revealing more clearly than ever Howells's dependence on the method of assembling a representative group of panelists to give *voice* to economic theory and analysis, and his difficulty in achieving effective integration of principle and story. At the end Howells refers all questions to the rule of Providence, to "the operation of a law so large that we caught a glimpse of its vast orbit once or twice in a lifetime."[50] This, however, is the rather easily won reflection of the young protagonist, and it therefore seems evasive, an almost desperate rationalization appended to the novel.

Ray learns in the course of the story that the acceptance of his novel by a publisher and its success with the public are entirely matters of chance, without relation to its quality as a work of literature. He also becomes involved with a variety of people representing diverse social and economic positions and attitudes. But there is no real interaction between the events which affect him directly and those which he observes happening to others. He becomes intimate, for example, with the Hughes family and is thoroughly exposed to the radical social and economic doctrines which the father, David Hughes, propounds. Ray's significant reactions, however, are not to the old man's ideas and their application to his own experience, but to the pathos of Hughes's personal situation as the *pater familias* of a disintegrating household, which includes an attractive unmarried daughter. It is to this daughter, Peace, that Ray naturally responds, and the story of their potential love, which never finds the fertile grounds it needs to come to fruition, proceeds along otherwise conventional romantic lines of liking, misunderstanding, and eventual parting by mutual agreement. Ray's other experiences—with the other members of the Hughes household, another daughter and her husband, Ansel Denton; with Kane, an impossibly witty sometime author of *Hard Sayings;* with his publishers and their wives—are part of the excitement and interest of city life. They strike the young author's consciousness as rich literary material, but they effect no funda-

50. *The World of Chance* (New York: Harper and Brothers, 1893), p. 375.

mental changes in his sense of himself and his relation to the world in which he lives; he might be described as remaining unselfishly egocentric.

Another kind of doubleness also works to make the economic criticism of the novel an intellectual abstraction rather than the implicit meaning of a deeply felt and powerfully represented drama. Lurid and commonplace catastrophes befall the Hughes household: the death of the Denton children by scarlet fever after threats on their lives by their father; the subsequent threat to Peace's life by Denton; Denton's macabre suicide by drinking the prussic acid used in the printing process he had invented; Hughes's death from diphtheria caught from exposure to his grandchildren. Not only are these events absorbed by the youthful resiliency of Ray, through whom they are observed or reported, but Howells himself seems curiously remote from them (as he was not from the experience of Basil March or Lindau). The chief reason for the effect of authorial detachment and coolness is that all the characters—with the exception of Peace—are treated with such an insistently double view of both their essential decency and their comic or pathetic ineffectuality that the irony becomes not an attitude but the refusal of an attitude.

It is not, for example, merely that Howells has his fun with Ray's literary ideals and with the kind of fiction represented by A Modern Romeo and accepted by "a reading public wearied and disgusted with the realism of the photographic, commonplace school" (p. 355). Howells had had his fun with romantic fiction before and would again. And there is good humor and undoubtedly a memory of his own youth in Howells's recording of Ray's naive and stuffy reaction to the motley collection of social revolutionaries Ray encounters at the Hughes home: "He abhorred all sorts of social outlandishness; he had always wished to be conformed, without and within, to the great world of smooth respectabilities. If for the present he was willing to Bohemianize a little, it was in his quality as an author, and as part of a world-old tradition" (p. 126). Never before, however, had Howells allowed such a central consciousness to remain so relatively unchanged. Lemuel Barker, for instance, is not only made thoroughly aware of the shallowness of his literary ideals and the inadequacy of his literary talents; he is given a social

education which returns him from Boston to Willoughby Pastures
with a tested self-understanding and a pragmatic conception of the
responsibility of the individual to the community. The structural
symmetry achieved in *The World of Chance* by closing with Ray
returning to Midland, dreaming dreams very like those which had
carried him into New York at the novel's beginning, may be taken
as the final circling of Howells's attempt to deal with economics
in fiction. Faced with an intolerable state of affairs which he could
yet see no way to change—he could *imagine* the possibilities of
the Australian ballot or the application of an immediate altruism
and therefore wrote the two Altrurian romances—Howells chose
to be ironic about it.

There are plenty of other viewpoints in the novel, which is
rich in individual characters. But each character is finally so ironically qualified that even in the aggregate they not only do not
offer any useful guide as to what can be done about the general
economic condition: they supply no reliable norm for individual
conduct within those conditions. The two extremes of possibility
exemplified by Denton and Kane are self-disqualifying; but even
within the broad range of choices that remains, no suggestions are
offered that compel emotional or intellectual commitment.

*The World of Chance* shows a clear difference, then, from the
other economic novels which used irony but were not brought to
a kind of moral stasis by it: Annie Kilburn could at least end by
adopting Idella Peck and working for the Social Union; Dr. Morrell
had all along refused speculation in favor of limited but practical
alleviation of suffering; and even Ralph Putney could put his
talents in the law at the service of the poor; Basil March, educated
to his own helplessness in the larger conditions, could at least
work for amelioration through the profit-sharing scheme of *Every
Other Week;* Brice Maxwell could attempt to educate the public
to the corruption of the capitalistic system through his journalism;
and Matt Hilary could write his theoretical tracts and set an
individual example of nonparticipation in the commercial enterprise
of his father. No one is more aware than Howells himself of the
inadequacy of these choices, but his irony is directed toward the
discrepancy between the palliative and the condition and not at

the egoism or cynicism or ineffectuality of the individual. In *The World of Chance*, on the other hand, the important characters— again with the exception of Peace, an exception that enforces the point—are either subjected to Howells's flicking irony or, like Percy Brandreth, are basically creatures of comedy in the first place.

In fact, one way of accounting for the flaws of this novel— which has such an abundance of materials Howells used more successfully elsewhere: varied characterizations, witty talk, social contrasts between salons and tenements, frequent opportunities for realistic descriptions of hotels, newspaper publishing offices, the streets of New York—is to recognize that Howells actually told one part of his story in comic terms and never settled in the other part on a tone beyond the ironic in the treatment of character. The story of Ray's discovery of the role of chance in determining the success of his novel is a comic one, and Ray himself is treated comically and ironically as the innocent abroad in the city, suffering agonies of suspense and despair in pursuit of fortune, and shock and delight in his social encounters. The point of view he brings to bear on his involvement with the affairs of the Hughes family undergoes no essential change: he can conquer his natural and understandable egotism to the extent of asking Brandreth to publish Hughes's socialistic tract in substitution for his own novel (feeling equally understandable relief when the proposal is rejected), but that is an expression of his natural generosity and his sympathy for a dying man rather than a sign of his conversion to or even interest in Hughes's ideas. His tentative romantic involvement with Peace has little to do with the quality of the ideas she holds. Indeed, his sympathy for the whole family must to some degree be willed in opposition to his instinctive reaction against their way of life. As the novel ends, Ray is determined to be a better novelist than he was in *A Modern Romeo*, but there are no clear signs that he wishes to become an essentially different kind of novelist.

One of the responses to the unjust economic system that Ray witnesses is that of Ansel Denton, former Shaker, member of Hughes's "Family" (p. 193), and now husband of Jenny Hughes. Denton, a wood-engraver by trade, has invented a printing process which could gain him great wealth but which would absorb the jobs of many workers. Tortured by the conflict between a man's right to the fruits of his own labors and his duty to his family and his larger social responsibility, Denton is driven to destroy both his invention and himself. The clarity of this indictment of the economic system is ironically blurred, however, by the fact that Denton is a religious fanatic, subject to visitations by "an inner Voice which governs his conduct" (p. 245). Therefore, when the destruction of his invention is followed by the death of his children and he comes to believe that merely the invention itself was a sin and that remission of sin requires "the shedding of blood" (p. 247); when he is led by the voices to attempt the sacrificial murder of Peace and then to commit suicide by drinking the prussic acid used in his new printing process, the parabolic significance seems to be directed more against unreasoning acts of revolt or expiation than against unjust conditions. (Hughes had tried to convince Denton that " 'Men have nothing to do with the remission of sins; it is their business to cease to do evil!' " [p. 247].)

At the other extreme from this kind of total (insane) commitment is the charming Kane, who long ago had given up the desire which had originally led to his acquaintance with Hughes to "transcendentalize" (p. 87) the world. His present condition is justly formulated by Hughes, who accuses him of taking "the mere dilettante view of life" and regarding "the world as something to be curiously inspected and neatly commented, instead of toiled for, sweated for, suffered for!" (p. 97). Howells invokes associations between Kane and Hawthorne's Miles Coverdale to indicate his awareness of the price that must be paid for the wit and detachment that enables Kane to produce a steady stream of "Hard Sayings."

Coverdale, for Howells, was "the minor poet . . . and self-conscious historian of a tragedy which he observes with cynical curiosity rather than a human sympathy."[51] Kane, too, never allows sympathy to become strong enough to affect his way of life or stifle an epigram. Typically, he pays for the funeral of his old friend Hughes but does not attend "because of a prejudice against

51. *Heroines of Fiction*, 2 vols. (New York: Harper and Brothers, 1901) I, 176.

such events" (p. 326). Such a negative answer to life or to the conditions which men create in which to live their lives is no more effective than Denton's fanatical striking out against it. Like Coverdale, Kane finally pays for his detachment by being cut off from significant relationship and experience. In lieu of friends, he has a wide acquaintanceship, which he eagerly expands through chance encounters like that with Ray. But " 'Nobody knows how he lives' " (p. 63), and no final accounting is made of him at the end of the novel. Presumably he will just go on pleasing himself with his own sallies of wit until the truth of one of them overtakes him: " 'The earth is a dangerous planet; the great question is how to get away from it alive' " (p. 255).

The ambivalence which lay behind the creation of Denton as both madman and selfless believer in the common good, and of Kane as a brilliantly intelligent observer of the defects of modern civilization and a pathetic nonparticipant in human affairs, also affects the central range of characterizations in such a way as to turn the novel back from economic criticism to another study of the lives that people live. The evidence of Howells's life and work clearly puts him emotionally on the side of David Hughes's hopes for a benevolently monopolistic, noncompetitive society. Howells's own experience, however, and the demands of his realistic art also dictated that he show the fanaticism which makes Hughes both a selfless idealist and a practical burden to his family.

While Hughes devotes himself to holding court for what Ray and Kane agree are "a lot of cranks" (p. 127) and to writing a book called *World Revisited,* Peace and Ansel work in the capitalistic system and Jenny manages the household. They live, by Hughes's own admission, among "abominations of sight and sound . . . horrible discords, that offend every sense," but he is glad to be there for the sake of fully realizing "the hideousness of a competitive metropolis" and thereby getting "some color of it" into his book (p. 297). Moreover, according to Kane, he would not want to have himself and his family helped to live in a better place because " 'Any help of that kind would mean dependence, and David Hughes is proud' " (p. 129). In his self-absorption, he sees Ansel's progressive derangement as a lack of "common-sense" whose worst effects are to disturb the serenity of the household and prevent him from pursuing his writing (pp. 270–271). On the occasion of his outburst to this effect, Howells invokes authorial privilege to comment, "It was a moment of pain without that dignity which we like to associate with the thought of suffering, but which is seldom present in it" (p. 271).

Howells even undercuts Tolstoy by assigning his beliefs to Henry Chapley, senior partner in the firm which becomes Ray's publisher. Chapley is a decent, kindly man whom time has passed by: bewildered by the increasing complexities of modern commercialism, he has lost his grip on his publishing business. He wistfully clings to Tolstoyan ideas without having any notion of how to put them into practice. It is another ironic hit in the novel that his comic fool of a son-in-law, Percy Brandreth, rescues the firm by deciding for a variety of irrelevant reasons to publish Ray's novel and by having it become, by chance, a commercial success. Even Jenny Denton, who in her indifference to social theory and her interest in social gossip, in her casual treatment of both her husband and her children, in her desire for pleasure and excitement and her capacity for malice toward her husband for not providing them, seems a telling illustration of Kane's suggestion that "the world is quite good enough for the sort of people there are in it" (p. 86)—even she is made to participate in the pervading irony of Howells's view. She is actually her father's favorite daughter, and it is to her that he turns in his dying days for comfort because, surprisingly, "There was probably a reciprocal lightness in Hughes's own soul to which hers brought the balm of kinship and of perfect sympathy" (p. 292). Though Ray cannot quite forgive her for not evidencing a more tragic response to the deaths of her children and husband, she receives authorial extenuation in the suggestion that her "buoyant temperament served a better purpose in the economy of sorrow than a farther-sighted seriousness" (p. 293).

The insistently double—or realistic—view from which Howells draws this gallery of portraits is a reminder that he could not escape his sense of the final importance of individual character and ethical responsibility in order to explain the world in terms of its conditions. In the significantly named Peace, there is an even clearer reminder that the only answer to the world's ills that Howells could trust was a broadly Christian one, a Tolstoyan one, and that it was not a panacea but an individual answer. Howells betrays no trace of reservation or qualification in exhibiting the qualities of love, devotion, dependability, and moral strength by which Peace is enabled to demonstrate, through living rather than theoretical formulations, the beauty of a life of selfless service to family and sweet charity to all. Certainly for Ray she is the "peace that passes all understanding."[52] He marvels at her patience in the trying circumstances in which her father's convictions force them to live and at her tolerance of the foibles and even the fanaticism of others: "He could not yet understand how the girl's love was a solvent of all questions that harass the helpless reason, and embitter us with the faults of others" (p. 293).

All this is to say that Howells, too, "helplessly" recognized that he was making no real comment on the economic injustices his novels brought into evidence, except to deplore them, except to point out the necessity for a change in conditions and to confess despairingly that he could imagine their being changed only by a miraculous moral transformation of individuals or by an impossibly long evolutionary process. There are signs of that recognition in the characterization of Peace: she is able to lose herself in giving to others, but the effects of her goodness do not radiate much beyond the family circle. Hers is essentially a passive role. In a sense, she supplies what was given up by leaving the Family "where there was no failure, and no danger of it" (p. 193). Her absorbing love, her refusal to judge, her patient acceptance of her father's chosen means to the ideological ends which she tactily approves—

52. The character and life of Peace Hughes make tenable the association of her name with the blessing of the Protestant communion service: "The peace of God, which passeth all understanding, keep your hearts and minds in the knowledge and love of God." Howells makes the specific allusion in *The Son of Royal Langbrith*, introduction and notes by David Burrows (Bloomington, Indiana: Indiana University Press, 1969), p. 218, describing Dr. Anther as experiencing "something of the peace that passes understanding in his heart."

all have the effect of cushioning the shocks of reality for those around her.

But implicit in her story—in this case the irony is not critical —is a sorrowful awareness of the human cost of near-saintliness. Such goodness, for example, responds to Ray's attack for failing to recommend his book with no attempt at making "any answer in protest" and by sitting "passive under his irony" (p. 241); it cries out when Denton is threatening murder, " 'Oh, don't hurt him! . . . He isn't hurting me,' " and then sinking "senseless" (p. 273) to the floor when released. This is a goodness which can bring peace to the self but whose human effects are both limited and limiting. It can absorb the effects of, but not change, the egotism of Hughes; it can understand the emotional limitations of Jenny and supply the true grief the mother cannot feel for her dead children; it can preach to Denton the lesson of justice through the sacrifice of self and not of others, but the result is suicide rather than abnegation.

Such unearthly purity and goodness lift Peace out of the realm of more normal human relationships and fulfillments. Ray had had an intermittent perception of a "quality in her that awed him from all other sense of her" (p. 293). He finally feels compelled, however, to offer her marriage, not on the grounds of "love," but of "worship" and his belief that their "lives would be united in the highest things" and she would "save [him] from living for . . . himself alone." In refusing this offer, Peace explains that the love she had felt for him has gone and that she will never marry. Love, she explains in familiar Howellsian terminology, would not have been "enough of itself, but everything else would be nothing without it." She argues that " 'There is work in this world for me to do, and I can do it' " (pp. 367–369), but it can only be assumed that her "work" will be to provide alleviation of suffering and an example of a Christ-like ideal.

This last attempt, then, to relate the "phenomena" of the "outer world" of economics to such "miracles of the inner world" as love and conscience and character apparently convinced Howells that this was not "the material with which art would prosper most." It proved, at any rate, that the method he had been experimenting with since *Annie Kilburn* was not satisfactory. More openly than in any of the previous three novels, Howells, in *The World of Chance*, took the components, the unresolved conflicts, of his own thinking and assigned them individually to appropriate characters. The result was continued irresolution, for he withheld endorsement of any particular view by maintaining some measure of distancing irony in each presentation except that of Peace. The meaning of her story, however, its demonstration of the value of individual character, could not be appropriated to the purposes of clarification and resolution of the economic problems. Peace's limited version of the good life is not made to function in ironic contrast to the impracticability of her father's and the madness of her brother-in-law's actions because the contrast would be more striking than true. To offer her life as a solution to the immediate problems with which the whole family is involved would be analogous to reminding workers of the Australian ballot. Moreover, in terms of the novel's organization, Ray rather than Peace is the central character; he is the protagonist, she is part of his experience. That experience with her is purely personal, independent of the broader social meanings which the novel introduces; their love affair— except for her suggestion that if her family situation had not made her "so unhappy, it might have been different" (p. 368)—is neither in its beginnings nor its resolution a function of anything but their instinctive emotional responses. The environment in which it occurs does not become crucially relevant circumstance. Ray goes back to Midland as a published author and a somewhat more experienced man of the world, but the social attitudes he takes back with him owe as much to Kane as to Peace.

Howells does offer the suggestion of a link between the two orders of experience at the end, when he has Ray reflect that he has encountered the "rule of mere casualty" not only in the economic world but "in the world which we suppose to be ordered by law— the world of thinking, the world of feeling" (p. 374). The "chance" which caused Ray and Peace to love and to cease loving each other—producing, incidentally, in Ray, "a relief which he tried to ignore, though he could not deny himself a sense of the unique literary value of the situation" (p. 369)—is simply the nature of experience and not the effect of a *system* working against the possibilities of individual happiness. Moreover, as the resolution of the affair between Ray and Peace shows, in the realm of feeling there is still the possibility of individual control and adjustment to the effects of the originating chance.

What is lacking, then, in *A World of Chance* is not a solution to the general economic ills of the world or of the capitalistic system, but a resolution which would provide a controlling attitude, which would establish a view of the relationship or the lack of relationship between the inner and outer worlds. Instead of inter-relation, however, the novel offers an account of the variables on either side of the equation. The effect is a novel filled with certified critical attitudes toward the dehumanizing conditions enforced by an economic world of chance, with wry recognitions of man's individual frailties, and even more with civilized appreciations of man's capacities for sacrifice, for love and compassion, for self-deflating wit. The difficulty is that these components do not sufficiently interpenetrate to achieve an artistic and moral unity.

This result cannot be attributed to any lack of awareness on Howells's part, for, as has been indicated, the question of whether art should serve a social function is specifically introduced. It is, however, debated to no resolution. Again the extremes are represented by Hughes and Kane, with Ray, humorously apologetic, holding an intermediate position close to the ground Howells himself helplessly occupied. Hughes, as might be expected, challenges Ray to "justify" his novel by asking: " 'How does it serve God and help man? Does it dabble with the passion of love between a girl and a boy as if that were the chief concern of men and women? Or does it touch some of the real concerns of life—some of the problems pressing on to their solution, and needing the prayerful attention of every human creature?' " (p. 154). He insists that literature must not be merely "aesthetic" but must be imbued with "an ethical quality" and serve as "the handmaid of reform" (p. 290). Kane, for Hughes, is "a mere frivolous maker of phrases" and *Hard Sayings* is "a bundle of phrases—labels for things" (p. 98). Howells, too, though he obviously enjoys coining witticisms for Kane's delivery and even has Ray pay Kane the compliment of emulation, is finally severe with such "heartlessness which so easily passes for wit" (p. 185). Howells's own view is recognizable when he has Hughes say, " 'We can have no true art, no real literature, no science worthy the name, till the money-stamp of egoism is effaced from success, and it is honored, not paid' " (p. 132).

Howells's concern in *The World of Chance* and the other economic novels, however, is with what kind of fiction it is possible to write in present conditions. Like Ray, Howells could value the attitudes of a Hughes "aesthetically, but he could not make personal application of them" (p. 155) to his own fiction. As he did in *The World of Chance*, he could make his fictions "touch some of the real concerns of life," but no matter how urgently these problems pressed for solution, he could not make his art "the handmaid of reform." He could not do it because that would destroy the art and because the only solutions he had to offer were the Tolstoyan injunctions to selflessness that applied to every aspect of human relationships and human endeavor and not just to problems of economic maladjustment and injustice. Again like Ray, Howells could subscribe to the idea that "it would help . . . if every artist could express his feeling about . . . or represent somehow" (p. 186) the necessity for art to be free from "the fear of want" (p. 185), and thus to show as well the degrading effects of economic slavery on the whole of American civilization. The economic novels were the expression of this hope, but the risks to which he subjected his art in the process of writing them were greater than could be justified by their social value. He would continue to write what were, by his definition, "socialistic" novels; but his concern with specific questions of economic and other reforms he would consign to the pages of the Altrurian romances, his editorial columns, and his private correspondence.

# III

# THE REALISTIC CENTER

## More Contexts

HOWELLS's doctrine of complicity was first explicitly enunciated in *The Minister's Charge* (1887) and thereafter was an implicit and explicit factor in the economic novels. The specifically social implications of the concept have frequently been explicated as they appear in the economic novels and in incipient form prior to that time. It has generally been assumed, however, that the *absence* of dramatized complicity in the later novels is one of the reasons for their inferiority. When it has been noted in such novels as *The Son of Royal Langbrith* or *The Landlord at Lion's Head*, it has been regarded as evidence of the intermittent revitalization of Howells's creative powers.

For Howells, however, complicity was more than an accusatory explanation of the problems of social and economic injustice. Nor was it, as a recent commentator would have it, an abdication of individual responsibility or, at best, an exonerating diffusion of it: "All it seems to have meant to him was that since nobody is *uninvolved* in what goes wrong, there is consequently no ground for any one person's assuming responsibility, no individual reason to feel guilt."[1] Such a view of complicity as entirely negative and

1. Warner Berthoff, *The Ferment of Realism* (New York: The Free Press, 1965), p. 58.

escapist fails to take into account its Christian and Tolstoyan foundation. In that context, its assignment of communal guilt is the
negative aspect of a polarity. It also includes the moral and psychological postulates of man's freedom and accountability. It is this
larger context which relates complicity to the assumptions which
governed all of Howells's mature work, and if it is recognized,
the later fiction need no longer be passed over on the grounds of
a lack of moral seriousness and social relevance.

Unfortunately, even informed and favorably disposed discussions
of complicity have seen it almost entirely in its negative aspects.
For example, Arnold Fox has provided this summary statement of
Sewell's sermon in *The Minister's Charge:*

No one is actually apart from his fellows: all, regardless of position, are
joined to each other in a brotherhood which stems from the fatherhood of
God. No man's sin can affect himself alone as a result; it necessarily affects the whole community. Even the good are responsible for the sin
which exists, for they have neither stamped it out nor endeavored to find
out how they themselves have contributed to it. It is not the one evil man
who is to be held culpable, but the evil of the time and place, for that is
what shaped him. Every man must accept the responsibility for his
brother, and he must seek it out, must accept it voluntarily, for in doing
this he will come to know God.[2]

The clearest exemplification of this theory, according to Fox, is the
account of Northwick's crime in *The Quality of Mercy:* "Society
is responsible for such defalcations because it supports an economic
system under which the accumulation of money is the highest aim
of man, and as Howells became more acutely aware of the existing
economic injustices, he came to attribute a greater share of the
guilt to the environment rather than to the individual."[3]

One context for the later fiction established by this view of
Howells's developing thought has already been commented on at

2. "Howells' Doctrine of Complicity" in *Howells: A Century of Criticism,*
edited by Kenneth E. Eble (Dallas: Southern Methodist University Press,
1962), p. 197. The essay originally appeared in *Modern Language Quarterly,*
XIII (March 1952), 56–60.

3. *Ibid.,* pp. 200–201.

length: since the "environment" could be changed only by a millennium, Howells was turned back to an examination of the individual life within the given conditions. More important, such views
of complicity do not sufficiently take into account the moral posi-
tives that can at least associate it—though Howells out of his final
scepticism stops short of specifying the connection—with a moral
government of the universe, with Providence itself. Under the
control of the pessimism which resulted from his personal experiences and his intellectual and spiritual response to Tolstoy and such
socialistic writers as Gronlund, he naturally emphasized the negative
aspects of the doctrine. But even in *Hazard*, Basil March, after
venting his despair with a viciously competitive world in which
men are "covered with blood and dirt and sin and shame" (p. 486),
comes back to a view that "we can put our evil from us with
penitence; and somehow, somewhere, the order of loving kindness,
which our passion and our wilfulness has disturbed, will be restored" (p. 506).

That "order of loving kindness" may often—even usually—be
obscured to the merely human perception. To the human sense,
the world most often seems a place of mere "casualty" rather than
"causality," as *The World of Chance* demonstrates. Such a view
may, indeed, be a cause of the complicity of society—the permis-
sively complacent or ignorant assumption of its individual members
that they have no connection with or responsibility for the actions
of their fellowmen—and this complicity must bear the blame for
the Northwicks. That, however, is not the whole story. It is the
present condition, but there is evidence available to show that
when individual men *do* assume their responsibilities toward not
merely other individuals, but toward the community, the mass of
men, there are powerful effects. This is the positive aspect of
complicity, complicity in the sense of *acceptance* of one's ties with
the brotherhood of men, and it is connected with Howells's insistence, discussed earlier, that morality must "refer itself to a belief in
some life after this," that our "ideal of conduct" must not "restrict
itself to time and space" but must look "to its origin in Christ and
its effect in eternity."[4]

4. *Harper's Monthly*, LXXIX (August 1889), 479.

There are many examples throughout Howells's posteconomic fiction of a complicity for good—a decision or an action by an individual or group which takes into account more than private morality, more than what would by any reasonable standard be personally "right." If "we see the development of Jeff Durgin as the logical result of his contact with a world which seeks constantly to relegate him to an inferior social position,"[5] we should equally see Cynthia Whitwell's development as a force for good affecting her brother Franky, Westover, and even Mrs. Durgin. Cynthia is an equally important "illogical" proof that character as well as conditions may count, and that it has the power to refuse to ally itself, even passively, with the standards Jeff has taken over from the society he is trying both to repay and to join. The whole life of Clementina Claxon, in *Ragged Lady* (1899), is an exemplification of the connection between moral and religious ideals and of the acceptance of an ideal of duty toward the world rather than a goal of personal happiness or social success. In the last of Howells's novels published during his lifetime, *The Leatherwood God* (1916), Nancy Dylks Billings is forced to remain silent about the identity and fraudulence of the self-proclaimed God, Joseph Dylks. Yet her true religious faith saves her from the guilt which eventually attaches to her brother David and to Squire Braile for their evasions of their responsibility actively to oppose the evil they recognize.

Even at the time Howells was offering his most pessimistic versions of complicity in the economic novels, there were at least small signs of returning balance. In *The Shadow of a Dream,* which immediately followed *Hazard,* Basil March supplies a version of complicity, phrased in alternately serious and self-protectively flippant terms, which embraces the double implications of its application: " 'We suffer every day for our sorrows, and for the sins of men we never saw or even heard of. There's solidarity in *that* direction, anyway.' " From this negative beginning, however, he goes on to suggest the possibility that good as well as sin and sorrow may be absorbed in and felt by the mass of men:

"It's all a mystery; and I don't know but we *are* rewarded for our happiness, quite as much as we're punished for our misery. Some utterly

5. Eble, *A Century of Criticism,* p. 198.

forgotten ancestral dyspeptic rises from the dust now and then, and smites
one with his prehistoric indigestion. Well, perhaps it's some other forgotten ancestor, whose motions were all hale and joyous, that makes me get
up now and then impersonally gay and happy, and go through the day
as if I had just come into a blessed immortality."[6]

It is in *The Son of Royal Langbrith*, however, that Howells
most explicitly makes the point that an unblazoned goodness has
pervasive effects far beyond the ken of its perpetrators, a good
benefiting those who have no knowledge of the decision made in
their behalf. The decision by the minister, Dr. Enderby, and more
meaningfully by Dr. Anther, not to reveal the secret of the dead
Langbrith's wicked private and business life has more than the
effect of permitting the son to revere his father's memory and to
court the daughter of his father's victim (until the revelation is
made by another agency). Anther becomes convinced that the
"publicity which his revolted instincts had long demanded for
Langbrith's sins . . . would have been the wildest and wantonest
of errors" (p. 267). It would have destroyed to no purpose the
moral sense of the community; it would have caused useless and
harmful passions of hate, revenge, shame, guilt, and the like in
the dead man's victim and in his innocent family. It is true that
the failure of disclosure prevents until too late the marriage of
Anther and Mrs. Langbrith, but even that might have been the
greater wisdom. It is possible that "her happiness was never essentially involved" (p. 271), and Anther, we are told, continues
about his "daily duties which were always full of interest and had
the variety which keeps men from stagnating" (pp. 231–232).

In such a light, Enderby's rather desperate reasoning to a justification which even his wife's devoted confidence in him cannot
quite accept is not even necessary: " 'It may be the complicity of
all mortal being is such that the pain [Langbrith] inflicted was
endured to his behoof, and that it has helped him atone for his
sins, as an acceptable offering in the sort of vicarious atonement

6. William Dean Howells, *The Shadow of a Dream and An Imperative
Duty*, edited by Edwin H. Cady (New York: Twayne Publishers, Inc., 1962),
pp. 92–93.

which has always been in the world'" (pp. 276–277). Whether the individual sinner is thus benefited or not, the doctrine of complicity has been shown to be both an accusation of man's communal guilt and an affirmation of the modifying force of his individual acts of larger than personal goodness.

In the course of his condemnation of the plutocratic system and of the complicity which permitted its evil, Howells had yet always insisted that "the potentialities of goodness implanted in the human heart by the Creator forbid the plutocratic man to be what the plutocratic scheme of life implies," and he had marvelled at the modifying effects of "the personal equation."[7] It was this perception of goodness in the midst of corruption, voluntary and involuntary gropings toward moral law and order amidst disorder, that led Howells back to affirmation of "the order of loving kindness" or, with a frequency that achieves a kind of choric effect in his fiction, to an at least tentative affirmation of a moral government of the universe. As late as 1910, he was still debating whether "the power of an awful force" which is felt in every life was one of "fatherly love" or something more sinister. But the pressures of his will and temperament always returned him in the direction of faith. In the letter to his father in which he speaks in these terms of his wife's death, he could not resolve the question. Echoing the words he had used at the end of The Undiscovered Country thirty years before, he said simply: "I submit, and we must all submit." He immediately added, however, that if there were no divine plan, no immortality in which loved ones would meet again, "It seems to me that it would not be fair from the creator to his creatures."[8] The expressions of hope, then, that Howells assigns to major characters like Basil March, Jere Westover, Clementina Claxon, Hugh Breckon, Dr. Anther, and others are a counterbalance to the negative side of complicity. They are also a sign that the psychological

7. William Dean Howells, The Altrurian Romances, introduction and notes by Clara and Rudolf Kirk (Bloomington, Indiana: Indiana University Press, 1968), p. 290.

8. William Dean Howells, Life in Letters of William Dean Howells, edited by Mildred Howells, 2 vols. (Garden City, New York: Doubleday, Doran and Company, Inc., 1928), II, 285.

studies of his late fiction do not exhibit an abandonment of principle or seriousness.

Complicity, in these terms, is one element in Howells's essentially balanced reading of the human experience. He saw character surviving conditions, the American democratic man modifying the worst potentialities of plutocracy, individual goodness leavening the lump of complicitous apathy and permissiveness, faith (or hope) in a universal moral government sustaining will in the face of an apparent law of casualty. These considerations afford a basis for further preparatory contextual observation. Again what seems appropriate is a reassertion and restatement of the comic vision which governed Howells's fiction. So many of Howells's novels have been dismissed as mere comedies of manners[9] that the reputation of even those which must be taken "seriously" has suffered from infectious association. Conversely, some readers have found a tragic vision (in selected novels), with the effect of seeing Howells's career as a preparation for and a falling away from the great period of the nineties. *The Shadow of a Dream* (1890) is one that has been read as a tragedy. To establish the grounds for a differing view of it—and, indeed, a view of all the noneconomic novels between 1890–1920—the following comments are made.

The question of Howells's artistic intention—whether he meant to write tragedy or not—first arose early in Howells's career, when Henry James reviewed *A Foregone Conclusion* (1875). James objected to the denouement. The story should have ended, James felt, with the death of Don Ippolito, a Venetian priest who had tried to leave the priesthood for worldly success and earthly marriage.

---

9. It has already been pointed out that Howells used *comedy of manners* and *realistic fiction* as interchangeable terms. If *comedy of manners* is used to designate what he called *society fiction*, he would reject its application to his own work. In an "Editor's Easy Chair" appearing in the same year as *Fennel and Rue* (1908), one of his novels most susceptible to such a pejorative designation, he described the English variety as novels that "deal most with their social varieties and complexities, with their classes and the differences which their classes create"; and, he added, "They are the most tiresome of their novels" (*Harper's Monthly*, CXVII [October 1908], 796).

In the denouement, however, Howells went on to account for the marriage of two other principals, and thus blurred the tragic focus.[10] This criticism came at a time when Howells was admitting that "No man ever felt his way more anxiously, doubtfully, self-distrustfully than I to the work I'm doing," so that his reaction against it must be regarded as more defensive than convinced. After admitting that editorial pressure had dictated the ending, he continued, "I feel pretty sure that I deepened the shadows by going on, and achieved a greater verity, also."[11] Yet, if this was rationalization, his habitual practice thereafter seemed to confirm that it was also artistic discovery, that it was a method appropriate to his sense of proper realistic emphasis. For example, in the very next novel that offered tragic possibilities, *The Undiscovered Country* (1880), Howells deliberately refused them, though the character of Dr. Boynton offered greater tragic potentiality than did that of the pathetic Don Ippolito. Here again there was a "going on" beyond the death of Boynton, the seeker of proofs of immortality, to the marriage of his daughter and her sceptical suitor.

The value of this ending, however, was not the conventional romance of the happy ending, but its meaningful contrast to the alternatives posed by the preceding action: Boynton's attempts "to surprise immortality" (p. 419), and the attempt of the Shakers, in whose community much of the action takes place, "to make the other world of this world" (p. 201). Against these possibilities, the young couple willingly choose a "life in the full sunshine of common day" (p. 419), and Howells ended with their story because that gave the truer realistic weight. He chose neither the abnormality of Boynton nor the mere romance of youth. His interest was in the mutual definition of terms on which the young couple chose to base their *living*: their "undiscovered country" is not merely the love they hesitantly are brought to admit to, but the totality of their future life. From Boynton's country, Howells well knew, no message could be received: "They wait, and we must all wait" (p. 419).

10. *North American Review*, CXX (January 1875), 213–214. See also "Howells's 'Foregone Conclusion,'" *The Nation*, III (January 7, 1875), 12.
11. *Letters*, I, 197.

Whatever the tentativeness with which Howells extenuated the denouement of *A Foregone Conclusion,* then, from *The Undiscovered Country* on he never varied his practice, and by 1904 it was an explicit part of his theory of realism:

"In art, the catastrophe must be the close of the work, for otherwise there will be what is called an 'anti-climax,' a thing to be avoided. Life, on the other hand, is not afraid of anti-climaxes; it produces them daily. No tragedy in real existence but has its tomorrow, unheroic, perhaps, artistically, but unavoidable, inexorable. Art may stop where it pleases, life must go on. Realism endeavors to take note of the continuity which nothing can arrest for long, and considers it more important to the individual and humanity at large than the violent interruption."[12]

Realism must go on beyond the "culmination of a tragedy" which "does *not* reveal character to the full" but "rather stuns all the faculties, all the emotions except a single one—defiance, perhaps, or fear, or despair" so that "the interaction of life and human character ceases."[13] There is a connection here with Howells's familiar attack on the "romanticistic" which, however, is often understood to be merely a rejection of contrived incident, exaggerated emotion, or lurid passion. He was also rejecting the imposition of a *controlling* tragic attitude and a management of materials to produce a final effect of tragedy. In fact, the language Howells used often seems to make a direct association between various forms of excess and the tragic. Discussing the French novel, he remarked:

No one will pretend that there is not vicious love beneath the surface of our society; if he did, the fetid explosions of the divorce trials would refute him; . . . it exists, and it is unquestionably the material of tragedy, the stuff from which intense effects are wrought. The question, after owning this fact, is whether these effects are not rather cheap effects.[14]

12. Quoted in Edwin H. Cady, *The Realist at War* (Syracuse: Syracuse University Press, 1958), pp. 136–137, from A. Schade Van Westrum, "Mr. Howells on Love and Literature," *The Lamp,* XXVIII (February 1904), 26–31.

13. *Ibid.*

14. "Editor's Study," *Harper's Monthly,* LXXIX (June 1889), 152.

A few months later, he took over another term from the Spanish novelist, Armando Palacio Valdés, who defined *effectism* as "'the itch of awaking at all cost in the reader vivid and violent emotions.'"[15] On several occasions, Howells explicitly dissociated his own work from any intention of seeking after such effects. He said of *The Son of Royal Langbrith*, one of the later novels that has enjoyed some critical favor as a "dark novel,"[16] that though the materials for a tragedy were clearly evident in it, "the tragedy finally seemed too easy, and I shrank from it."[17] And he added, in further revelation of his association of tragedy and the unrepresentative, "Besides, I have always loved the sweet face of Nature, the divine look of Probability."[18] In a more surprising comment, but one which again shows his constant concern to establish the realistic—it even seems possible to say antitragic—standard by which his fiction should be judged, he said of two novels, *The Coast of Bohemia* (1893) and *The Story of a Play* (1897), about which there would seem to be little question, "They threaten to become tragical, but with their utmost seriousness they keep within the bounds of comedy."[19]

Howells thus defined the poles of his realistic and comic spectrum. The expressions of that judgment in a series of rich and complex novels extending from *The Shadow of a Dream* through *The Vacation of the Kelwyns* (1920) disclose a range of perception from the profoundly serious to a deliberately relaxed amusement with mere vagaries of temperament and complications of manners. The operative tests were that realistic fiction must always do more than amuse; and it must not portray experience in such a way as to indicate that the "momentary arrests of life" are the most "productive of revelation of character."[20]

Basic to Howells's affirmation of this view of life as serious comedy was his conception of the nature and power of evil. Given

15. "Editor's Study," *Harper's Monthly*, LXXIX (November 1889), 964.
16. Cady, *The Realist at War*, p. 239.
17. George Arms, editor, "Howells's Unpublished Prefaces," *New England Quarterly*, XVII (December 1944), 585.
18. *Ibid.*
19. *Ibid.*, p. 588.
20. Quoted in Cady, *The Realist at War*, p. 136.

that conception, there was no place in his ontology or ethic for a tragic formulation of man's condition and fate. The consistency of his view is again demonstrable. In *The Undiscovered Country*, the man most opposed to Dr. Boynton's fanatical psychic experiments with his own daughter finally arrives at a judgment that Howells was not essentially to modify for the rest of his life. After harshly condemning the fanaticism which is in danger of turning Boynton into a Rappaccini, this sceptic, who loves the daughter, formulates a more general moral philosophy. He concludes that actions which are not of the will, which are the result of passion or error, are not evil but are merely "misguided" and belong "to the great mass of impersonal evil." An individual cannot do "essential injury" to others: he " 'may make others unhappy, but . . . can't destroy the possibility of happiness in them; we can only do that to ourselves' " (p. 319). Conscience, therefore, must be concerned with motives, and we must believe that " 'Forgiveness *does* somehow right a wrong! It must be so, or else this world is not a world of possibilities and recoveries, but a hopeless hell' " (p. 362).

Even at the time of his greatest personal distress and his most pessimistic view of the American system, Howells never accepted the alternative of the world as "a hopeless hell." The Basil March of *Hazard* can still opt for the belief that penitence can restore a moral order based on love and kindness. Dr. Anther, in accounting for the dead Langbrith's depravity, uses words almost identical with those Howells had supplied his *raisoneur* in *The Undiscovered Country*: Langbrith was "part of the vast sum of evil, not personally detachable and punishable" (p. 356). In an even later statement, assigned to a persona in an "Easy Chair" essay but typical of the position Howells had reflected in his fiction over the years, the pronouncement is made that in " 'a world pretty full of evil there isn't any purely voluntary evil among the sane.' "[21]

This is a question which Howells treated specifically in developing his theory of realism in the articles that were to become *Criticism and Fiction*. In his notorious argument for the treatment

21. *Imaginary Interviews* (New York: Harper and Brothers, 1910), p. 5.

of "the more smiling aspects of life" in American fiction, he commented, "Sin and suffering and shame there must always be in the world, I suppose, but I believe that in this new world of ours it is still mainly from one to another one, and oftener still from one to one's self."[22] This is evil domesticated, brought at least under the possibility of human control. Moreover, the practice or the combating of this kind of evil is not productive of a malignity or a heroism suitable to any received sense of tragedy. This evil is not a demonic principle which must be accommodated in a religion or a philosophy; it is an element in the human character and personality which is obscured by a dominating tragic view: " 'By all means, let us have tragedy in fiction as part of life; but the study of human character is best pursued in the normal daily round, with its endless variety of revelation of traits and formative influences, its gentle humor and gentler pathos, its ills for which it even has its uses and cures.' "[23]

A belief in these "uses and cures" of evil is not an easy optimism, an escape to a trust in some system of perfect compensation for individuals. The same Basil March who believes in an ultimate order of "loving kindness" also knows that " 'We can never atone for the wrong we do; the heart we have grieved and wounded cannot kindle with pity for us once it is stilled' " (p. 506). But Howells could claim the "utmost seriousness" for a work which yet stays within "the bounds of comedy" because individual suffering ultimately has meaning: "In the moral world as in the material world, Nature takes care of the wrong done; she softly covers it up, transmutes it, turns it even to use and beauty, not for the doer indeed, and usually not for the victim, but for the race."[24]

Within this cosmic plan, in the moral order of the living, there is no place for purely tragic figures. The fact of calamitous death does not make a tragic hero, and the tragic attitude among the

22. William Dean Howells, *Criticism and Fiction and Other Essays*, edited by Clara Marburg Kirk and Rudolf Kirk (New York: New York University Press, 1959), p. 62.

23. Quoted in Cady, *The Realist at War*, p. 137.

24. "Editor's Easy Chair," *Harper's Monthly*, CV (November 1902), 967.

living is a distortion and exaggeration.[25] Howells knew that the "hopeless and helpless" grief such as he himself had known at the death of his daughter "passes over us like a black wave, but it doesn't destroy us."[26] As for the heroic efforts to do good or the saintly desire to live the good life, the realist is compelled to qualify his admiration with an honest report of the humanly mixed motives which prompt the efforts and the mixed results they may produce. Lindau dies "in the cause of disorder" trying to correct an injustice that "could not be reached in his way without greater wrong" (p. 502). Conrad Dryfoos dies "thwarted and disappointed, without even pleasing the ambition that thwarted and disappointed him" (p. 480). Peck, in *Annie Kilburn,* dies without noticeably effecting a change in the economic system through an appeal to justice rather than alms. Dr. Grace Breen is compelled to a life of service by a morbid sense of duty from which she is never able to escape completely even through marriage. The selfless idealism of Dr. Boynton leads him to play the "vampire" (p. 319) with his daughter. In such a world, an intelligent and sympathetic modera-tion, a humorously reductive perception of limitation, an active awareness of the positive dangers of excess in any form, a willingness to accept the modest rewards and the heavy enough responsibilities of the rational life become the highest virtues. These are not the virtues of great romantic heroes or tragic Titans, but of a realist's protagonists who show that men "are more like than unlike one another."[27]

25. Such a view, Howells was aware, had to be achieved over the in-stinctive will, especially among the young, to regard oneself as the center of the universe: "It is hard for the young to understand that the world which seems to stop with their disaster is going on with smooth indifference, and that a little time will carry them so far from any fateful event that when they gather courage to face it they will find it curiously shrunken in perspective. Nothing really stops the world but death, and that only for the dead" (*The Coast of Bohemia* [New York: Harper and Brothers, 1893], p. 278).

26. *Winifred Howells* (n.p., 1891), p. 4.

27. *Criticism and Fiction* (1959), p. 87. Howells's disgust with the forms of romanticism stemming from an insistence on the sacred rights of the indi-vidual personality is conveyed by his expression of admiration for Emerson's "impersonality," maintained during "a period still reeking with gross romantic

In calling his realism "comedy," then, Howells was placing it solidly in the center ground between two common standards of artistic and moral judgment: the conception of tragedy which sees the defeat of an individual's noble aspirations and ideals by forces within himself or his environment as productive of a revolutionary change of character and reverberating effects in society; and an opposite view, which sees the individual as an essentially insignificant creature whose career, whether benevolent or malign, is of little ultimate significance and whose final fate is of importance only to himself. Howells disqualified himself from a controlling tragic attitude by his refusals: he refused to make an absolute judgment about the fact and conditions of an after-life; to believe in a principle of absolute evil in human nature; to believe in the transforming or redemptive power of catastrophic suffering; to accept personal happiness as a legitimate final goal of man's activities. He similarly rejected a purely comic or absurdist attitude by his affirmations: he affirmed a benevolent God who has decreed that man shall make his own moral choices; a morality that is not relativistic and temporal but refers itself to its origin in Christ and its effect in eternity; a moral system by which individual acts of both sinfulness and goodness are absorbed and diffused by the mass of men; and the capacity of man to reason to an understanding of himself, of his relations to others, and of the conditions in which he lives, and thereby to contrive an equitable personal and public polity or at least a rational accommodation to the unreason of those circumstances.

A key to these affirmations, clearly, is reason. In Howells's terms, it is an "ideal" which men through selfishness or passion fail to reach, which through vanity or sentimentality they reject as inadequate to the resolution of their problems, or which, through abstractly admirable motives of personal nobility and public idealism, they actually try to exceed. All of Howells's treatments of these various possibilities give his "comedy" such moral seriousness that

individualism, when so many were straining to retch out the last rinsings of their sick egotism upon their fellows" ("Editor's Study," *Harper's Monthly*, LXXVI [February 1888], 478).

his characters in the third category—Peck, Lindau, Conrad Dryfoos, James Nevil, Rhoda Aldgate, Ansel Denton, James Langbrith, to name some—have often seemed to move his work toward full-fledged tragedy. Yet there is not an instance in the whole body of Howells's work of an unqualified hero, either romantic or tragic. His point is always that tragedy—except that which "comes in the very nature of things," such things as "death . . . and disagreeable and painful disease"[28]—is excessive. The rational ideal *is* available to men if they will only adopt it, and hence that which is called tragedy is more accurately and realistically revealed as needless waste and suffering and inequity. The social and economic conditions which cause suffering cannot, of course, simply be reasoned away by the individual. That being the case, however, they are in effect part of "the very nature of things" which the individual must exercise his reason to endure and adjust to until they are changed by evolutionary process and a more widely practiced altruism.

As an ideal, Howells recognized, reason is both an affirmation of man's power over himself and an admission of human limitation. Mere reason cannot supply answers to certain questions which men have always persisted in asking about the meaning of suffering and death, about the fact and nature of an after-life. The question of whether Howells's resigned acceptance of their ultimate mysteries is a tragic or nontragic attitude is, perhaps, not susceptible of final answer. But the question of Howells's most characteristic attitude toward this limitation of human understanding as it is given dialectical and dramatic expression in his fiction is crucial to an interpretation of his governing view of man's fate and man's responsibilities. Howells always found (even willed himself to find) a sufficient measure of objectivity about the facts of sin and catastrophe and injustice in the world, and of hopefulness, both about the other world and its supernatural operation in this one, to preserve a comic (used simply in broad opposition to tragic) view. Even if this means that he was in fact simply evading the whole question of the meaning of man's existence by remanding it, too, to the

28. *Criticism and Fiction* (1959), p. 62.

area of the unknowable (and if that evasion is itself regarded as a comment on the tragic predicament of man in being forced on a blind pilgrimage through experience), the effect was not to make of Howells an existentialist *manqué*. Its effect was to make him a *realist* in his concern for "the way things are now" and a moralist in his assumptions about the grounds on which human behavior could be evaluated.

One of these assumptions—Howells's repeated assertion that mere personal happiness was not a defensible life-goal nor a permissible standard of moral judgment[29]—had the effect of precluding a frequently applied norm for tragedy, at least for sentimental or romantic tragedy. Since happiness may be a by-product but not the dominating objective of human endeavor and relationships, suffering and death are not equivalent to tragedy; for Howells, in fact, they may simply be assumed to be the normal, the conditions inevitably concomitant upon the pursuit of the right and the good rather than the pleasurable and the gratifying.

To the realist's sense of things, the process of those experiences conventionally described as tragic is from extremity to normalcy, aberration to sanity, irrationality to rationality. What is present to the tragic experience but lacking here is the sense that the gain has justified even the most fantastic cost, that a blinded Oedipus, a blasted Lear, have attained a knowledge of self and the cosmos which exalts the human spirit over the human cost. Howells's realistic protagonists are at most returned to, or elevated to, a sense of their rational capacity to order their lives more effectively; to a recognition of the wrong they have needlessly committed, the harm they have needlessly inflicted on others; and to an acceptance of the necessity of putting aside self in favor of righteousness. These are by no means small gains, but they are inherently limited by man's nature, and their cost need never be paid.

29. See, for example, "Leo Tolstoï," introduction to *Sebastopol* by Count Leo Tolstoï (New York: Harper and Brothers, 1887), p. 5. Reprinted in William Dean Howells, *Prefaces to Contemporaries* (1882–1920), edited by George Arms, William M. Gibson, Frederick C. Marston Jr. (Gainesville: Scholars Facsimiles and Reprints, 1957), pp. 3–10. (This volume hereafter cited as *Prefaces*.)

To describe the process in a realistic novel, therefore, is to offer a normally ironic picture of the discrepancies between man's capabilities and his conduct: he may overvalue himself and his right to happiness or misjudge his duty to a more than human ideal; or he may fail to exercise the human capacities of reason and love and goodness, which would give him peace, if not happiness, and thus bring suffering and even destruction upon himself and others. But in either case the lesson is reductive: the "ideal hero" would be the man who perfectly understood and perfectly expressed in action the truth that "goodness brings not pleasure, not happiness, but it brings peace and rest to the soul and, [sic] lightens all burdens: the trial and the sorrow go on for good and evil alike; only, those who choose the evil have no peace."[30] In a sense, this is a heroism within the grasp of every man, and therefore no heroism at all. It is the condition under which man must live, and it is the realist's business to make him aware of it, to teach him that he may share in both its unspectacular burdens and its unpublicized rewards.

The ideal which is being proposed here as Howells's is something more, however, than sterile rationalism. A man does not reason himself to a performance of such a standard of conduct, though he may reason himself to a consciousness of it. Man is also a creature of love as well as of reason, and this fact makes the practice of goodness and selflessness possible. He is also capable of an objective, self-deflating, perspective-giving humor which enables him to bear the unknowableness toward which human life is directed and the frequently terrible circumstances which he is powerless to control but must suffer along the way.

The goodness and love of which man is capable, and the basis in his own experience of Howells's faith in their reality and force, are nowhere better illustrated than in the lightly fictionalized memorial Howells offered to his father and mother in the "chronicle" New Leaf Mills. These portrayals of Owen and Ann Powell are a memorial tribute, but they are unique only in the special quality of tenderness which Howells imparts to them. Varied degrees of these qualities in various combinations with other attributes may

30. Prefaces, p. 23.

be seen in a whole gallery of Howells's characters: in the Shaker lovers of *The Day of Their Wedding,* in Clementina Claxon of *Ragged Lady,* in Peace Hughes of *The World of Chance,* in Nancy Billings of *The Leatherwood God,* to mention only a few.

The humor which Howells valued was the kind of double vision permissible to realism but not to tragedy. It was far more than mere wit or situational comedy. It was a perspective, a clarity and completeness of vision, which neither ridiculed man nor exalted him, but measured him and his circumstances. It is, moreover, a valuable clue to Howells's instinct toward balance and accommodation that he provided such a definition just at the time of his deepest pessimism about those circumstances. A humorist, he said, in an "Editor's Study" of 1891, "is one who beyond other men sees both sides of every question and is haunted by the consciousness of the absurdity that lurks in all aspects of human affairs."[31] So, it seems hardly necessary to add, does a realist.

## Shadows and Illuminations:
### *The Shadow of a Dream* and *An Imperative Duty*

The problem of terminology becomes especially slippery in application to such works as *The Shadow of a Dream* because it is self-evident that whether this novelette is called tragedy or comedy it is a deeply serious study of tangled human relations which end disastrously for its three main actors. The choice of the designation *comedy,* then, is as important for its implications concerning the totality of Howells's fiction—the direction of his development as a realist and the quality of his achievement—as it is for its use in defining certain emphases in the single work.

The critical approach to *The Shadow of a Dream* as a tragedy goes back to the characterization of it by O. W. Firkins as a "picturesque and romantic tragedy."[32] It has since gone through a

31. *Harper's Monthly,* LXXXIII (June 1891), 153. A fuller discussion of Howells's conception of humor and its importance to the realistic writer is included in Chapter V of this volume.

32. Oscar W. Firkins, *William Dean Howells: A Study* (Cambridge: Harvard University Press, 1924), pp. 135–136.

modern appraisal of its power as a psychological tragedy[33] back to a mixed but basically hostile description of it as "a psychological thriller of considerable intensity" whose use of a "gratuitous accident" allowed Howells "to end the book without having to finish it."[34] A more equivocal ground is taken by the comment that it "wavers somewhat unsuccessfully between romantic tragedy vaguely reminiscent of Shakespeare in tone, and psychological analysis inevitably recalling Hawthorne."[35]

Whatever the varying merits of these evaluations,[36] the general agreement on the romantic and psychological and tragic elements is clear and is not in dispute here. What is being brought into question is the nature of the resultant mix:[37] whether, for example,

33. See Cady, *The Realist at War*, pp. 113–121, and *The Shadow of a Dream* (1962), pp. 1, 12–13.

34. Berthoff, *The Ferment of Realism*, p. 55.

35. Alexander Cowie, *The Rise of the American Novel* (New York: American Book Company, 1948), p. 686. Firkins (*William Dean Howells*, p. 135) also mentions "the Shakespearean title" (see *Hamlet*, Act II, Scene II) and the Hawthornian character of the story (comparing it to *The Blithedale Romance*). Cady (*The Realist at War*, p. 118) names Keats's *Endymion* as the source for the title. Everett Carter (*Howells and the Age of Realism* [Philadelphia: J. B. Lippincott Co., 1954], p. 30) asserts that it is Shakespeare. Given Howells's frequent references in his fiction to Hawthorne, and the description of Arthur Dimmesdale as "the shadow of a dream" (Chapter XII, "The Minister's Vigil"), William G. Gibson's choice of *The Scarlet Letter* carries conviction (*William Dean Howells* [Minneapolis: University of Minnesota Press, 1967], p. 33).

36. Cady's discussions, including his comments on the psychic turbulence of the time immediately before the writing of *Shadow*, are the fullest and most persuasive. But if greater significance is attached to Howells's *winning through* that turbulent time to a personal and artistic control, a somewhat different emphasis on biographical details and artistic results is possible. For example, the early part of *Hazard* was written as a kind of drug against consciousness. But after that, Howells recalled, it "came . . . so easily from the pen that I had the misgiving which I always have of the things which do not cost me great trouble" (*A Hazard of New Fortunes* [1890, reprint edition, New York: E. P. Dutton and Company, Everyman's Library, 1952], p. xxiii). The primary suggestion here is of a regained mastery over the original plan of the novel.

37. *Hazard* had become "the most vital" of his fictions through "quick-

Howells's ironic treatment of both the romantic and the tragic elements has been given sufficient attention; whether the psychology is confined to the victims of the "shadow of a dream"; whether the tragic is not deliberately moved toward the melodramatic and the comic; whether, in short, both the context of its composition and the particulars of its artistry do not allow—and then support— a reading of *The Shadow of a Dream* as another piece of balanced realism in which Howells deliberately refused the tragic mode as he had before and would again.

Firkins's analysis of *The Shadow of a Dream* as a flawed tragedy makes a convenient beginning for this discussion because it is a perceptive and accurate statement of the problems which the novel poses. Firkins distinguishes between what he believed to be Howells's strong "tragic sense" and the "drama" actually conveyed by *The Shadow of a Dream*. The first is confined to "the tone of certain passing allusions or observations" which express "a Shakespearean depth of awe and wonder in the face of the mysteries and pain and guilt that embitter and enlarge our lives"; the "drama" of the novel, on the other hand, by which is designated "in the broad, general sense . . . the interaction of human beings by speech and conduct," Firkins believes, "had its sources in lighter phases of . . . [Howells's] being." The reasons, then, for the novel's falling below the standard of tragic greatness are "precise": the major characters are not given adequate tragic stature; the action is not sufficiently weighty, and its impact is softened by being "conveyed to us too uniformly by the circuit of the Marches"; the Marches are allowed to express feelings contradictory to and unworthy of their better natures and their conduct; finally, the dra-

---

ened interest" in life "at a moment of great psychological import" and the source of that vitality which Howells mentions was a "strong emotioning in the direction of the humaner economics" (p. xxii). There is little in *Shadow*, on the other hand, to parallel his own recent experience, and the complete absence of "economics," the shift from a New York locale and use of a *younger* Basil March, the controlled economy of the novelette form in contrast to the looseness of *Hazard*—all of these factors may be taken to suggest a quite different motivating impulse but a continuing and tested control of the creative flow that produced the two novels in the same year.

matic effect is muffled by excessive "analysis and commentary."[38] What makes these comments especially useful is that they are, indeed, "precise" in identifying the functioning of the novel's interrelated elements.

Yet all that is required to see these conditions as virtues rather than defects is an approach to the novel as conscious and emotionally poised realism. From that point of view the very conditions that Firkins takes exception to function to bring the whole under the control of an ordering art. That art implicitly advocates an acceptance of the broad sweep of experience which must go on for the living, and it testifies to man's potential power to modify through reason and love and goodness the sometimes devastating particulars of that experience.

It is for the purposes of control that Howells may be understood to have used the "circuit of the Marches." They function as a filtering device, a way of modifying the emotional impact of the persons most directly involved in the dominant action, of providing a commentary deflationary of the heroics latent in that action and the actors' views of their own motives and conduct, and of giving "distancing" to the whole—the sequence of disastrous events and the perfervid emotional relationships which were in large measure their cause.

Distancing is a device which can be used to treat a variety of materials and to indicate a variety of perspectives. Howells had long before experimented with it when he had little else but an attitude to use as an entree into fiction. One of the diversionary incidents of *Their Wedding Journey* had been a collision of steamboats which had caused a man to be badly scalded. When Basil had time to reflect on the experience, he did so "with a certain luxurious compassion" that made the poor wretch seem "of another order of human beings, as the calamitous always seem to the happy, and Basil's pity was quite an abstraction." Howells was working here toward a point of view which would simultaneously record what one "ought" to feel (the romantic response: exaggerated horror, excessive sympathy), what a completely detached observer would register (objective no-

38. Firkins, *William Dean Howells*, pp. 135–136.

tation of "mortal anguish," self-satisfaction at not being the victim), and, by implication, what the person of normal sensitivity and perception does feel (a complex modification of all these).[39] Howells would use the device again in such a novel as *An Open-Eyed Conspiracy* both to counteract the sentimental romanticism of the love affair between Julia Gage and Gerald Kendricks and to puncture the complacent superiority of the supposedly detached Basil March himself.

Here, in *The Shadow of a Dream*, Basil and Isabel March are not the intimates of any of the dramatic principals; their involvement in the catastrophic events is sporadic and their roles variously advisory, observational, and peripherally functional (Mrs. March is helpful in the funeral arrangements for Faulkner; March chaperones Hermia Faulkner on a train trip from Boston to the midwest). Therefore, their limited responses to the individual events and the ultimate "interpretation" by which they accommodate the total experience to the business of going about their own lives provides the only real emotional gauge for the reader.

March is brought into relation with the principals when he discovers that a friendly acquaintance of his youth in the midwest, Douglas Faulkner, is being treated by his friend, Dr. Wingate, for heart trouble and a general nervous condition, and has expressed a wish to renew the acquaintance. March, accompanied by his wife, journeys from Boston to Swampscott for the duty call. They find an obviously dying man in the care of his wife Hermia, and the friend who had first introduced them, the Reverend James Nevil, whom March had also met at Faulkner's in the past. The anomalous nature of the "three-cornered household" strikes the Marches immediately and is the subject of discussion during their first privacy. It is not a sexual liaison, nor even strikingly unusual—in fact, they agree, "It was the innocence of our life that made it so common"—but "It was undignified and silly and mischievous" (p. 35). Though not fully recognized as yet, the consequences of the arrangement are already more serious. The Marches are quick to perceive the fact,

39. *Their Wedding Journey*, edited by John K. Reeves (Bloomington, Indiana: Indiana University Press, 1968), pp. 49–50.

which Nevil and Hermia have been living with for the past six months, that Faulkner is subject to intermittent but intense feelings of repulsion from his entirely devoted wife which express themselves in a "deadly look" (p. 34).

It is out of this foreboding context that the events of Part One of this stripped-down three-part novelette rapidly develop to the climax of Faulkner's fatal seizure. And it is an early instance of Howells's method of controlling the emotional tone to have it come with almost the effect of an anti-climax. Howells manages this effect by engaging March in a series of contretemps which, though they originate in the pervading atmosphere of anxiety and gloom caused by Faulkner's physical and mental instability, generate a frenetic activity and misdirected emotionalism which becomes comically absurd and whose very excess robs the culminating actuality of Faulkner's death of much of its normally legitimate dignity. The sequence begins after March is released by the arrival of Dr. Wingate from a conversation with Faulkner about terrible dreams. The conversation took place in a picturesque garden conducive to such talks, and there Faulkner obviously indulged his own emotions by comparing the flower beds to graves and by "magniloquent" pronouncements on its "melancholy," "desolation," "crazy charm and dying beauty" (p. 44). March now is glad to join his wife and the others on the beach, but when Hermia sees March without her husband, in her alarm she immediately imperils life and limb in clambering over the rocks to reach him. His waving her back is ineffectual, and when she discovers there was no need for haste, she remarks, " 'Oh, then, I'll go at once' " (p. 52).

Now Mrs. March and Nevil, who were farther away, repeat the mistake, with such comic effect that Mrs. Faulkner laughs hysterically, then cries, then dashes off to join her husband with the effect of causing Nevil and Mrs. March to redouble their efforts. When, finally, Mrs. March and Nevil are reassured that there is no crisis, the three walk back to the cottage, and in the course of the conversation make known to each other their awareness of Faulkner's aberration. Nevil reveals an additional irony in the fact that Faulkner's heart condition may have been developed by selfless nursing of Hermia during a long illness.

Now it is Mrs. March who would indulge in heroics and sentiment by exclaiming, " 'Ah! . . . how cruel life is! But how beautiful, how grand!' " (p. 56) March quickly exposes the exaggerated response (realistically, he is also salving his own "personal grievance" [p. 53] resulting from the confusion caused by his appearance at the beach) by turning his wife's earlier jaundiced appraisal of Faulkner back upon her: " 'A nature . . . that might impress the casual observer as a mere sop of sentiment, is often capable of that sort of devotion' " (p. 56). In a more serious, but equally reductive reflection, when Nevil comments on his dread of seeing once more Faulkner's aversion to Hermia and her bewilderment at it, March can pity him but only as "the victim of a situation which he ought never to have witnessed, which should have been known only to the two doomed necessarily to suffer it" (p. 57). The point of the reflection is not really to excuse Nevil as "victim": this is a development of the Marches' view of "the evil of that disgusting three-cornered domestic arrangement" (p. 57) for which ultimately all three are responsible. Nevil had earlier admitted that his year in Europe as the guest of Faulkner and his continuing stay with them was an evasion of other "duties, interests, claims" which were his "proper work." His concluding outburst—" 'And yet I can't tear myself away from him—from them' " (p. 42)—suggests a giving in to desire as much as an inability to reject the claims of friendship. Mrs. March later accuses all three of being "weak" and "sentimental" and asserts that Hermia " 'ought to have put a stop to it' " (p. 69).

Such insights into the deeper, complex motivations beneath the externally ideal relationships of selfless love, perfect friendship, and heroic self-sacrifice make the inadequacy of Mrs. March's retrospective attempt to attribute the situation to "Fate, in the old Greek sense" (p. 92) apparent. When, for instance, the trio return to the arbor just in time to see Faulkner die, that death comes as merely another instance of "heart-breaking comedy" (p. 31) which the Marches are obliged to witness. For the chief actors, in this melodramatic circumstance, the effects are, of course, "heart-breaking." The larger view, however, sees what the principals cannot or will not see: the degree of their own responsibility for at least the complication of their circumstances; sees how easily even genuinely serious circumstances and legitimate emotions can lead fallible and inept mortals into actions and statements which reveal them as helplessly absurd; and sees from later events in the novel that what from one point of view is noble and heroic is from another irrational; and never loses sight of the mixed nature of human experience in which a "grotesque and squalid element is . . . apt to mar a heroic situation, in order apparently to keep human nature modest" (p. 94).

The death of the man whom all the observers, including Dr. Wingate, agree was a "sentimental idealist . . . [who] tried to live the rather high-strung literature that he might have written" (p. 63), whose "silly, romantic clinging to sentiment" was responsible if not for the dream itself, "for the occasion of his dream" (p. 92) of an illicit relationship between his wife and Nevil, seems at first to have freed them to prove its falsity. Six months later, Nevil's engagement to one of his Kansas parishioners is announced. But this announcement, as relayed to the Marches by Hermia's letter, reveals that there are still many ambiguities remaining. Faulkner's mother is "reconciling" herself to losing one who has been like a son, and Nevil's ecstasies are tempered by the hint that if the old relationship were possible he would not be getting married (p. 71). There quickly follows his rejection by the girl and his collapsing return to Mrs. Faulkner and Hermia. Instead of being "tragically permanent" his situation proves a "transitory phase" (p. 77), and, following a year in Europe, Nevil returns to become engaged to Hermia. Now Hermia's conscience takes control, and she is compelled to come to Boston to learn from Dr. Wingate whether Faulkner's "dream" was a belief that she meant him physical harm.[40] Overwhelmed now to

40. This is a reversal of her original resolve to pry no further into the mystery of her husband's aversion to her if Dr. Wingate can assure her that the decision would best serve her husband's memory. Concerning the nature of that original decision, opinion is unanimous if not identical: March wishes that in her interest Hermia "had been a little less heroic"; Dr. Wingate can only characterize it in untypical superlatives such as "super-human" (p. 67); and Mrs. March comes to see the reversal as Hermia's "punishment" resulting from "trying to bear more than she could. For trying not to know what she must know" (p. 82).

learn that the dream involved jealousy of her relation with Nevil, she returns home, deciding on the way to let him be the final judge of whether it is now possible for them to marry. His decision is that they must part. March, who has chaperoned Hermia, apparently persuades Nevil to reconsider, but as Nevil leaves March's train, he is crushed between it and a stone archway.

The bare recital of a story involving so much suffering and death does not suggest its actual effect on the reader. That effect is curiously muted and softened; the glare of disaster is dimmed by a curtain of speculation about character and motivation woven by the Marches. The point is not merely that Howells did not choose to have one of the fated triangle tell the story. In using Basil as his narrator, and in having much of the story "philosophized" through Basil's conversations with Isabel, Howells deliberately made it possible to adopt a tone at variance with the tragic force of the events themselves.

For one of the chief characteristics of these familiar personages from the earliest days of their marriage (*Their Wedding Journey*) was the flow of their sometimes witty, sometimes trenchant, sometimes fatuous talk, which only rarely proceeded from involvement with experience and characteristically took its tone from their roles as detached observers and commentators on it. This, at any rate, is a role which March insists upon now, and it is one of his most frequent functions to deflate the swollen romantic or tragic sentiments in which the other characters tend to indulge themselves.[41] This is not to suggest that March is merely light or irresponsible: he is a thoroughly intelligent and sensitive commentator on the drama which plays itself out before his interested gaze. Basil's interest, however, is that of a man who finds in his observation of life materials for philosophizing or picturesque representations.

The Basil March of *The Shadow of a Dream* is still an insurance

---

41. On one occasion, Basil punctures a formulation of Hermia and Nevil's involvement as "an affair of the soul" of the kind ladies demanded from popular novelists. He says, " 'It's a plain, earthly affair, for this life, for this trip and train only' " (p. 121). Given the circumstances of Nevil's death, the remark would also seem to show Howells engaging in ironic foreshadowing and providing an anticipatory gloss.

man in Boston whose literary tendencies have not yet found even modified expressions in his writing for *Every Other Week*. Though *A Hazard of New Fortunes* was written first, it does not seem logical to assert that the New York Basil, "newly sensitive and responsive to life, was in the foreground of Howells's consideration"[42] in the writing of *The Shadow of a Dream*. There is a beginning of Basil's education in complicity in *The Shadow of a Dream,* but when he first arrives in New York that lesson is not yet a part of his *own* experience. Having given a coin to a man feeding on garbage heaps, he tells his wife that the case is surely an exceptional one and their concern is not to change the conditions which make for such degradation but to "go to the theatre and forget them." Much later, he wanders the East Side taking impressions of the squalor and the poverty, a "man who had always been too self-enwrapped to perceive the chaos to which individual selfishness must always lead." He is capable of "a vague discomfort," but his dominant impression is "a sense of the neglected opportunities of painters in that locality."[43]

It would have been easily possible to make the narrator of *The Shadow of a Dream* the initiated Basil March who had himself risked his livelihood for principle and who had come to all sorts of new knowledge and awareness by his experiences in the great city, if Howells had been intent on providing the kind of interpreter who would establish the tone proper to a profound psychological tragedy. He actually chose the younger Basil, who would consciously think of himself as mere observer of the events and dissecter of the variously true and false emotions, the variously good and reprehensible motives which produced them. Since, however, Basil, in the process, *is* to some degree educated in complicity, the effect is not to satirize him as lacking in the compassion to feel the tragic import of the events, but implicitly to propose a realistic standard which Basil actually finds exemplified in Dr. Wingate: "a sympathy for human suffering unclouded by sentiment, and a knowledge of human nature at once vast and accurate" (pp. 24–25). This, of

42. Cady, *The Realist at War,* p. 114.
43. *A Hazard of New Fortunes* (1952), pp. 73, 200.

course, is a partial standard: love must be an element in such relationships as March and Dr. Wingate merely observe.

It is Basil's function, therefore, to show the essentially romanticistic nature of that drama, to show that its tragedy is in large measure
self-induced, the product of various attitudes struck by the players.
The more that March is forced to become entangled in Hermia's
affairs, the greater is his sense of excess. By the original connection
of a really slight past relationship with Faulkner, he is forced to
become a party to matters which should have remained inviolate
between husband and wife. In witnessing them, he is consistently
forced to an awareness of their hysterical character, even when they
are most serious, and of their potential and often actual grotesqueness and ludicrousness.

The reaction to Basil's appearance at the beach, just prior to
Faulkner's death, was merely a minor and primarily comic instance
of the potential of unreason which is nurtured by the characters'
lack of self-perspective. When Basil finds himself journeying west as
chaperon to the tormented Hermia, he is filled with "a keen sense
of preposterousness" at the "fantastic exaggeration of the whole
business," which is itself a "gossamer nothing, which might perhaps
accountably involve the lives of those concerned through a morbid
conscience" (p. 95) but which is actually none of his affair. Just
prior to their arrival at their destination, it is apparent to him that
Hermia has arrived at some decision (though she does not communi-
cate it to him) that gives her relief and should, logically, release him
from any further function. She insists, however, that he stay with
her and Faulkner's mother, and the latter immediately begins to
treat Basil with an intimacy which she must have known had no
basis in his relationship with her dead son. It is she who informs
Basil that Hermia has gained relief from her intense emotional tur-
moil by deciding simply that, after Nevil has been informed of
Faulkner's jealous dream, he must decide whether they will marry.
Basil finds himself histrionically putting a "trick of surprise" (p. 111)
into his reaction to this disclosure of the dream. Moreover, he dis-
cerns her appreciation of "the literary quality of the situation" and
suspects that she is "rather proud of a passage in her family life

which was so like a passage of romance" (p. 112). On this occasion, however, he is able to insist that his relationship to the affair does not qualify him to be the intermediary who should inform Nevil of Faulkner's dream.

But for a final time mere accident forces him into a more active role. He has bid Mrs. Faulkner good-bye and is about to leave without even seeing Hermia when he becomes the involuntary witness of a passionate scene of renunciation between her and Nevil. He now offers to detour on his way to the depot and take the distraught Nevil home in his carriage. In developing the following action, which comes to a climax with Nevil's death, Howells skillfully plays on a variety of ironies, not the least of which is the accidental pointlessness of that death, with the clear effect of reducing the tragedy to a more rational measurement by the exercise of common sense and the perception of the distortions of relationships, facts, and judgments induced by even the noblest of passions.

They repair to Nevil's church study, "a kind of Protestant confessional," where March quickly becomes aware of its ironic inappropriateness. March assumes the unwanted role of priestly confessor and spiritual and moral preceptor, convinced that the confessions Nevil must have heard there "stain and blacken the facts of his own experience, and prevent him from seeing them aright" (p. 126). In attempting to counteract Nevil's "morbid introspection . . . that never ends in anything but self-conviction" (p. 127), March is himself drawn into arguments which he immediately recognizes as embodying "the romantic view . . . celebrated in many novels as something peculiarly fine and noble and high, something heroic in the silently suffering lover" (p. 129).[44] Recovering himself,

44. Earlier, as the observer of the parting of Hermia and Nevil, March was moved to feel "that there could be only one good in the world, and that was the happiness of that woman" (p. 123). That March succumbs on occasion to the intensities of the moment is part of Howells's realism. Howells is not arguing that the passions are not real and important; he certainly has no intention of depicting March as an absolutely detached and impossibly rational man who "interprets" the meaning of the novel for a romantically deluded reader. March's final view of the "tragedy" gains weight by being *achieved* rather than ready-made. It is this fact which makes Cady's comment

he attacks Nevil's "raving" (p. 130) as an "infernal juggle of the morbid conscience" (p. 131) and apparently, at least temporarily, convinces him that the dual grounds of a clear conscience and responsibility to Hermia should permit their marriage. Were it treated as anything other than merely a gratuitous irony, Nevil's death, under these circumstances, would be gross melodrama. As it stands, even if it is interpreted as an indication of Howells's view that the marriage could never take place, that is not the same as saying that Howells was proposing that the tragic view of the predicament which would prevent their marriage was the appropriate one. Howells privately admitted that he had at first "meant to have him marry Hermia, but he convinced me, as he wormed it out, that this was not possible." But the reason was that "Nevil was a helpless prisoner of his traditions."[45] It was precisely those traditions which, in the absence of any proof of guilt, yet made him so merely "afraid" (p. 131) of being guilty that he would have been unable to act rationally.

Also acting as a tonal control of the catastrophic events and emotional intensity generated by them is another significant pattern of reference and imagery operating throughout the novel. From a general insistence on his function as reporter, March slips into a more specific characterization of himself and his wife as spectators of a dramatic production, who are sometimes embarrassed by the overwrought character of the performance. When Hermia returns to Boston for the confrontation with Dr. Wingate, she insists on the Marches' presence as though it were a scene which could only be played before the same audience which had witnessed her husband's death. March feels "from the first an odious quality in the part . . . [they] had been obliged to bear" (p. 87) and reflects in charitable extenuation: "In some of the most intimate affairs and sentiments, in which women are conventionally supposed to play a veiled and hidden part, they really have an overt, almost a public role, which nature no doubt fits them to sustain, without violence to their

---

that Basil and Isabel are merely "Good Victorians" defending civilization open to demurral (Cady, The Realist at War, p. 119).

45. Letters, II, 11.

modesty, without touching susceptibilities that in men would be intolerably wounded" (p. 88).

It has already been noted that March found a histrionic note in Mrs. Faulkner's presentation of her request to him to act as intermediary and found himself giving the anticipated responses to her cues. And that request had suggested to March a retrospective question whether Hermia might have been capable of a kind of innocent duplicity in her sudden change of mood at the end of their journey: "Could that exquisite creature, in that electrical moment of relief from her trouble have foreseen my usefulness by the same flash that showed her the simple duty she had in the matter?" (p. 116). At dinner on the previous evening, March had suspected Hermia of costuming herself as a way of communicating to him the decision she had reached but not yet announced.[46] When he witnesses "the tragedy of . . . renunciation," his thought is that "The play suddenly ended" (p. 123), and when he is thrown together with Nevil outside the house, "It was if we had both just come out of the theatre, and actor and spectator had met on the same footing of the common-place world of reality" (p. 124). The obvious explanation is that these are appropriate terms of reference to the "dramatic" action of the novel. But the references seem also a pointed comment on the quality of much of the action, its tendency to become melodramatic or self-deflating because of the fevered emotionalism of its actors, their half-open or half-concealed pleasure in assuming postures and attitudes derived from sentimental and romantic literature and the popular imagination.

The final groping of the Marches to put the events into a larger pattern of meaning suggests to them the idea which Howells began

46. If this was intended, it was in a language too subtle for Basil's understanding. But it is characteristic of Howells's reductive realism, his constant reminder that mere mortals cannot sustain for long the tragic or heroic attitude. March is so struck by Hermia's youth and loveliness, her womanliness, that he cannot prevent himself from wondering if Nevil ever had this "unruly sense of her" and feeling something "perversely comic" mixed with his remorse at this thought. Shortly before this, impressed by the luxury of the Faulkner home, he had wondered "how much the invitation of such luxury might tempt a man fagged in heart and mind," as Nevil was (p. 103).

by calling "complicity" in *The Minister's Charge* and here characterizes as "the necessary solidarity of human affairs from the beginning to the end, in which no one can do or be anything to himself alone" (p. 62). The alternatives to believing in some such ultimate balancing—that is, negatively all men, not merely the immediately guilty, are responsible for the sin and suffering in the world; but, positively, no physical or spiritual suffering "is lost or wasted, but is suffered to the good of someone, or of all" (p. 40)—is to accept mere meaninglessness and chaos or to prefer a cruel and unjust providence to none at all. It is to this formulation that Howells has March recur at the very end of the novel in attempting, now that Hermia is also dead, a summary evaluation. Nevil's death, "violent and purely accidental," was a "most vague and inconclusive catastrophe" (p. 113) which did nothing to solve the theoretical problem. Hermia had inevitably regarded it as a judgment and had died of a "broken heart"—actually, of course, of the prolonged physical and emotional strain she had suffered in her marriage and subsequent engagement—and that too was an ending and not an answer. But the Marches do conclude that the dream would always have had the power to prevent or to spoil their marriage and can, therefore, come to "regard their death without regret," in the faith that "all suffering is to some end unknown to the sufferer or the witnesses, and no anguish is wasted" (pp. 133–134).

Howells, it should be emphasized in conclusion, is always outside of his fictional characters. He is as capable of noting the Marches' foibles as he is of detecting the characteristic emotionalism of the three characters who are destroyed. Their foibles do not disqualify the Marches, however, from representing something close to Howells's own view, any more than the essential sincerity of the other characters and the actuality of the effect of the dream gives them an emotional impact beyond the pathetic. Though he has March point out Nevil's misapplication of the formulation in a particular case, Howells had no quarrel with the description of man's role as "submission, renunciation, abnegation, here below" (p. 130). If there is a tragic sense in Howells, it was certainly in the novels of this period that it found expression.

Those novels may also be read, however, as a willed denial of ultimate tragedy, and something like "sense of limitation" would more accurately describe their quality. It could even be said that the affirmative attitude being proposed here as a foundation stone of Howells's fiction approached at this point in his career the kind of "tragic sense" which has been found in Emerson—"a not unconscious *answer* to his experience of life, rather than an inference from it," "an act of faith, forced on him by . . . 'the ghastly reality of things.' " What is admittedly being overstated as a "tragic sense" by this interpreter of Emerson was really a "tension of faith and experience" that determined "the quality of his affirmation."[47] A similar tension is certainly part of Howells's realism, and is perhaps most clearly evident as forced upon him, for all the reasons that Cady and others have demonstrated, in the two novels of 1890. But the stabilizing of that increased tension into the taut equilibrium which Howells effected in *The Shadow of a Dream* made it a significant factor in all the subsequent fiction. It finds expression, for example, in carefully controlled and varying modulated ironies in apparently "idyllic" fictions like *The Vacation of the Kelwyns* as well as in the most profound novels of Howells's later career, *The Landlord at Lion's Head* and *The Son of Royal Langbrith*.

*An Imperative Duty*, the second of the very brief novels with which Howells followed the broad complexity of *A Hazard of New Fortunes*, is even more compact than *The Shadow of a Dream* and, structurally, more simple. This tale did not invite a division into parts with the aim of producing an intensified focus on each major character in turn. The single narrative line of this story concerns

47. Stephen E. Whicher, "Emerson's Tragic Sense," in *Interpretations of American Literature*, edited by Charles Feidelson Jr. and Paul Brodtkorb Jr. (New York: Oxford University Press, 1959), p. 158. This essay originally appeared in *The American Scholar*, XXII (Summer 1953), 285–292. A few months before the *Shadow of a Dream* began to appear in *Harper's Monthly*, Howells commented on Edward Emerson's *Emerson in Concord* in terms that emphasize his own will to faith and optimism. He responded to the book's report of Emerson's "sense of a tranquil and joyous religion, of a steadfast faith in good as the only reality, and in life as necessarily continuous from the implications of all experience" ("Editor's Study," *Harper's Monthly*, LXXIX [August 1889], 478).

the "imperative duty" which is passed from Mrs. Meredith to her niece, Rhoda Aldgate, when, after years of secrecy, she informs Rhoda of her Negro ancestry.[48] It then becomes Rhoda's duty to determine how such knowledge shall affect her future, specifically and immediately the question of her marriage with the already declared Mr. Bloomingdale and quickly thereafter with Dr. Edward Olney. Even the occasional reader of Howells will correctly suspect that Rhoda's first hysterical reaction, which sends her on a nightmarish visit to the Negro district of Boston and then makes her resolve to go to New Orleans to find her octaroon mother's people and "try to educate them, and elevate them,"[49] is not permitted to determine her fate. Instead, after a few months of sheltering with the conveniently available Clara Kingsbury Atherton, she is married to Olney and dispatched to Italy.

As Howells himself said of one of his own commentaries, "this outline of the story gives no just sense of its quality,"[50] and, of course, it is the problem of defining the "quality" of *An Imperative Duty* that is crucial. The treatment of the general problem of racial prejudice and a specific instance of miscegenation within the brief scope of one hundred or fewer pages would suggest that the result must be either the most lurid kind of melodrama or a vastly oversimplified exemplum. In Howells's own terms, "the first germinal impulse . . . recognizes the essential simplicity or complexity of the motive" of a fictional work, and "what contains the germ of much conditioning or characterization belongs to the novel."[51] By this

48. It has been suggested that Howells named the book from "its minor issue of morbid conscientiousness" rather than from the major problems of racial segregation and miscegenation (Cady, *The Realist at War*, p. 156). The evidence of the novel itself and of Howells's general fictional practice argues that the title is a valid indication of Howells's own sense of the relative weight of these elements in his fictional compound; the novel views the racial issue as the concrete (and especially harrowing) but subordinate form in which the problem of "dutiolatry" poses itself.

49. Cady, editor, *The Shadow of a Dream and An Imperative Duty*, p. 229.

50. *Heroines of Fiction*, 2 vols. (New York: Harper and Brothers, 1901), I, 52.

51. *Literature and Life* (New York: Harper and Brothers, 1902), p. 119.

standard, then, it hardly seems appropriate to approach *An Impera-tive Duty* as a profound psychological study of racial and sexual relations. Equally, the lack of "conditioning" (i.e., the accumulation of social detail and significant environmental pressures) and "char-acterization" (i.e., the study of the protagonists in a representative *variety* of social, ethical, and psychological contexts) disqualifies the novelette as an examination in depth of a festering social condition or as an individual tragedy of racial injustice. On the other hand, the solution which sends the married couple off to Italy and thus merely begs the larger social issue, and Howells's pointed collapsing of the potentially sensational implications of the situation to the dimensions and tone of the *opera bouffe* effectively save the novel-ette from the damaging charges of being nothing more than a pro-grammatic moral fable or a superficial exploitation of social and sexual taboos.

After such denials, the obvious question is whether there is any-thing left for serious attention and intelligent enjoyment, and the equally obvious answer is that it has been for the purpose of establishing some acceptable grounds for both that these demurrers have been proposed first. *An Imperative Duty* is one of several of Howells's novels which have the appearance of problem novels but which have not fulfilled the expectations raised by that initial im-pression. It is hard to imagine a novel which is not in some way a "problem" novel, if the dictionary sense of the term—"presenting a problem of human conduct or social relationships"—is taken; but as applied to the drama, a more specific and limiting meaning is normally understood: "A problem play invites attention to a socio-logical problem of some sort. . . . A problem play may or may not be tragic or comic, but the emphasis is on the social problem rather than on the destiny of particular characters."[52]

In this sense, Howells's conscious determination to deal with human experiences, rather than to propose solutions for human problems, precluded the writing of problem novels. *An Imperative Duty* is no exception, though it clearly attacks the cruelty and un-

52. Sylvan Barnet, Morton Berman, and William Burton, *A Dictionary of Literary Terms* (Boston: Little, Brown and Company, 1960), p. 32.

reason of racial segregation and is just as clearly in favor of the particular instance of miscegenation which it describes. What it deals with is "the destiny of its particular characters," and its manner of doing so invites its easy dismissal with yet another familiar term: *comedy of manners*. Again, a borrowing from a discussion of drama will show the inadequacy of that term and, what is more important, help to define the real virtues of the attitude and the method of expressing and controlling it which Howells adopted in *An Imperative Duty*.

The discussion which offers assistance is Joseph Wood Krutch's distinction between the comedy of manners and high comedy.[53] The problem of terminology was created by the persistent assumption that superficiality, witty badinage, and indecent repartee unrelated to character or serious social purpose, entertaining but merely frivolous or reprehensible characters were not only the distinguishing characteristics of all comedies of manners, but were in fact their entire substance, and that such plays had nothing whatever to do with the serious and important aspects of human conduct and with significant ideas. Moreover, the "higher" a comedy became, the conventional assumption maintained, the more artificial and less "real" it became, the more its people became impossibly witty and sexually daring and less tied to the actualities of the known experience of its audiences. Krutch believed that a certain kind of comedy was "high," not merely because it employed the restricted setting of the drawing room, introduced characters who were witty and intelligent enough to understand themselves and their problems and to comment on them, and divorced its characters from the normal economic and social conditioning, but because it dealt with fundamental and universal aspects of human nature in basic seriousness; therefore, a new term seemed necessary to describe it. Krutch chose *abstract comedy* and offered as a measurement of the "abstraction" which was attained the degree to which the comedy was purged of sentimentality and merely conventional or fashionable morality.

53. The following discussion of abstract comedy is based on J. W. Krutch, *American Drama Since 1918*, revised edition (New York: Random House, 1939), pp. 160–163.

A classic example of such comedy in American drama is S. N. Behrman's *The Second Man,* in which the hero, Clark Storey, a self-acknowledged second-rate writer determined to enjoy the civilized pleasures of good food, wine, talk, and sex supplied by the money and person of his mistress or any other congenial source, preserves the only integrity he has by resisting the romantic and sentimental appeal of a beautiful young girl to marry for love and art. Such a definition of integrity is established by acceptance of honest and humorous self-appraisal, charm and wit, a rejection of cynicism for a kind of gallant gaiety, and a denial of romantic love, sentimental idealism, and individual importance as the positive and negative virtues of an imperfect world. Such high comedy then makes that imperfect world "perfect." Such people as Storey and his mistress, Kendall Frayne, freed from economic considerations, from the arbitrary demands of sentiment and conventional morality by friendship, sexual compatibility, and intelligence, can solve their own problems in a way which gives complete emotional and intellectual satisfaction to themselves. They are "abstracted," not merely because they are idealizations of those qualities established as admirable by the context of the play itself, but because in the world of the play they are perfectly free to express those virtues and do so with complete self-consistency.

No novel of Howells matches these conditions of abstract comedy, but *An Imperative Duty* adopts a sufficient number of similar assumptions to be called by analogy an example of abstract realism. The most important and evident difference between this purely comic view and that of Howells is that while he time and time again challenged sentimental or merely unexamined morality, he never completely discarded the traditional assumptions; he wanted to get back to them rather than to rewrite the rule book. His realism, therefore, proposes no radical moral reconstitution, but a radical return to commonsense and good will in the application of recognized standards for human behavior.

The primary abstraction which Howells introduces in *An Imperative Duty,* as has already been suggested, comes from the refusal to treat the dual question of racial prejudice and miscegenation as a sociological problem.[54] The dramatic focus is kept on Rhoda Aldgate's individual dilemma in dealing with the knowledge of her ancestry in relation to the question of marriage, and even that is treated in largely abstract or theoretical terms. Rhoda's "Negro-ness" is actual, but it is not real: it has played no part in her life or consciousness. In spite of her emotional attempt to establish her identity with the Negroes in the church which she attends and her later attempt to intellectualize the relationship on the basis of responsibility, it is clear that she cannot will herself to be black nor do circumstances force her to any further attempt. In the same context, the knowledge of the fact of her ancestry produces its effect on Olney, and he experiences a "profound and pervasive" disgust. But this is merely an "impulse," a kind of conditioned reflex which momentarily overcomes his previously untested open-mindedness and which he immediately masters "with an abiding compassion and a sort of tender indignation" (p. 165). After these reactions, the condition represents an emotional problem for Rhoda and a problem of social management in her marriage (which Olney offers to solve by proclaiming the truth to Mrs. Atherton and to anyone else). The effect of this treatment is to generalize it to the status of any problem of social difference, to abstract it from the realm of a tragic social condition to a merely theoretical obstacle to married love and social ease.

This is not to dismiss the novel as merely superficial, to condemn it for failing to be a scathing protest against racial prejudice. *An Imperative Duty* is an indictment of the stupidity which governs racial relations, but that indictment is formulated in its own terms, which recognize their inadequacy as a corrective program. Neither Olney nor Howells could prescribe for the general social ill, but in the world of this kind of novel Olney could be both "real" and an almost idealized embodiment of rationality and compassion. He could refuse

54. The special circumstances of Rhoda's problem were what made it susceptible of abstraction. There is no intention to argue here that all of Howells's fiction should be read in these terms. Some pressures, in some lives —the kind of economic circumstances Howells had been treating in the other novels of this period, for example—were too strong and pervasive for such treatment.

to accept as effectively operative the confusions out of which Rhoda "had dramatized his instant renunciation of her when he knew the fatal truth." He could reduce such "tragedy" to "ruin" to "be reconstructed, if at all, upon an octave much below the operatic pitch" where it would have to "be treated in no lurid twilight gloom, but in plain, simple, matter-of-fact noonday" (p. 227).

Olney thus performs a comic but entirely serious function in cutting through the inconsistencies and illogicalities of conventionally romantic or heroic or "conscientious" attitudes to a more sensible idealism. Olney's conceptions of love and honor and responsibility and even propriety are not iconoclastic, but he differs from the average individual in keeping those conceptions tied to the actualities of experience and circumstance and in acting on that basis. The results of their novelistic representation, of this kind of realism, have their own kind of value, which is analogous to that of abstract comedy:

Comedy first deflates man's aspirations and pretensions, accepting the inevitable failure of his attempt to live by his passions or up to his enthusiasms. But when it has done this, it demonstrates what is still left to him—his intelligence, his wit, his tolerance, and his grace—and then, finally, it imagines with what charm he could live if he were freed, not merely from the stern necessities of the struggle for physical existence, but also from the perverse and unexpected quixoticisms of his heart.[55]

The "deflation" which occurs in a novel by Howells is not as total as that produced by this pure comic spirit, nor are his major characters "so triple plated with the armor of comic intelligence"[56] that they are freed entirely from human limitation. But a character like Olney is sufficiently endowed with reason, humor, and his own kind of grace to illustrate that there is a potential world—not yet, to be sure, a reality—in which such qualities would be the norm. And since love and marriage rather than a mutually agreeable sexual liaison is still the approved male-female relationship, the "quixoticisms of the heart" are not eliminated. But they should have their

55. Krutch, p. 190.
56. *Ibid.*, p. 189.

origin in honest respect rather than blind chivalry, in reasoned
rather than romantic idealism, in character rather than mere temperament, a point which Howells had realistically documented in *April
Hopes*.

Thus Olney's "solution" to the particular problem with which he
is faced is to marry Rhoda and take her off to Italy. It offers no
hope that the endemic disease of racial prejudice will be cured by a
universal adoption of a similar compassionate rationality or by an
infusion of indignant tenderness and love into the social body. On
the other hand, neither is it an evasion: it has the effect of forcing
a responsive reader to a re-examination of his merely conventional or
fashionable attitudes toward the specific and general situations, and
that was as far as Howells would go toward accepting a responsibility
of the novelist to grapple with human problems. It is precisely what
may be called Olney's grace under pressure that subjected Howells
to the accusation of evasion of the social question; and if the novel
were read in the present-day atmosphere of antiintellectual activ-
ism and emotional absolutism, mere accusation would surely
become outright excoriation. Olney's refusal to accept a specific individual guilt for the social condition when even anguished self-
accusal can effect no change, and his refusal to accept Rhoda's
determination to make herself miserable as a solution either to the
racial problem or to her own personal one is not simply indifference to general injustice or a lack of emotional sympathy in his
personal relationships. It is a willed and responsible balance between
intellectual and emotional extremes, and it is not maintained without
certain costs: the marriage which results is forced to foreign shores,
and it does not produce "more than the common share of happiness"
(p. 233).

Howells's abstract realism is thus more "real" than abstract
comedy in which solutions may be achieved which give perfect
intellectual and emotional satisfaction. Such realism still responds in
a controlled and limited degree to the presence of social and economic actualities; it acknowledges in the considerations of its protagonists a greater degree of vulnerability to illogicality and passion;
and it shows that at least some of the effects of these conditioning
factors carry over into the "comic" solution arrived at. Moreover, the

familiar charges of evasion and timidity would not, perhaps, be as frequent if this abstraction of reality for the clarification of art were understood to obtain, not only in the resolution of such works as *An Imperative Duty,* but in their very textures (which are sometimes deceptively smooth: *April Hopes,* again, superficially seems all youth and gaiety and romance in ideally pleasant settings).

There may be grounds for arguing that the texture is too closely knit, that the deception is too successful and the proper communication of art is not achieved, but there is little basis for accusing Howells of a failure of nerve. He may throw away lines which are his means, but he does not undercut the ends toward which they are directed. For example, he leads into the assessment of the Rhoda-Olney marriage by saying: "There are few men, who, when the struggle of life is mainly over, do not wonder at the risks they took in the days of their youth and strength" (p. 233). The reader who has been infuriated by the cavalier treatment of social injustice, the reader who has been mildly amused by the ephemeral difficulties of relatively privileged people, the reader who has testily accused Howells of dealing with "average" people in a disappointingly unexciting fashion, the reader who has noted only a too obvious dissection of a Puritanical "hypochondria of the soul" (p. 233)—all will surely ask, "What *risks?*" They will thereby reveal that they have missed Howells's seriousness, Olney's difference from the average, and the novel's refusal to distort in the service of romance, humor, heroics, or sociology—in short, have failed to understand Howells's realism.

Yet, just as that realism pushes at times in the direction of pure comedy, but deliberately stops short of it, so there is still another direction it takes which is a mark of the seriousness and complexity of Howells's vision. The scenes in which Rhoda compulsively tries to force upon herself an emotional acceptance of her Negro ancestry, tries to "concentrate and intensify the fact to her outward perception; . . . densely to surround herself with the blackness from which she had sprung, and to reconcile herself to it, by realizing and owning it with every sense" (p. 196) show that realism which is intense and honest enough far exceeds the limits of the representative average Howells is so often accused of being satisfied with[57] and moves to include the compassionately comic or is even pressured by its inner force into the grotesque. The Rhoda Aldgate who had liked to exhibit her broad-mindedness and sensitivity by finding Negro waiters charming because of their "soft voices and gentle manners" (p. 153) now is forced to a reappraisal:

She never knew before how hideous they were, with their flat wide-nostriled noses, their out-rolled thick lips, their mobile, bulging eyes set near together, their retreating chins and foreheads, and their smooth, shining skin; they seemed burlesques of humanity, worse than apes, because they were more like (p. 191).

This reaction is part of her hysteria, but it is also part of Howells's realism. It is an example of the "fatal gift of observation" which will not permit the reader's emotional reaction to be generated by a distortion of the facts. It includes an awareness of how easily even legitimately intense emotions can issue into absurd or grotesque expressions, the forced consciousness of which returns the observer (sometimes also the participants) to a more balanced and objective attitude. Or, as here, the relentless inclusiveness compels a renewed recognition that broad social issues have their roots in particular lives and particular facts, and that at this level the powerful impact of what *is* dominates the consciousness: "The night was warm, and as the church filled, the musky exhalations of their bodies thickened the air, and made the girl faint; it seemed to her that she began to taste the odor" (p. 197). Rhoda sees "repulsive visages of a frog-like ugliness," an old woman with a "mouth like a catfish," and in her "frenzy of abhorrence" thinks of these "hideous" people as "animals" (p. 197). Yet, moments before, she had been touched to tears by the "motherly kindness" of an old woman whom she accosted and asked to accompany to church. And, though Rhoda is too preoccupied with her misery to take it in, a genuine pathos is achieved by Howells's portrayal of the simple faith and humility of this former slave. When

57. See Berthoff, *The Ferment of Realism*, p. 56, for an example of the persistence of this kind of critical attitude.

Rhoda rejects the idea that God will lighten her burden and argues God's indifference by asking why He doesn't make the woman white, she replies: " 'I reckon He don't think it worth while, if He can make me *willing to be black* so easy' " (p. 195).

It is because Howells's awareness—unsatisfactory as it may be to either militant liberalism or illiberalism—is thus both broadly sympathetic and honestly particularized that he can introduce genuine humor into his treatment of it and then modulate to the halftones of the ending by which Rhoda and Olney achieve not romantic bliss and evolutionary social example but a "common share of happiness" and expatriation. It is surely no accident that in the process of reporting Rhoda's experiences in the Negro church, Howells begins to play with some descriptive contrasts of black and white, has the "light" of a Christian and Tolstoyan doctrine of love issue in Negro accents from almost total darkness, and causes that broad doctrine to be reduced to its immediate application to the collection plate. The speaker

was entirely black, and he was dressed in black from head to foot, so that he stood behind the pulpit light like a thick, soft shadow cast upon the wall by an electric. His absolute sable was relieved only by the white points of his shirt-collar, and the glare of his spectacles, which, when the light struck them, heightened the goblin effect of his presence. He had no discernible features, and when he turned his profile in addressing those who sat at the sides, it was only a wavering blur against the wall (pp. 196–197).

The theme of the lecture that peals out of the darkness with "a plangent note, like some rich, melancholy bell" (p. 197) is that love is " 'the one way out of all the trouble in the world. You can't fight your way out, and you can't steal your way out, and you can't lie your way out. But you can *love* your way out' " (p. 198). If the source of this exhortation is both literal and figurative darkness— the atmosphere of the church and the limited perception of the speaker—the effect on Rhoda may also be described as obfuscating. She empties her purse and rushes back to her hotel resolved on forgiveness toward Mrs. Meredith, only to find her aunt dead. She takes refuge in the shadows of self-pity and the enclosing walls of

Mrs. Atherton's summer place in Beverly. Now it is that it devolves upon Olney to bring the illumination of reason to her problem. He succeeds in showing her that it is she who needs forgiveness for forcing a new deception from Mrs. Meredith—the assurance that she had told no one of Rhoda's ancestry when in fact she had unburdened herself to Olney—and that her plan to make herself miserable in New Orleans is no solution either to the race problem or her personal one. What is offered is merely resolution, and that in terms which continue the imagery: "Their love performed the effect of common-sense for them, and, in its purple light they saw the every-day duties of life plain before them" (pp. 231–232). If there is little that is conclusive in all this, that lack is attributable to realistic design. Howells would insist that such realism, spanning the spectrum of pathos and comedy,[58] carries its own ethical effect and is thus self-justifying.

### Art and Life: *The Coast of Bohemia* and *The Story of a Play*

If *The Coast of Bohemia* (1893) had received the critical attention given to some of Howells's earlier novels which are also lightly regarded but which have been studied as important to his developing realism—such as *Dr. Breen's Practice* or *A Woman's Reason,* superficially obvious comparisons because they all deal with women's attempts to practice a profession—his remarks about it might well have haunted him even more than they have and rivalled the notoriety of his advocacy of the smiling aspects of American life. Even in the present state of criticism, it is probably safe to assume that those comments have contributed to the neglect of this novel,

58. Some years later, reviewing a novel called *An Eagle Flight,* Howells again linked the "humorist," as he called its author, with the realist, and insisted on a middle ground between tragedy and mere comedy as the realist's domain: "His story has the reliefs without which a world where death is would not be habitable; but even in the extreme of apparent caricature you feel the self-control of the artistic spirit which will not wreak itself either in tears or laughter. It is a great novel, of which the most poignant effect is in a sense of its unimpeachable veracity" ("Editor's Easy Chair," *Harper's Monthly,* CII [April 1901], 806).

have played a tacit part in generalizations about the decline of
Howells's achievement after the greatness of the economic novels,
and have influenced adversely such judgments of *The Coast of
Bohemia* as have been proposed. While he was writing the book,
Howells complained that the work would not go smoothly, and his
immediate reaction on its completion was apparently complete dissatisfaction: "Today I finished the story which has been lagging so
long, and I think I have ended an epoch of my literary life. I doubt
if I shall ever write another story in which mating and marrying
plays an important part."[59] However, the countertendencies of his
comments in two prefaces on the book's composition and value
have been largely ignored or summarily discounted. It is probably
true that his later recollection that the "story ran glibly from the
point of my pen"[60] is a softened memory. Yet it is merely an extension of a claim made closer to publication that the novel was
written with pleasure. Moreover, under the guise of letting the book
rehearse its own history, Howells had it say: " 'You think that I
have form, and that, if I am not very serious, I am sincere, and that
somehow I represent a phase of our droll American civilization truly
enough.' "[61]

If these latter remarks are not taken as outright misrepresentations
and deceptions, then the "mating and marrying" outburst may be
taken to embody an understandable degree of impatient exaggeration
as well as a measure of truth. The point is important only as it asks
that the novel be given an open reading. If it is a failure, a specifi-
cation of its weaknesses should at least provide some possibilities of
judging the relevance of this work to Howells's more favorably
received novels of this same period and, indeed, of his entire career.
It is, for example, a critical disservice to reason from Howells's immediate reaction and the fact of the novel's publication in *The Ladies
Home Journal* that it may simply be discounted as the performance

59. *Letters*, II, 29.
60. Arms, "Unpublished Prefaces," *New England Quarterly*, XVII (December 1944), 589.
61. "Introductory Sketch," *The Coast of Bohemia*, biographical edition
(New York: Harper and Brothers, 1899), p. vi.

of a popular novelist like his Mr. Twelvemough.[62] When he deprecated the novel as "not very serious," he did not intend to imply that it was merely frivolous, or that by pandering to a popular audience it was a violation of an artistic responsibility he had long practiced and long after continued to practice and defend. He was perhaps acknowledging that *The Coast of Bohemia* did not involve the kind of social and economic issues that he had just treated in *The World of Chance* and certainly that the emotional involvements were such that "Nobody's heart will be wrung by them, or, at least, not for a long time." Again, however, before it is assumed that Howells is admitting the triviality of the novel, it should also be remembered that he spoke of the novel's threatening to become "tragical" though it finally with the "utmost seriousness . . . [kept] safely within the bounds of comedy."[63]

All of this is to suggest that whatever else it is, *The Coast of Bohemia* is a deliberate and serious part of Howells's "realism" and that a possible key to his impatience with its "mating and marrying" was that such matters played an *important* part. There are many signs in the novel itself that what caused his dissatisfaction was that the sheer machinery of his story—" 'Have a nice village girl, with a real but limited gift, go . . . to study art in New York! And get in love there! And married!' " (p. iv)—took a degree of managing disproportionate to the amount of "heart-wringing" that could be achieved by it.[64] And this was at the sacrifice of the more interesting possibilities of the subject: the "veridical representation of the ardent

---

62. See Clara Marburg Kirk, *W. D. Howells, Traveler from Altruria* (Brunswick, New Jersey: Rutgers University Press, 1962), pp. 71, 90. Mrs. Kirk merely makes this suggestion and does not argue it. She is primarily interested in enforcing the seriousness of the ideas in *A Traveler from Altruria* by the comparison, but it is because that work is frankly a "romance" and an inferior artistic performance that the basis of criticism should be kept clear.

63. Arms, "Unpublished Prefaces," *New England Quarterly*, XVII (December 1944), 588.

64. Lending support to the idea that it was the machinery and not the fact of "mating and marrying" that caused Howells's dissatisfaction is the obvious point of the continuing appearance of this element in the subsequent fiction.

young life of the New York Synthesis of Art Studies" (p. iv); the "coast of Bohemia" (p. vi); the relationship of art to life; the artist's democratic responsibilities.

The fact that *The Coast of Bohemia* was published in the same year as *The World of Chance* makes it natural to look for some link beneath their wide divergences in subject matter and motive. The only economics involved in the later novel concern Cornelia Saunders's efforts to be a self-supporting art student in New York. The concern with art, however—its character and its function— might well be a continued exploration of that question which had been introduced but not resolved in *The World of Chance*. To read *The Coast of Bohemia,* then, as a novel which worked toward be- coming an investigation of the relationship between art and reality (including, by implication at least, the art of the novel) does not seem merely arbitrary or eccentric. And it has the positive result of granting the serious intent Howells claimed for all of his fiction without making any predeterminations about its quality as a literary performance.

In Cornelia Saunders, the young girl from Pymantoning, Ohio, who goes to New York to develop through study at the Synthesis the genuine artistic talent recognized by Walter Ludlow; in Ludlow, him- self, a practicing impressionist who painted the trotting match at the annual fair of the Pymantoning Agricultural Society as though it were being held in France; and in Charmian Maybough, rich young Synthesis student, theoretical Bohemian, and befriender of Cornelia, some of the possible attitudes toward the relationship between art and life are represented and brought into play. Diffi- culties are occasioned, however, by the fact that the *story* which in- volves these three characters is not dependent in any significant way on their concern with art. The result is disjunction between the serious *subject* of the novel and its fable, the developing love affair between Cornelia and Ludlow, which is outfitted with the usual complement of hurts and misunderstandings and ecstatic moments before it eventuates in marriage.

This disjunction is most apparent in the role of Charmian, who is independently a triumphant comic creation. Howells's own pleasure in her is clearly shown in the "autobiographical preface": " 'You gave me two heroines, and you know very well that before you were done you did not know but you preferred Charmian to Cornelia" (p. v). But amusing as she is in her determination to throw off at properly prescribed intervals her "badge of slavery" (p. 17)—her corset laces and her fashionable Parisian hats—and give herself "to the truth of art" (p. 129) in her contrived garret, she really has nothing to do but be amusing. Mrs. Maybough's salon provides the occasions of some meetings between Cornelia and Ludlow, Charmian is always eager to receive Cornelia's confessions and encourage "Hawthornesque" (p. 312) transformations of reality into "artistic" suffering and purification. But she has no active influence on the events. More importantly, Howells deliberately confined her to the "coast of Bohemia" and refused to report on those "shady places inland" (p. vi) where a more profound questioning of the obtaining social and moral values might be expressed in art and behavior.

Yet even amidst his fun with Charmian's combination of radical naïveté and essential warmheartedness, Howells was led by her playing with art to an oblique admission of his own frustrated helplessness in trying to find a "direct and obvious means" (p. 209) of using his art for social purposes. When Ludlow expatiates on "art, its methods, its principles, its duties to the age, the people, the civilization; the larger moral uses," Charmian immediately conceives "a scheme for the relief and refinement of the poor on the East Side by frescoing the outsides of the tenement houses . . . with subjects recalling the home life of the dwellers there" (p. 208). This absurdity forces Ludlow to large generalities about "the gradual growth of a conscience in art" (p. 209) and to a theoretical position not much more practical than Charmian's.

Cornelia's story, in contrast to Charmian's, is ostensibly that of a sincere attempt to develop a genuine artistic talent and presents itself, therefore, as a suitable vehicle for Howells's representation of the value and function of art in both a personal and public sense. The disjunction occurs here because what actually gets dramatized is simply the story of Cornelia's affair with Ludlow. It begins with their meeting in Pymantoning when she is fifteen; continues through the period of her artistic training at the Synthesis and her social education at Mrs. Maybough's and Mrs. Westley's; is complicated by a renewed relationship at her boardinghouse with one of Howells's bounders, the drummer Dickerson; and culminates in a June wedding in Pymantoning and married contentment, unmarred by any problems of social acceptance, in New York. The difficulty is that Cornelia's pursuit of art is merely the agency which brings her to New York; it has no real function in determining the quality of her significant experience there, though it does provide the occasion for the "veridical" local color of the Synthesis.

The difficulty was inherent, apparently, in Howells's conception of Cornelia. Her devotion to art is, finally, not so much a conscious intellectual commitment or a passionate aestheticism as an unavoidable expression of her character and temperamental qualities. She never, for example, formulates to others—and apparently not even to herself—a goal of critical acclaim or commercial success. Her stated objective in going to New York is simply to settle the question of whether she can paint or not: "And the only way is to go and find out. It'll be easy enough to come home" (p. 53). Though her practice of art takes a realistic form of which Howells approves—a fact which is important in the scheme of the novel—she never articulates a theory: "She had learned to be faithful to what she saw, which is the great matter in all the arts." The judgment is Howells's own, for he adds: "She had never formulated this fact, even if she knew it" (p. 45).

In a real sense, also, a strong element in Cornelia's desire to paint is revealed to be simply a desire to assert her independence and individual worth. Art tends to become merely the means to that end (in contrast, for example, to schoolteaching, which she dislikes intensely). Thus she is scornful of becoming "just a great *woman* painter," and she sets out on her venture insisting that " 'now that I've made up my mind, I don't want to be discouraged, and I don't want to be helped. If I can't do for myself, I won't be done *for*' " (p. 48). Ultimately, however, it is the ease with which Cornelia gives up not merely a career, but the serious study of art for marriage, that disqualifies her from functioning in any of the several exemplary roles for which she might have been cast: the poor but dedicated artist in an indifferent world; woman struggling to break the artificial barriers of a male profession; the practitioner of an uncom-

promising and unappreciated realism; or the person caught in the
irreconcilable dilemma between the opposing claims of the happiness of love and the aesthetic rewards of painting. But all these
possibilities simply fade away with Ludlow's proposal—even the last,
which seemed to have real substance in Cornelia's initial determination to labor on for years, if necessary, at the Synthesis—and
though Cornelia continues to paint after her marriage, even her
art is merged with her husband's.

Ludlow is one of several portraits of the cultured young artist in
the Howells gallery and, like Henry Ferris of *A Foregone Conclusion* before him or Westover soon to follow in *The Landlord at
Lion's Head,* he can act spokesman for Howells when such a
strategy seems desirable. Ludlow, however, is quickly established as
having been trained in a school of art, impressionism, with which
Howells would have only qualified sympathy. It is, in fact, his attempt to apply this theory to a portrait of Charmian which results
in his failure, while Cornelia's instinctive penetration to the reality
of Charmian's nature beneath her Bohemianism produces an effective likeness. Ludlow's artistic standards are succinctly represented by his proud possession of one of Manet's "most excessive"
(p. 159) paintings, but Howells uses even Ludlow's departures from
his master's theory to insinuate an argument for objective realism.
Wetmore, a fellow painter, accuses Ludlow of trying in the portrait
of Charmian " 'to *interpret* her; to come the prophet! . . . You
would naturally like to paint the literature of a thing' " (p. 218),
by which one supposes he means the *morality.* Finally, Ludlow
abandons the portrait but does a sketch which is presumably a combination of the impressionistic method and the imposed moralizing.
The results bear little relation to reality, for the picture depicts "an
idealized Charmian, in which her fantastic quality expressed itself as
high imagination, and her formless generosity as a wise and noble
magnanimity" (p. 264).

On one point, however, Ludlow advances an ideal with which
Howells clearly would agree,[65] that of proving not just to "the few"

65. In the "Editor's Study," *Harper's Monthly,* LXXVII (November
1888), 963, Howells lamented that literature was universally regarded, with
the other arts, as mere "amusement, a distraction" and wished that it might be

but to "the many" that "our life is full of poetry and picturesqueness," and to prove it by "a real work of art that asserts itself in a good way" and not by a prettifying and falsifying "chromo" (p. 154). However, the same general criticism that applied to the other major characters applies to Ludlow as well: there is a disjunction between Ludlow the artist and Ludlow the suitor for Cornelia's hand. His love for her is in no sense caused by the fact that she is also an artist, and we are given no sense that his commitment as an artist is in any way threatened by marriage and its responsibilities. Indeed, the fact of his being an artist remains largely an abstraction: it is simply one of the "circumstances" in which we find him and leave him; and while that circumstance conditions his view of the world and experience, it remains simply a given constant of his being, rather than, say, the precipitating factor of a struggle for self-definition or self-preservation.

These are damaging but not totally disabling admissions. *The Coast of Bohemia* fails, not because it is a romantic triviality, but because the details of sheer story work to obscure even the relatively light burden they were intended to carry. One theme which was central to Howells's theory of art is introduced but cannot accumulate decisive weight in this kind of slight realistic exercise. Henry James in "The Art of Fiction" had made the point that the morality of art would be determined by the quality of the artist's mind, that intelligence would control the "beauty and truth" of a work of art. Howells went beyond mind or intelligence as the determinant: a "work of art . . . was a growth" of all an artist's "thinking and feeling about it,"[66] was an expression of the total person. He even admitted that his "way of thinking and feeling . . . about literature and life" might cause "a confusion as to which is which."[67] One implication of such a remark is that the individual life is itself an art, an expression in action of the same conditions of character an

---

made to serve something more than "the taste, the aesthetic pride, the intellectuality of the reader." He rather wistfully remarked: "Literature is an art like the rest; and we do not ask people to be vitally concerned about a picture, a statue, an opera, a building; but it sometimes seems as if it ought to be unlike the other arts, since if it would it could speak so frankly, so brotherly, so helpfully, to the mass of men."

66. *Imaginary Interviews*, p. 288.
67. *Literature and Life*, p. iv.

artist inevitably expresses in his imitations of life. From this view-point, *The Coast of Bohemia* becomes a demonstration of the inter-acting value of the "simple, natural, and honest" in both life and art and provides a moral test of the "performances" of all the char-acters in the novel.

Cornelia is instinctively faithful to what she sees, and her own rectitude allows her to penetrate both the deceitful sham of a Dickerson and the mere self-dramatizing of a Charmian. Her "saving simplicity" (p. 234) allows her to appreciate the beautiful in the commonplace—the Pymantoning County Fair, for example—without wanting to change it, to make it look "as if it were somewhere else" (p. 161). That is Ludlow's problem in both art and life: he tries to heighten the impression, to make the American scene look French, to "interpret" rather than to understand Charmian, and the results are distorted prettifyings of reality. Similarly, for a time, his superior sophistication gets in the way of his knowledge of Cornelia's virtue and of his love for her, and he acts rather on the false impression created by Dickerson's machinations. Charmian is pretending, not only as an artist and a Bohemian, but as a person. Her youth and privileged circumstances have prevented her from having as yet a life of her own, and though she vicariously lives in Cornelia's experi-ences, she transforms them to happenings in a romantic novel rather than accepting their reality.

Even Mrs. Saunders is claimed among the ranks of artists by virtue of her skill as a "woman who drapes the human figure in stuffs" rather than "drapes it in paint or clay" (p. 30), but she illustrates the relationship between life and art in a different way. Her "art," though it is a natural expression of her love of beauty and her simple taste, is not raised to the full level of consciousness. It is, thus, a rather exact expression of her easygoing approach to life itself. It is she who originally involves her daughter with Dickerson by her willingness to accept his projection of himself as simply a charming, entertaining, well-intentioned, and honorable person.

Dickerson himself is a master of the arts of a commercialized culture in his chosen profession of drummer and in his personal relationships. In spite of herself, Cornelia can find that she is taking "pleasure in the apt slang, and sinister wit and low wisdom" with which he is capable of making "everything higher and nobler seem ridiculous" (p. 246). By sheer effrontery he is able at times to transform reality by ignoring it: by refusing to recognize Cornelia's aversion, by artfully describing his past relationships with Cornelia and Mrs. Saunders in slanted terms which distort but do not abandon fact, and by all the while being so amusing and humble that he gains conviction and acceptance. Such arts, however, require the screening of his forceful presence, for when he attempts them in the subliterary form of a letter to Cornelia, the "low cunning, the impudent hypocrisy, the leering pretence of reverence, the affectation of penitence, the whole fraudulent design, so flimsy that the writer himself seemed to be mocking at it" (p. 256) is clear to her.

It is some such texture in all of Howells's novels—even in those, such as this one, which do not cut a completely symmetrical and functional pattern from the woven materials—which makes them more than romantic draperies, more than flimsy transparencies, which gives them durability, if not perfect elegance.

Howells felt a sufficient "tie of common temperament" between *The Coast of Bohemia* and *The Story of a Play* (1898) that he would have published them in a single volume of the unfinished Library Edition of his works,[68] and the juxtaposition seems fruitful enough to excuse the violation of chronology in this study. One effect is to show why the first is a comparative failure, the other a comic creation of a high order. *The Coast of Bohemia* is so weighted down with "love-business" that it cannot realize its full potential as a fictional proof of the relevance of art to life, or morality to art. *The Story of a Play*, on the other hand, has just enough plot to support the novel's real concerns. Howells told Henry James that "the husband-and-wife business was the chief thing,"[69] but there are many other interests besides that of detailing the vicissitudes undergone by Brice Maxwell and shared by his wife (the former Louise Hilary) in writing a play and getting it successfully produced, which is the narrative line.

The personal "husband-and-wife business" expands to an amus-

68. Arms, "Unpublished Prefaces," *New England Quarterly*, XVII (December 1944), 588.
69. *Letters*, II, 94.

ing consideration of the larger social strains of a "mixed" marriage; the story of Maxwell's determined attempt on the theater allows for both interesting comment on the drama as literature and for telling comic portraits of theatrical personalities; Maxwell's attempts to satisfy his artistic conscience and to achieve a popular success offer some direct insights into Howells's own problems as a semipopular novelist; and the depiction of the instant feline animosity between the leading lady with smoldering eyes, Yolande Havisham (or, more prosaically, Mrs. Harley), and Louise Maxwell is a fine piece of comic business. This diversity is unified, not by plot,[70] but by tone, by skillful modulations within the range established by the same kind of "light, semi-comic motive of the love-business" that Maxwell identified as in conflict with "the sin-interest"[71] in his play. This diversity Howells undoubtedly had in mind in remarking that the title was "rather more outright than I liked the titles of my books to be,"[72] and the problem of tone he remarked on in both his preface and in a letter to Henry James. To his literary friend, he said, "You know my experience of the theater was comic, rather than tragical, and I treated it lightly because it was light."[73] In the preface, his comment was undoubtedly directed to the management of the "husband-and-wife business" when he spoke of curbing the tendency toward the "tragical" and keeping well within the limits of comedy.

Howells had long since shown in *The Rise of Silas Lapham* that the "silken texture of the marriage tie bears a daily strain of wrong and insult to which no other human relation can be subjected without lesion."[74] What gives new force and painful intensity to this latest demonstration is not merely that it disperses the conventional

70. In fact, as O. W. Firkins has amply and amusingly demonstrated, Howells was positively "reckless" in his use of coincidence in a work in which "there is no plot and no process, nothing but an irregular movement with a fortuitous culmination" (*William Dean Howells*, pp. 177–178).

71. *The Story of a Play* (New York: Harper and Brothers, 1898), p. 70.

72. Arms, "Unpublished Prefaces," *New England Quarterly*, XVII (December 1944), 588.

73. *Letters*, II, 94.

74. *The Rise of Silas Lapham*, Rinehart editions (New York: Rinehart and Company, 1951), p. 50.

acceptations with regard to newlyweds, not merely that it plays the easy game of puncturing clichés, but that it does so almost casually in the course of depicting an "idyllic" marriage based on real love and shared ideals. What strikes the renewed consciousness as both terrible and comic is not that this nice young couple can so easily pass from bliss to deadly insult, but that the injuries are so easily sustained and absorbed.

However, the degree of pain engendered by the lacerations of spirit with which the Maxwells scourge themselves do not for several reasons really go "beyond that which literature is authorized to inflict,"[75] nor beyond the bounds of serious comedy. Brice and Louise have been honestly represented from the start, he "in his straightforward egotism," she in "her sinuous unselfishness" (p. 59), and their quarrels issue from temperament rather than character. Moreover, both are intelligent and generous enough to recognize their own folly and guilt and to wish "to meet and bind up one another's wounds" (p. 300). After one quarrel has driven Maxwell from his home, he is an involuntary witness on a walk along the "squalid waterside avenues" to a scene of domestic strife which "was his own in quality, if not in quantity." He is shamed by his "human identity" (p. 164) into a resolve to practice whatever forbearance might be necessary to prevent any recurrence in his own marriage.[76]

Most important, these tempests are not the normal weather of the Maxwells' marriage. The flashings of his intelligence and sometimes searing wit usually serve to highlight their interdependence through self-disparagement and fond mockery of her impossible ideal of him, which is inextricably and unavoidably mixed with the sense of his differing social origins. Her passionate involvement in his writing and life in the theater can sometimes lead to absurd jealousy and finicky protests against the literary use of their private experience. Yet it is the measure of her commitment to their life together and

75. Firkins, *William Dean Howells*, p. 179.
76. Part of the interest developed by the characterization of Maxwell as a literary man is in Howells's sketching of the double consciousness of the artist. In this scene and in others, Maxwell, miserable or happy, continues to take objective note of his own feelings and the motives behind the actions of others as possible material for his art. See, for example, pp. 26, 165.

her defense against the difficulties experienced by her family and friends in comprehending her marriage at all. Thus, Howells's remarks about the tragic potentiality which he declined in his preference for the utmost seriousness of comedy—remarks which, as applied to *The Story of a Play* and *The Coast of Bohemia,* could only seem pretentious exaggerations to those readers content to dismiss most of the later novels as pallid repetitions of the themes of his earlier period—are justified by his fresh penetration of familiar materials and by the sustaining comic tone with which those materials are represented. It is clearly part of the point that *The Story of a Play* is not another *A Modern Instance,* and it is equally part of the point that it does not belong to the generic type of the imaginary *Slop, Silly Slop* (more literally, but not more charitably, *Tears, Idle Tears*) that Howells was fond of castigating."[77]

A different but similar shading of tone controls the effects achieved in dramatizing Maxwell's high ambitions for producing drama which is great literature. In fact, in dealing with this theme, Howells provides almost a gloss for the reading of his own novel, a fictionalized expansion of his prefatory comments and remarks to Henry James. At one point, for example, Maxwell explains to Louise his current difficulty in proceeding with his play along the lines they have previously agreed upon:

"Don't you see that the love-business is the play now? I have got to throw away all the sin-interest, all the Haxard situation, or keep them together as they are, and write a new play altogether, with the light, semi-comic motive of the love-business for the motive of the whole. It's out of tone with Haxard's tragedy, and it can't be brought into keeping with it. The sin-interest will kill the love-business, or the love-business will kill the sin-interest" (p. 70).

Moreover, there can be little question that Howells was speaking for himself as well as for Maxwell in having the playwright reflect on his literary objectives: "It was not the drama merely that Maxwell loved; it was not making plays alone; it was causing the life that he had known to speak from the stage, and to teach there its serious

77. See *The Rise of Silas Lapham* (1951), pp. 211–213.

and important lesson. In the last analysis he was a moralist, and more a moralist than he imagined" (p. 217). But this basic seriousness is merely the support for all kinds of fun Howells had in following out not merely the evolution of the play, but its passing from the effective control of the playwright to the status of a "vehicle" for the competing players.

It is this latter process which bring Maxwell, first, into intimate relations with Launcelot Godolphin, and, later, somewhat less intimate relations with Yolande Havisham. For Maxwell, Godolphin is a bundle of contradictions, an alternate sorrow and joy. He is capable of delicate literary perceptions which fully appreciate the most beautiful and meaningful passages of Maxwell's play, but he exasperates the playwright by attaching no more importance to them than the "crudest verbiage" (p. 98) which offers histrionic possibilities. Indeed, his whole vision is concentrated by the single focus of his selfish interest in his own art, but that selfishness is so open and ingenuous that he remains attractive.

There is no malice or intentional deception in Godolphin's frequent withdrawals from association with the play after the most extravagant avowals to make it his lifetime career; there is no intellectual pretension in his barrage of suggestions as to how the play should be written. These are suggestions which are so bad as almost to make "Maxwell shed tears" (p. 99) or so good as to make him marvel, but Godolphin values them equally as providing fine dramatic effects for the star role. In his life outside the theater, what there is of it, Godolphin is "chaotically generous" (p. 100), an effective teller of comic tales without a sense of humor, a punctilious performer of gentlemanly services to Mrs. Maxwell without quite being a gentleman. In his business relation with Maxwell he proves scrupulously honest in his financial accounting, if not in his more imaginative reporting of the houses attracted to and moved by his performances of Maxwell's play. Maxwell finally formulates him as "mere human material, waiting to be moulded in this shape or that" (p. 100). It is a nice comic touch that that moulding is presumably to be accomplished, as the novel ends, by his marriage to Miss Pettrell, the leading lady who replaced Miss Havisham. The comic irony is that the replacement, which was effected because Miss

Havisham was stealing the play from Godolphin, has resulted in Miss Pettrell's acclaim by the critics, so that the marriage makes irrelevant the question of Godolphin's professional pride and also saves Maxwell from still another production crisis.

Miss Havisham is one of those apparently effortlessly turned out cameos[78] which variegate Howells's novels. (Other examples easily come to mind: Mrs. Faulkner of *The Shadow of a Dream*, Mrs. Saunders of *The Coast of Bohemia*, the carriage driver in *The Day of Their Wedding*, Mr. Orson of *Ragged Lady*.) She is a kind of Howellsian *femme fatale*, and from the first moment Maxwell sees her in bathing costume on the beach and notes that her eyes seem "to smoulder under their long lashes" (p. 81), she becomes a comic complication in both his vocation and his marriage. From this first appearance as a dramatically interesting personality to Brice and a sexual threat to Louise, she becomes successively a resident in the Maxwell apartment house, an encountered customer in the butcher shop patronized by Louise, the applier of first aid when Louise falls and sprains her ankle in the lobby of the apartment house, the receiver of duty calls of thanks from Brice and then the Maxwells together, and finally the engaged star for Brice's play.

Howells's amused expertise in recording the genteel cat-fighting produced by the clash of two instinctively and implacably hostile feminine temperaments is illustrated when Louise tries to maintain control over her "distasteful" duty call on Miss Havisham by repairing "to her presence in rather overwhelming virtue." But that thoroughly self-possessed and self-conscious woman "contrived with a few well-directed strokes to give her distinctly the sense of being a chit" (p. 231). Miss Havisham triumphs by turning her complete attention and the full force of her smouldering eyes on Maxwell: "If this had all or any of it been helpless or ignorant rudeness, it could have been borne and forgiven; but Louise was aware of intention, of perfect intelligence in it; she was sensible of having been even more

78. Miss Havisham's manager is too slightly sketched even to be called a cameo, but it is part of Howells's playing with the relationship between literature and the uses to which literature may be put to designate the "dark bulk" which "was not somehow a gentlemanly bulk" (p. 252) by the name of L. (Lawrence) Sterne.

disliked than disliking, and of finally being put to flight with a patronizing benevolence . . . that was intolerable" (p. 232). These two spar again when Louise visits a rehearsal and afterwards pays Miss Havisham some barbed compliments on her performance as Salome, a character her husband has partially modelled after herself. Miss Havisham is fully able to return these social barbs in kind, and Maxwell's subsequent comment on his wife's duplicity evokes an angry rejoinder which clearly reveals the nature of the undeclared warfare:

"She knew from every syllable that I uttered that I perfectly loathed it, and I know that she tried to make it as hateful to me all through as she could. She played it *at* me, and she knew it *was* me. It was as if she kept saying all the time, 'How do you like my translation of your Boston girl into Alabama, or Mississippi, or Arkansas?' " (p. 297)

The superiority of *The Story of a Play* to *The Coast of Bohemia* stems from the unity of effect achieved in the former by having everything in it relate to the problem of engaging art with life. In *The Coast of Bohemia,* there was a wavering from Cornelia's concern to prove herself as an artist to her love affair with Ludlow to the sheer fun of Charmian's masquerade. The mating and the marrying diminished the significance of the first motif and both motifs revealed the irrelevance of Charmian's attempts to manufacture experience, so that the rich potentials of the diverse materials of Pymantoning, the Synthesis, and the coterie of artists in New York society did not achieve effective thematic and tonal fusion. In *The Story of a Play,* on the other hand, the relation of art to reality is not merely a technical problem which controls the various versions of Maxwell's play; it is the central fact of his own experience. The writing of a play (which will not be just a commercial success but literature of genuine realistic merit) is the fact around which all the conditions of his marriage take shape: how and where he and Louise will live, how they will spend their time, what will be the nature of their talk together, who will be their mutual friends.

Thus, the marriage itself comes to stand for one side of the conflict between the creative artist and society. That battle involves getting the artist's work before the public through the offices of producers and manager-actors and still preserving its artistic integrity, refusing "any sort of catchpenny effectivism in it" (p. 89). It is also a battle against the ignorance and indifference of the public to which it is offered, represented in degrees of magnitude by the opposition of Louise's family to the marriage itself and more specifically by the Boston to which Louise belonged and to which she cannot help at times returning, the Boston that "never hears of American books till they are forgotten" (p. 247) and which "did not in the least know what . . . her husband did" (p. 247). It is an advantage to the comic tone to have much of this presented from Louise's point of view. Her superior social and economic background, her intense loyalty to her husband, her desire to contribute to his creative consciousness while excluding their private passions from the artistic product, all combine in an attitude sufficiently mixed for sympathetic detachment. She exhibits a partially willed devotion which brings Maxwell's dedication to art into a perspective showing its strong roots in egotism as well as idealism. Such firm basic control of his subject allows Howells not only to produce, in contrast to the diffusion of *The Coast of Bohemia,* integrated and relevant comic characterizations like Godolphin and Miss Havisham, but to deal with the Maxwell marriage in comic terms which fully account for its real complications and stresses. The total result is, indeed, an example of the seriousness Howells could maintain in realistic comedy, and one more sign that all the novels of his later career are products of conscious artistic choices and very often effective justifications of those choices.

# IV

## REALISTIC VARIATIONS

### Minor Realities: *The Day of Their Wedding* and *An Open-Eyed Conspiracy*

THE novelettes which closely preceded and followed *The Landlord at Lion's Head* (1897) are fictions of a different order from that major novel. It is again useful, therefore, to violate chronology to pair them for discussion. The purpose is not just to clear the ground for *The Landlord at Lion's Head*—though that is a worth-while result—but to take advantage of their similarities and differences. In using the same fictional form and a common setting—Saratoga—the novelettes offer some interesting contrasts of the uses to which that form can be put. Moreover, each is a skillful exercise in tonal control. Even as minor performances, then, they illustrate the range of Howells's realism. The first, *The Day of Their Wedding* (1896), glosses the sympathetic response to the gentleness and simple goodness of the Shakers which Howells had recorded in *The Undiscovered Country;*[1] the second, *An Open-Eyed Conspiracy* (1897), offers fresh evidence that when Howells wished to confine his fiction within the limts of a conventional comedy of manners, he could do so with wit and

1. The story "A Parting and a Meeting," *Cosmopolitan*, XVIII (December 1894; January, February 1895), 183–188, 307–316, 469–474, however, gives some indication of Howells's reservations about the life which the Shakers practiced.

charm and without compromising the realistic literary principles on which his more serious work was based.

A summary of the action of *The Day of Their Wedding* does not seem to promise very much. A Shaker couple, Lorenzo Weaver and Althea Brown, having decided to leave the order and marry, travel to Saratoga, where they apend the day in several stages of indecision before resolving the conflict between their personal and their religious feelings. But the concentration on the emotions and the *experience* of this unworldly couple as they encounter the obtaining realities of the "world-outside"[2]—of which, Saratoga, with its elegancies and idle diversions and mixed humanity of vacationers and exploiters, serves as a particularly effective symbol—produces a small triumph of sensibility. Howells's documented aversion to meretricious or exaggerated emotionalism insures that the term, in this case, refers to an intelligent and perceptive response to the moral and aesthetic values inherent in the simplicities of this story and these characters. It serves, also, to indicate the crucial artistic problem of the novel: its management of tone so that "intelligence" governs the degree of permissible "perceptiveness" and results in valid emotion rather than bathos.

The structural and thematic singleness of *The Day of Their Wedding* is apparent from a listing of its elements: as narrative, it describes the train trip of Althea and Lorenzo from Fitchburg to Saratoga and gives an account of the little incidents—a carriage ride, some shopping, the choice of a hotel—of their day there; as drama, it concentrates on the single question of whether they will renounce "the angelic life" (p. 9) and marry; technically, it relies heavily on the colloquial and unsophisticated dialogue of these two innocents for its tonal and dramatic effects. These components, together with some evocations of Saratoga scenes which produce reactions of guilty delight and disapproving wariness in Althea and Lorenzo and with some etchings of such worldlings as their carriage driver and the honeymooning Mrs. Cargate, add up to a surprising effect of richness

2. *The Day of Their Wedding* (New York: Harper and Brothers, 1896), p. 9.

of texture. When Howells had offered an explicit comment on his much fuller treatment of the Shakers in *The Undiscovered Country*, he had distinguished "their truth, charity, and purity of life, and that scarcely less lovable quaintness to which no realism could do perfect justice."[3] *The Day of Their Wedding* might be said to be Howells's attempt to execute that perfect justice and to do it, not by abandoning realism, but by a careful selectivity, a controlled focusing on the uniquely "real" qualities of this latter-day Adam and Eve.

Perhaps the reason Howells did not also subtitle this work, along with *An Open-Eyed Conspiracy*, an "idyl," is that it does not have a conventionally happy ending. It is an effective realistic modulation that has Althea and Lorenzo overcome their final doubts about marriage after their day of hesitations, only to have Althea then decide, after the ceremony, that she must return to the Family for the simple reason that, whether it taught her right or wrong, " '*It's too strong for me now*, and it would be too strong as long as I lived' " (p. 153). That the whole affair has not been merely a silly escapade indulged in by two pleasure-seeking simpletons but a movingly sincere attempt at full human sharing is made apparent by the quiet dignity with which Lorenzo receives this announcement, his lack of recrimination or reproach, and his own decision to resume the Family life rather than live in the "world-outside" without her.

Working well within himself, Howells admirably sustained a deliberately low key while introducing sufficient harmonic variation to avoid monotony. His snapshot of the carriage driver, whose "wicked wisdom" (p. 55) easily penetrates to the truth of the Shaker couple's mission in Saratoga and tempts him to a display of superiority and exercise of wit at their expense while at the same time being restrained by a basic kindliness and fraternal feeling, is a fine distillation of experience. Mrs. Cargate, the honeymooner, does not even possess such a saving capacity for amused sympathy: she is all show and gush; in Lorenzo's word, she is "sickish" (p. 134), and she serves as an important deterrent to the choice of the "earthly order" (p. 155). The realistically observed scene includes a restaurant, which, in spite of its splendid mirrors and marble-topped tables,

3. *The Undiscovered Country* (Boston: Houghton Mifflin and Company, 1888), p. 161.

is largely inhabited at an untimely morning hour by angrily buzzing flies; a fashionable dress shop where Althea makes bridal purchases under the desperately courageous urgings of Lorenzo; and the Grand Union Hotel with its upholstered and chandeliered splendors.

In each of these settings, and others such as the dim parlors of the minister with whom the young couple counsel about their marriage, they undergo the "adventures" which innocence must always experience in encountering superior knowledge and sophistication, alien manners and attitudes. Through them all, they are often comic but never ridiculous: Howells always succeeds in showing the sweetness of their devotion and the uprightness of their characters without making them either saccharine or priggish. The comic tenderness of Lorenzo's saying to Althea, "'I *want* you should cry'" (p. 30), or remarking in helpless inarticulateness after Althea's decision to default on their marriage, "'I declare . . . that hat's got to look like you'" (p. 156), delicately negotiates the perilous path between legitimately evoked sentiment and indulgent sentimentality. And the intrinsic seriousness on which Howells bases his compassionate humor is an appropriate fulcrum of the novel: the sacramental ideal of marriage as "the death of the individual" (p. 87), which is enunciated by the minister, is actually fulfilled in the different terms of mutual agreement which they reach in renouncing the world, not merely because it is strange and confusing, but because "the light of the world" (p. 155) would have the effect of "shutting . . . [their] eyes to the light" (p. 154).

A far more experienced and indulgent view of the "earthly order" of Saratoga is provided by the narrator of An Open-Eyed Conspiracy, Basil March, who is taking his first vacation from his duties as editor and part-owner of Every Other Week. The common setting and equal simplicity of story—the introduction and rapidly following engagement of Julia Gage, rural beauty of DeWitt Point, and Gerald Kendricks, literary contributor to Every Other Week and New York City cosmopolitan, all under the accidental and somewhat uneasy aegis of Basil and Isabel—are, however, the extent of the similarities between The Day of Their Wedding and An Open-Eyed Conspiracy.

The earlier novelette is all simplicity: the uncomplicated natures of Althea and Lorenzo required no deep subtleties of interpretation. Their directness of selfless concern for each other and their unsophisticated reactions to the conditions of the glittering resort were fully caught by the objective lens of the dramatic method. In contrast, *An Open-Eyed Conspiracy* is all artifice, all deliberate elaboration for its own sake of a love story which encounters only the mild threat of opposition in the girl's father. The embroiderings of Isabel are thoroughly familiar and derive from her liking for Kendricks, her naturally sympathetic interest in such affairs, and her practical responsibilities as volunteer chaperon.

Basil's function is more complex. It is no surprise to find Howells using March to record his own mild amusement at the contrasts offered by the situation and the Marches' enforced relation to it: between such oppositions as youth and age, innocence and sophistication, emotionalism and rationality, appearance and reality, literalness and imagination. But March himself also becomes a means through which Howells registers his awareness of the tenuousness of the structure being erected in *An Open-Eyed Conspiracy,* his awareness of the limitations and exclusions necessary to make this "An Idyl of Saratoga." In short, the comedy of *An Open-Eyed Conspiracy* lies not merely in its report on the clichéd inanities of young love as viewed by the weary antiromanticism of March, but in its conscious offering of itself as a literary artifice in which that total cliché is justified by the cleverness of its presentation. In this context, March is both a device used to indicate Howells's conscious playing with the role of (realistic) writer-observer and a comic figure whose intellectual complacency and sense of superior sensibility are given some mild shocks.

Those unconscious roles are deftly insinuated by Howells at the very start when March strolls Congress Park to observe the scene and to employ the "sophistication which enabled . . . [him] to taste pleasures which would have been insipidities"[4] to less delicate palates than his own. His attention is first attracted by "a young French-Canadian mother of low degree" who is spanking her dirty little boy

4. *An Open-Eyed Conspiracy* (New York: Harper and Brothers, 1897), p. 8.

with "insensate passion" (pp. 2–3). It is in his relief at their departure that he first notices the beautiful young girl who will prove to be Julia Gage and with whom March will become involved as putative chaperon. In contrast to his reaction to the mother and child, he immediately begins to "weave about her a web of possibilities" (p. 4) and to speculate about the couple who join her. He is "overjoyed" to be drawn into conversation, not because he is really interested in them in their own persons, but because he is "poignantly interested in the little situation . . . [he] had created" (p. 11) in his imagination. Having had conversation enough to supply a few facts with which to buttress his fantasy, he is impatient to report to Isabel on his "very rare and thrilling" (p. 19) adventure.

March *is*, of course, simply amusing himself and entertaining the reader in the process by endowing the commonplaces of incident and character with romantic significance and excitement. It requires no great stretch of the imagination, however, to realize that Howells is amusing himself as well by establishing March as a *persona* objectifying a partial conception of the authorial role. March uses these casually encountered people "conjecturally to give . . . [himself] an agreeable pang." He does not "want to know anything more about them than . . . [he] imagined" (p. 40). Howells uses the whole novel in precisely the same way. Just as March turned with relief from the aesthetically unpleasing spectacle of the dirty little boy— i.e., its "realism"—to imagined "romance," so Howells chooses the restricted scene of "the Saratoga world" (p. 6) and enjoys his power to savor its special conditions and its temporary inhabitants, including March, through the contingency of a vehicle involving nothing more serious than an acceptable if not ideal love match.

A more subtle and serious point is also exemplified by March's relations to these proceedings. He began by believing he could completely preserve the dilettante role, accepting only that part of reality useful to his fabricated enjoyment, but soon found himself, only half unwillingly, immersed in the wearisome actualities of performing as a chaperon at a round of luncheons, carriage rides, musicales, and dances. Pure detachment is obviously an inadequate—perhaps an impossible—state. A similar recognition of the weight of actuality qualifies the tone of the idyl, already shown to be totally idyllic only for the two lovers at its center: the final summing up by the Marches emphasizes that Kendricks was in love with Julia's "beautiful girl-hood," which will pass while "the girl will remain" (p. 181). And finally Howells uses March to suggest that any self-conceived role taken too seriously is at least comic, when it is not pernicious.

Basil is rather smugly confident, even as he is forced into more participation in the affair than he desires, that his intelligence, superior taste, and broader experience will be noted and valued, certainly by innocents like Julia Gage, and in a differing degree and quality by the more informed Kendricks. The skill with which Howells makes March both the vehicle of his own amusement at and tolerance of young love and a figure of the comedy is well illustrated in the account of an evening at a production of *East Lynne* by black performers. March waxes his most brilliantly "metaphysical" in commenting to Kendricks and Miss Gage on the misguided at-tempt of the actors to make the performances "white." He is amazed to discover that even Kendricks thought the play "pretty well done" (p. 105), and that the young lover is obviously indifferent to the imaginative ludicity of his discourse. With Howells, the reader shares in March's perceptions and enjoys his discomfiture as, faced with this inescapable proof of the generational gap which turns his aesthetic sensitivity and facile wit into so much intrusive gabble, he rational-izes that Kendricks was "either humbugging himself or he was humbugging me" (p. 106). Basil is guilty of assuming that because he and Kendricks share a literary sensibility their commonality of viewpoint extends much farther than the actualities of their differ-ences in age, experience, and temperament permit, and he comes close to being offensive to Kendricks in his remarks about Julia. He has allowed himself to forget, until reminded by this experience and others, that the adoption of an antiromantic attitude does not banish "romance" from life itself, that Kendricks, whatever his literary sensibilities and gentlemanly qualities, is a young man completely susceptible to Miss Gage's beauty and therefore capable of finding her general ignorance charming rather than boring.

Thus, while *The Day of Their Wedding* used simple means to simple ends, the artifice, the *working* of the simple materials of *An*

*Open-Eyed Conspiracy* is both the means and the ends. The Saratoga novelettes are fine examples of deliberately restricted fictions
which are nicely tuned adjustments of tone to material, controlled
exercises of art for desired effect. What makes them minor is that the
control is partially achieved by a deliberate narrowing of the scope
of the material. The Basil March who wishes to give himself entirely to his "impressions" of Saratoga, to the weaving of his gossamer adventures, has recently passed through some harrowing experiences in New York. That world of ruthless economics and political
and economic and social strife does not intrude, however, into the
picturesque, gracious, and well-ordered milieu of *An Open-Eyed
Conspiracy*. This is an "idyllic" world, not merely for the lovers,
but for their observers and sponsors as well, precisely because it does
not.

## The American Dream Re-Examined:
### *The Landlord at Lion's Head*

Late in his career, Howells publicly declared that the proverbial
"great American novel" or, as he called it, "the novel of the United
States," could never be written. His argument was that to attempt to
reduce the enormous complications of American industry, finance,
and politics to the "stuff of an imaginative work" would be to try
"to extract sunbeams from our mammoth cucumbers." The formula
for realistic fiction that he offered was: "First the provincial, then
the national, then the universal." The "provincial," which was the
foundation stone, however, was not to be mistaken for mere local
color. Correctly seen, the "parochial" elements in American life
would be revealed as the true gauge of national character and would
also, therefore, adumbrate the universal:

The simple structure of our society, the free play of our democracy in
spite of our plutocracy, the ineradicable desire of the right in spite of the
prevalence of the wrong, the generous instinct of self-sacrifice, the wish to
wreak ourselves in limitless hospitality, the capacity for indefatigable toil,
the will to make our achievement commensurate with our opportunity—

these are the national things which the national novel might deal with, better than with Pittsburgh chimneys and Chicago expresses.[5]

If some such formulation was taking shape in Howells's mind following the period from 1889 to 1893, when he tried to deal directly with the iniquitous effects of the plutocratic system, some light may be shed on the novelistic hiatus between *The Coast of Bohemia* and *The Day of Their Wedding*. Though this statement of "national things" could be applied to *The Coast of Bohemia,* that novel did not achieve the kind of imaginative expansion that Howells was suggesting as possible in dealing with such "common, crude material . . . ; the right American stuff,"[6] as he had earlier called it; and *The Day of Their Wedding* was even more limited in intention. The time between the publication of these two works of fiction was not, however, merely idle: Howells occupied himself with two farces, with *A Traveler from Altruria,* and with articles for *Harper's Weekly.* He also wrote a series of essays which became *My Literary Passions* (1895). That account of the formation, through emulation and reaction, of his own literary tastes and principles might well, also, have produced some second thoughts on what he had been attempting in his economic fiction. At any rate, *The Landlord at Lion's Head* marks a return to this sense of the "parochial," and it is a thoroughly successful validation of his analogous claim, in *Criticism and Fiction,* that "breadth" might be "vertical instead of lateral." The social range in *Landlord* reaches from the rural Durgins to the Bostonian Lyndes, but the lateral limits are determined by the focus on Jeff Durgin, and its expansions are generally only enough to accommodate his experience. The result of this kind of concentration, which Howells preferred to call "thorough rather than narrow,"[7] was one of the finest novels he ever wrote.

5. William Dean Howells, *Criticism and Fiction and Other Essays,* edited by Clara Marburg Kirk and Rudolf Kirk (New York: New York University Press, 1959), pp. 347–348.
6. William Dean Howells, *Life in Letters of William Dean Howells,* edited by Mildred Howells, 2 vols. (Garden City, New York: Doubleday, Doran and Company, Inc., 1928), II, 173.
7. *Criticism and Fiction* (1959), p. 67.

*The Landlord at Lion's Head* employs a relatively simple narrative structure; but in the course of covering some dozen years in time and tracing in greater or lesser fullness the histories of a variety of characters, it develops a great deal of significant detail. Since a knowledge and understanding of that detail is the best approach to the accumulated meanings which give *The Landlord at Lion's Head* its permanent value, a survey of its principal lines of action and relationships is a proper beginning for analysis and evaluation.

The primary focus traces Jeff Durgin's career from boyhood to his eventual assumption, in fulfillment of a long-time purpose, of the role of landlord at the inn which had originally been the family farm. The novel divides itself into five units, each of which details a stage of Jeff's development and works to some sort of climax or crisis. The first (Chapters I–VIII) shows Jeff as a boy on the farm at Lion's Head, already evidencing the strength, willfulness, and egotism which will characterize the man, and encouraged in the development of his unamiable qualities by the indulgence of his otherwise stern and morally severe mother. The keynote of his relationship with the artist Westover is struck when, after apparently accepting without ill will some deserved corporeal and verbal chastisement from the visitor, Jeff seizes the moment of Westover's leave-taking, when reprisal is unlikely, to revenge himself: he pelts him with apples and thus endangers the canvas of Lion's Head which has been several weeks in the painting.

After a transitional chapter, which allows for the passage of five years and the transformation of the Durgin farm into a successful summer resort, the next unit (Chapters X–XIX) deals primarily with aspects of Jeff's social education. He is administered a humiliating snub by one of the inn's summer residents. He enters Harvard—his mother's ambition is for him to become a lawyer—and his failure to gain social acceptance there culminates in his arrest for a drunken prank with some other "jays," a night in jail, and his suspension from college. He works his way to Europe where, among other activities, he studies hotelkeeping with a view to his future proprietorship of Lion's Head Inn (his own ambition, rather than the law). Prior to returning to Harvard, he continues a somewhat tentative country romance with Cynthia Whitwell, a childhood playmate now in charge of the resort's dining room. His return to Harvard is marked by no real change in his general social relationships, but he renews an acquaintance with a former summer resident of Lion's Head, Genevieve Vostrand. His eventual proposal to her is, to his surprise and chagrin, rejected because she regards herself as engaged to an Italian count.

The third section (Chapters XX–XXVII) shows Jeff becoming more and more dissatisfied with the idea of a career in law and more and more committed to becoming manager of the family business. Claiming to himself that he is reconciled to Genevieve's foreign marriage, he resumes his affair with Cynthia, and they become engaged. It is she who insists that he take his degree, for Mrs. Durgin, in finally surrendering her dream of him as a lawyer, has no further interest in Harvard. This decision by Cynthia has important consequences, which are detailed in section four (Chapters XXVIII–XLII).

An unusual set of conditions brings Jeff into Boston and Cambridge society enough to allow him to make the acquaintance of Bessie Lynde, an unconventional and flirtatious girl of twenty-five. Fascinated by her wit and daring, but fully conscious that their relationship is a contest of wills, Jeff pursues her at a variety of social affairs and ends a thoroughly unconventional late evening call at her home by sweeping her into his arms and kissing her. This is the end of the game, and Jeff's subsequent brutally frank admission to her that he has simply entered into the sport of her flirtatiousness, that one of his gambits had been to get her brother drunk, and that he had been engaged to another girl throughout the affair, initiates the action of the final major unit (Chapters XLIII–LII).

His confession to Cynthia results in the breaking of their engagement, and he discovers that he is relieved not to have to live up to an ideal. Bessie's part in an apparent renewal of their flirtation during Jeff's Harvard Class Day is made ambiguous when, later that day, Jeff is taken unawares by her brother and horsewhipped. When Jeff's older brother and then his mother die, the way is open to him to put into effect all his business plans. A chance meeting with Alan Lynde, who is taking a cure for his chronic alcoholism in the vicinity of the Lion's Head, enables Jeff to even that score by almost killing the horsewhipper. He now goes to Europe, where a meeting with the widowed Genevieve eventuates in their marriage.

The remaining chapters (LIII–LV) tie up the loose ends. Jeff is thoroughly successful as an innkeeper. Westover, who has been in constant touch with the events as a fairly regular visitor at Lion's Head and as a Cambridge resident who early became involved in Jeff's affairs there, pays court to and wins Cynthia Whitwell.

The vital core of *The Landlord at Lion's Head* is the characterization of that new American man, Thomas Jefferson Durgin (Howells thought of the surname as "strong" and "rough" and right for the personality to which he assigned it,[8] and the ironic implications of the given names are self-evident). The disciplined, probing power with which Howells searches for an understanding of both Durgin's distinctive individuality and those qualities which he apparently absorbed from the times in which he lives and which thus makes him a representative man as well, opens up a broad range of profoundly serious religious, moral, social, and psychological aspects of American experience. This management of his story allowed Howells to avoid both the split between the personal and broader meanings which marred the rich circumstantiality of *The Minister's Charge* and the schematic tendency of *A Hazard of New Fortunes*. Westover is the principal point of view, but since his knowledge is often limited and his judgment affected by his own bias and involvement, he provides merely *one* perspective, a way of formulating rather than solving the enigma of Jeff's personality and moral nature and the meaning of his conduct and fate.

Howells clearly indicated his own feelings toward Jeff by valuing his "aesthetic success" in portraying "a true rustic New England type in contact with urban life under entirely modern conditions" and apologetically admitting that he therefore liked him "more than

8. *The Landlord at Lion's Head* (New York: A Signet Classic, the New American Library, 1964), p. vi.

I have liked worthier men" (p. vi). It is one of the strengths of the novel, however, that it is open, that it refuses moral pronouncements in favor of the dramatizing of situations which inescapably reveal the inadequacy of the conventional acceptations or the necessity for finding fresh validation for them. The major dramatic confrontations which most clearly define the moral issue are between Jeff and Westover, though there are many other dramatically exemplified instances of this theme. Howells singled out Jeff's "anti-Puritan quality" (p. vii) as a clue to his own understanding of the character, but it not precisely this which is the basis of the conflict with Westover, since the artist is in his own way anti-Puritan also. He is a western man whose acquaintance in Italy with "Boston people" led him to choose "to live where that kind of people lived" (p. 204), and he professes an "agnosticism so common among men in towns" that he shocks both the Yankee Whitwell and Jeff's older brother, Jackson, by voicing it "quite simply and unconsciously" (p. 68).

Westover's unorthodoxy, however, still leaves him with a strong moral sense and a belief in a moral government of the universe which will, at least in some ultimate state, enforce a law of cause and effect which decrees that if a man has "sowed evil . . . he must reap evil. He may never know it, but he will reap what he has sown" (p. 303). For Jeff, such a belief in the relationship between good and evil is another of Westover's "old-fashioned superstitions" (p. 233), the kind of thinking that makes Westover an "idealist" (p. 191), by which he really means that the artist exhibits feminine scrupulosity and impracticality. His experience of this world—which is the only world he is concerned with and which has offered for his emulation only standards of social and materialistic success—has led him to the conclusion that the secret to personal satisfaction and worldly acceptance is strength:

"You pay, or you don't pay, just as it happens. If you get hit soon after you've done wrong, you think it's retribution, and if it holds off till you've forgotten all about it, you think it's a strange Providence and you puzzle over it, but you don't reform. . . . Prosperity and adversity, they've got nothing to do with conduct. If you're a strong man, you get there, and if you're a weak man, all the righteousness in the universe won't help you" (p. 234).

   Though some suggestions are made that Jeff's "cussedness"— evident in his adolescent pranks and vindictiveness and developed in this rationalized view of his behavior with Bessie Lynde—may be explained as literal deviltry, or original sin, or inherited propensity (p. 29), Howells's focus is more on what he is than on how he got that way. In Westover's view, Jeff's "conscientious toughness" is even less reprehensible than the kind of masked hypocrisy evidenced in Whitwell's "self-applausive rapacity" and "remorseless self-inter-est" (p. 306), or "the sentimental insincerities" (p. 289) of Mrs. Vostrand. Howells has no interest in portraying Jeff as Satanic or even as the carrier of some kind of blood taint: evil, for Howells, is a matter of the will, as it had always been, and there is no purely voluntary evil among the sane. Voluntary or uncontrollable evil is a matter for alienists and offers no temptation to the realistic novelist, who wishes to address himself to that area of human experience sub-ject to the ordering laws of rationality and therefore to the judg-ment of moral principle. Moreover, Jeff is never represented as com-pelled to wickedness for its own sake. He repays real or imagined af-fronts to his sense of his own dignity and rights (and from whatever instinct of self-preservation or moral principle, refuses the oppor-tunity to kill the man who attacked him unawares with a whip). He responds to social and sexual challenges. He rebels against his fam-ily's attempt to map out his life for him, but he is never simply malign.
   The image which seems best to embody Howells's controlling at-titude toward Jeff—as distinct from Westover's—is that of a "broken shaft." This is an image first introduced as a message from the planchette which Jackson Durgin spends most of his leisure time experimenting with. As interpreted by Whitwell and skeptically re-interpreted by Westover, it is taken when associated with the further revelation "Thomas Jefferson—," to mean that the ship on which Jeff is returning from Europe has been delayed by such a mechanical failure. This theory is exploded by Jeff's unexpectedly early appear-ance, in the very course of the theorizing, but the association with

Jeff is clearly established (pp. 69–73).[9] That association is enforced
when Whitwell and Westover return, at the close of the novel, to
this image in an attempt to bring some kind of judgment to bear
on Jeff's history, which is now shaping itself in what appears a mutually satisfying marriage with Genevieve Vostrand and the spec-
tacularly successful proprietorship of a renovated and reorganized
Lion's Head Inn. Westover cannot accept Whitwell's speculation
that the image exemplifies the change in Jeff (proven by his sparing
of the life of Alan Lynde), and he applies the metaphor to his general theory of the human condition and ultimate justice. He suggests that " 'Perhaps we're all broken shafts, here. Perhaps that old
hypothesis of another life, a world where there is room enough
and time enough for all beginnings of this to complete themselves
—" (p. 304) is the most convincing application.

Howells, however, has skillfully adumbrated throughout the
novel a more specific association with Jeff which accounts for his
own mixed feelings about this most virile and forceful of all his
protagonists. When Jeff characterizes Westover as an "idealist" (p.
191), the artist is given a perception, which he does not develop in
the closing statement. Yet it carries conviction as an exact measure
of the difference between a "primitive" (p. 90) Jeff Durgin and people who believe in or pay lip service to the individual responsibility
for the perpetuation or betterment of "civilized" life: "The acceptance of the moral fact as it was, without the conscious effort to
better it or to hold himself strictly to account for it, was the secret of
the power in the man which would bring about the material results
he desired" (p. 192). Jeff's moral naure is "broken"—incomplete—
and he is simply incapable of understanding or being motivated by
the "goodness" which is natural to his brother Jackson or to Westover:

9. It would be possible to introduce other applications of the image to
Jeff's characterization. For example, it is an apt image of Jeff's truncated and
powerful physique: "Jeff Durgin's stalwart frame was notable for strength
rather than height. He . . . was massive without being bulky" (p. 39). It
could be associated with his male aggressiveness which is "broken" by not
being allied with tenderness or reverence: his view is that "any man's fit for
any woman if he wants her bad enough" (p. 263).

Jackson had been a good man; he realized that with a curious sense of novelty in the reflection; he wondered what the incentives and objects of such men as Jackson and Westover were, anyway. Something like grief for his brother came upon him; not such grief as he had felt passionately enough, though tacitly, for his mother; but a regret for not having shown Jackson during his life that he could appreciate his unselfishness, though he could not see the reason or the meaning of it (p. 277).

Such an understanding of Jeff Durgin by Howells makes condemnation irrelevant: there is nothing to be gained by a thundering denunciation of a man incapable of understanding the grounds of judgment. Moreover, Howells clearly shares Westover's reaction to Durgin's "earthbound" temperament: his "simplicity of motive . . . had its charm. Westover was aware of liking Durgin . . . much more than he ought and of liking him helplessly" (p. 192). One reason is that Jeff's selfishness is "good-natured" (p. 192), and when he is measured against the actualities of motive and character that prevail in the world, he at least exhibits strength rather than weakness, amorality rather than immorality, a kind of healthy selfishness rather than a hypocritical or sick egotism, an absence of religious feeling rather than a decadent religiosity or attenuated or merely fashionable piety.

These are the terms, with little alleviation, in which Howells pictures the current moral and religious conditions of America. The alleviations are provided by Westover and Cynthia Whitwell, and to a lesser degree by Mrs. Durgin and Jackson. All of them, however, have personal limitations which make them something less than an ideal, and none is possessed of the kind of religious faith or moral force that could significantly modify the general condition. The religious context is established primarily by brief references to the practice or state of belief of the individual characters and by the constant reference of the problem posed by that "comical devil," as Whitwell habitually refers to Jeff, to a supernatural moral government, an enclosing plan which can be trusted to balance Jeff's achievement of worldly success by an ultimate exaction for his insensitivity and egotism. This context serves, then, not to supply a true religious answer to the questions raised—those illustrated are not merely inadequate, they are usually debased—but to direct attention to the connection between the absence of a vitalized, informing religious faith in the daily lives of the characters and the present conditions in all aspects of the social body, including the relationship between the sexes (which even Westover thinks of as "innate enmity" [p. 231]).

Westover's agnosticism, as we have seen, includes a belief in God and at least a desire to believe in a more justly ordered future world, but he is basically moral rather than religious. That is one reason his pronouncements have so little effect on a Jeff Durgin. They merely represent one possible interpretation of mundane reality, and Jeff's sometimes more experienced conclusions (as in his ability to see Bessie Lynde's character and motivation as they are and his refusal to explain her in terms of conventionally accepted womanly attitudes) can rather easily withstand the opposition. Westover's moral idealism tends to crumble into mere gentility and even priggishness because it issues from merely tentative religious principles and from an imperfect grasp of reality. The latter, in fact, sometimes approaches a denial of reality—as, for example, in his wish to believe in the Mrs. Vostrand known to his youth and inexperience in Italy rather than the present Mrs. Vostrand of Lion's Head and Cambridge—and this is a tendency which is fostered by his life as an artist. That role as a painter encourages him to be an observer rather than an actor, to prefer the "aesthetic" view which, for example, determines his early reaction to life at Lion's Head as "Arcadian" (p. 53).

Cynthia's Puritan heritage continues strong in her and gives her the moral force and courage to survive her affair with Jeff with dignity and without undue bitterness. She is, however, early described as a "pure, cold beauty" (p. 48). Something of that coldness finds expression in the moral certainty which enables her to dismiss Jeff by imposing conditions which it is obviously not in his nature to meet and in turning for marriage to the less aggressive man whom she has known since she was a child. Her father's religion has become largely a social exercise in the evenings spent with Jackson over the planchette and in "philosophical" discussions about the

origins of the idea of immortality (pp. 132–133). It is also a commercial asset, for he has found a congenial occupation as a natural
philosopher and guide to the feminine patrons of Lion's Head. As
Jeff contemptuously remarks, " 'He talks religion to 'em,' " because
" 'women seem to like religion, whether they belong to church or
not' " (p. 41). His truest character is that of a "Yankee" (p. 306)
of the type who takes full financial advantage of Jeff's need for his
otherwise modestly valuable property.

Jeff's indifference to religion and his greater energy and business
acumen allow him to exploit it in more imaginative and ambitious
terms. In expanding and renovating Lion's Head Inn, he incor-
porates the graves of his parents and brother into the landscaping
by having an "architect *treat* the place" (p. 301) and is even con-
templating the erection there of a picturesque little chapel for religious services. Mrs. Durgin exhibited in her lifetime a matter-of-
fact belief in a "spirit life" (p. 37) to which her husband and children had passed, but she was too absorbed in the problems of survival and then of furthering her dreams for Jeff to be really concerned with metaphysical questions. Bessie Lynde's aunt has shel-
tered herself in a "myopic optimism" which has allowed her to
evade a conscious realization of the truth about her alcoholic nephew
and neurotic niece and permitted them to grow "to manhood and
womanhood without materially discomposing her faith in the old-
fashioned Unitarian deity whose service she had always attended"
(p. 156). And Howells neatly ticks off the spiritual condition of
"good society in Boston" by his remark that "it goes southward to
indulge in a Lenten grief at Old Point Comfort" (p. 92) and the
further explanation that such summer sojourns are also a tax dodge
(p. 94).

These citations by no means exhaust the quantity of religious
reference which Howells weaves into his canvas, but they are more
than enough to support the introductory generalization: none of
these characters looks with any assurance, if at all, to a vital religious
faith for a supportive strength in the difficulties of earthly existence. By implication, at least, the corollary conclusion is that the
large majority of such people, thrown upon their own inner resources
by this lack of outside guidance, are either inadequate or distorted.

They are variously weak or shallow or corrupted or strong in their pursuit of wholly selfish and materialistic goals, or they are detached from the truly meaningful currents of spiritual or moral life—in short, they are indeed, in a more pessimistic sense than Westover intended, "all broken shafts" (p. 304).

The social meanings of the novel are more explicitly formulated and more carefully compounded by being natural developments of Jeff's romantic involvements with Cynthia, with Bessie Lynde, and with Genevieve Vostrand, each representing a distinct combination of social and sexual pressure. These relationships need, therefore, to be examined first in their psychological terms. Howells here specifically dealt with both love and flirtation as warfare in which "the innate enmity" could clearly be discerned: "its presence in passion that was lived" and "its prevalence in passion that was played" (p. 231). Such an insight contributes a great deal to the understanding of Jeff's conduct toward all three of the women with whom he becomes seriously involved. The earliest portrayal of Cynthia and Jeff, as children, for example, keys their relationship to a struggle for domination. Westover rescues Cynthia and little Franky Whitwell from being terrorized by Jeff and his dog. Not many days afterward, however, Jeff, apparently by assuming a kind of proprietorship of Westover and exhibiting him at work to the other children, has managed to restore "a good understanding" between himself and Cynthia of which she seems "ashamed . . . before Westover" (p. 31).

As the years pass, though, her self-control and intelligence give her an advantage. She tutors Jeff so that he can enter Harvard and even manages to keep up with him in at least some of his studies while he is there. When Jeff returns from his summer in Europe following his expulsion from Harvard, he is easily diverted from an incipient involvement with Cynthia, which she gives no sign of discouraging, by his acquaintance with Genevieve Vostrand. His mother recalls the insult he had suffered from an earlier guest and puts a stop to these attentions. Instead of turning back to Cynthia, he leaves Lion's Head and goes back to college. There, his renewal of acquaintance with Genevieve leads to the proposal which is rejected, and he goes once more to Cynthia, obviously in reaction and with the assurance that he will be welcomed. He does not propose to her until she has refused him certain freedoms formerly permissible, and involved in his motives is his desire to give up any notion of a legal career, leave college, and become a hotelkeeper, at Lion's Head preferably, but elsewhere if necessary. Their engagement offers Cynthia several immediate opportunities for dominance: she insists that Jeff shall finish at Harvard, that he shall inform his mother at once of their engagement, and that he complete the job by telling her of his resolve to give up the law.

The ambiguous character of Jeff's feeling for Cynthia is emphasized by his instant fascination with Bessie Lynde and his reckless conduct with her. And when this conduct has led to a formal break with Cynthia, the ambiguity is resolved. He feels relief, a sense of freedom: "He was sensible in his relaxation of having strained up to another's ideal, of having been hampered by another's will" (p. 251). He sees his affair with Bessie as proof that he simply does not care enough for Cynthia to continue the struggle to satisfy her conception of him without sacrificing his necessary sense of power over her. It is his view that any man's fitness for any woman is determined by the degree of his desire for her, and he is sure that he could win Cynthia back; he just does not judge the effort worthwhile. In terms of the original statement of the war between the sexes, Cynthia's "enmity" is present, but less obvious because she truly loves Jeff. Within limits, she can forgive and accept. But these limits are, at least unconsciously, indicative of the sexual battle. She breaks with Jeff because she claims she will not compel him to do what is right, that if she did he would make her suffer for it. What she really asks then is an even more complete domination which will involve no risk for herself: he must *want* to do what is right simply because he knows she wants it of him. Jeff is incapable of such selflessness and love, and it clearly will not be asked of him in his eventual marriage to Genevieve.

The contest with Bessie is far more openly recognized for what it is. She is a sophisticated habitué of society. By remaining single at twenty-five, she has outgrown the college boys whom she is forced to use as her escorts. With an avidity equal and analogous to her brother's drinking, she is seeking "excitement" (p. 183).[10] There is no mistaking the sexual component of the excitement she finds in deliberately taking up a daring relationship with a "jay." It is his "strange massiveness," the "rude force of . . . [his] face and figure" that first attract her notice. When he proves to be unimpressed with her social graces, she is "piqued" by his "indifference" and makes a deliberate "effort to hold his eyes" from wandering (p. 142). They engage in an unusually frank discussion, and she then leaves him "as if she had forgotten him"; but at her departure from the room, she directs to him "a brilliant smile that seemed to illumine him from head to foot, and before it was quenched he felt as if she had kissed her hand to him from her rich mouth" (p. 148).

As their intimacy progresses, Bessie continues to maintain her sense of superiority, while she indulges her sense of daring by describing Jeff to herself and others as barely humanized. He gives "a primitive effect in his clothes"; he is like a "prehistoric man that the barbers and tailors had put a *fin de siècle* surface on" (p. 159); he is "like an animal speaking French" (p. 161); he is "a bear who's gone so much with human beings that he thinks he's a human being" (p. 217). She also reveals the source of her excitement in encouraging this animal to believe he is human (for she unmistakably made clear to him, at their second meeting, that he was to walk her home, and she delighted him at a party by pretending he had committed her to a dance he had not asked for): she likes the danger which she knows to be present in playing with him. She admits, for example, that in his quality as a prehistoric man he gives her the "creeps . . . as if he were really carrying me off to his cave" (p. 159). And her reaction to their intellectual sparring is "mingled fear and slight" (p. 226). For his part, Jeff is under no illusion as to the kind of game they are playing, and very early "the will to domi-

10. The sexual character of this "excitement" in Bessie's case is made especially explicit in the scene where she is tempted to seek help from her brother's doctor but is beaten "back into herself" by his "fatally stupid" resort to a conventional cliché of language and feeling to describe her problem: to her remark that " 'Sometimes women get drunk, and then I think they do less harm than if they did other things to get away from the excitement,' " he replies, " 'You mean like breaking hearts and such little matters?' " (p. 183).

nate her began to stir in him" (p. 152). The force of Westover's accusation of him as a blackguard for having gotten Alan Lynde drunk is weakened precisely because it is based on a generalized, conventional attitude; he simply assumes an effect of shock and disgust like his own if Bessie were to know the facts of the case. Jeff's answer that he would be interested to know, not what she *said,* but what she *thought* is a far more realistic if less gentlemanly appraisal of their situation.

Similarly, though Howells judges Jeff's direct physical assault "a sacrilege" (p. 228), it is with full knowledge that sexual play invites this result and with the feeling that a woman's blame for the "betrayal" of love is "heavier" (p. 231) than that of the man whom she tries to play with. Moreover, Howells shows with complete honesty the degree of her responsibility and the mere snobbishness of her immediate reaction. She brought on the embrace by playfully barring Jeff's exit when he reacted with cold indifference to a final breaking off of their intellectual affair, and she is unable to sustain her poise. Whatever her outrage, Jeff knows she offered no resistance "and even trembled towards him." Her shock is not, it seems, that she has been kissed, but that she has been kissed like a maid by a grocery boy: "This man had abolished all the differences of family, of society, of personality, and put himself on a level with her in the most sacred things of life" (p. 228). Moreover, her own emotional confusion is so great that she cannot really decide whether she is outraged or not, and she thinks "that she must be in love with the man if she did not resent what he had done" (p. 228). Presumably, then, the decision to inform her brother, which leads to Jeff's horsewhipping, was specifically caused by his contemptuous break with her and is the revenge of a woman scorned as much as of a woman violated.[11]

11. Had Jeff Durgin raped Bessie Lynde instead of kissing her, presumably many would find the novel more realistic. But the kiss has the dramatic force of a rape in the context in which it occurs. It is carefully distinguised from the kisses Jeff exchanges with Cynthia both before and after their engagement; it is Jeff's impulsive reaction to "contact" (p. 227) with Bessie. It would seem, then, just as valid to regard it as an easily understandable convention as to explain it away as old-maidishness. Any gain from a

The fullness with which Jeff's affairs with Cynthia and Bessie are detailed made it possible for Howells to bring about the marriage with Genevieve Vostrand in much briefer compass. She is seen by contrast as Jeff's ideal mate. Her "exquisite gentleness" (p. 87), her habit of deference, do not obstruct but rather smooth the way to Jeff's sense of himself: she is of sufficient social rank for him to feel pride in winning her and to justify certain gentlemanly airs he adopts in his role as landlord. His feeling for Genevieve is sincere: in spite of his claims of being reconciled to her foreign marriage, his relations with Cynthia and Bessie have been affected by the fact that Genevieve was the "one woman in this world" (p. 263) he really cared for. Yet his first attraction to her, as his mother recognized, had been as a means of assuaging the hurt he had suffered by his ignominious rejection as a social equal by a guest. That injury was then compounded by Genevieve's refusal of his first proposal and his discovery that Mrs. Vostrand had been kind in order not to give the same offense. His marriage, therefore, is both a romantic triumph and a social vindication, and by it he gains a thoroughly complaisant wife and a perceptive mother-in-law in perfect sympathy with his materialistic ambitions.

This dramatically integrated awareness of the religious decay occurring in late-nineteenth-century New England, with its consequent effects on the moral characters of both rustic and urban inhabitants, and the probing in depth of the current forms of the war between the sexes are sufficient proofs of the continuing vitality and innovative modernity of Howells's creativity. *The Landlord at Lion's Head* supplies still more evidence in its exploration of the relationship between these facts and the general social condition.

In 1882, Howells confidently believed that Americans were a "thoroughly homogeneous people," believed that there was "such a parity in the experiences of Americans" that the average American was the man who had "risen." Fifteen years later, *The Landlord at Lion's Head* showed that his optimism about that common back-

---

more explicit detailing of the physical relationships would have been in dramatic verisimilitude and not in psychological truth.

ground and the value of "rising" had undergone modification. In 1885, he approved the moral rise of Silas Lapham, one of whose costs was the sacrifice of social ambition. The criticism, however, had been directed against the effects of wealth on Lapham, his swelling pride which sought to feed itself by buying acceptance from Boston society, rather than against the society itself. Howells was aware of the uselessness of a Bromfield Corey, the limitations imposed by mere propriety on a Mrs. Corey. In a Tom Corey, however, he had suggested the hope, it not for a radical reconstruction of society, at least for a revitalization of it through an honorable joining in commercial enterprise and an alliance with Penelope Lapham.

The Landlord at Lion's Head, on the other hand, is a convincing demonstration of the fulfillment of Howells's own prediction that the conditions he was describing in 1882 might, "in another generation or two . . . be wholly different."[12] Now, the society toward which men like Jeff Durgin attempt to rise is more than self-satisfied and punctilious: it is decadent and sick. The infusion of the strength of a Jeff Durgin, directed as it is toward wholly materialistic and selfish ends, will provide no moral restitution. The marriage of a Westover and Cynthia Whitwell is only in a very restricted sense an example of the "simple structure of our society, the free play of our democracy." Even the possibility of a spiritual restoration by a return to the pastoral simplicities (Lapham could go back to Vermont, Lemuel Barker could go back to Willoughby Pastures) is denied. In the first place, Lion's Head represented a life of grinding poverty and intellectual and spiritual impoverishment; in the second, it had now been thoroughly urbanized and commercialized.

The story of Jeff Durgin's climb to material success and a certain amount of social acceptance was no longer the kind of story that could be proudly offered as an example of the American dream. (Indeed, it might be seen as a realist's ironic answer to any of the enormously popular renderings of that myth by Horatio Alger, with whom Howells was contemporaneous for sixty-two years.) Additionally, the fate which the Vostrands suffer in Boston reveals the

12. "Mark Twain," Century, XXIV (September 1882), 781–782.

character of the social conventions which they themselves began by
invoking against Jeff.

He is at first treated as an object of social condescension, a jay
who can be invited to a second-rate affair and hopefully used in
the service of more openly characterized charitable "work at the
North End" (p. 149). He contemptuously refuses to allow himself
to be used for such purposes, but avails himself of any entree which
offers an opportunity of meeting Bessie Lynde. After a time, his
"social acceptance" gains "a sudden precipitance; and people who
wondered why they met him at other houses began to ask him to
their own" (p. 214). Mrs. Vostrand, who had been kind to Westover in Italy, and who has none of the obvious financial and personal disqualifications of Jeff, is briefly launched in Boston through
Westover's intervention with friends, but not even Genevieve's
"beauty and . . . grace" (p. 92) can make a lasting break in the social hierarchy. It is an interesting complication of theme that it is
their common roles as social pariahs that bring Jeff and Genevieve
into the intimacy which culminates in his first rejected proposal.
Mrs. Vostrand completely accepts the social system, and she fights to
win entrance into it through the purchased marriage of Genevieve to an Italian count, the almost continuously absent Mr. Vostrand supplying the money. However, the eventual marriage of Jeff
and Genevieve does not furnish, as it might have in an earlier
Howells novel, a contrast between American and European arrangements that is favorable to democratic love marriages. Mrs. Vostrand's
"mawkish hypocrisy" (p. 292) in furthering this result, and Mr.
Vostrand's relieved and long-distance approval of Jeff's being a "busi-
nessman" (p. 288) like himself, make for little distinction in the
two affairs.

It is through the Lyndes, however, that Howells pronounces on
an American society which is decadent, useless, and self-protective.
The maiden aunt with whom Bessie and Alan live perfectly typifies
the impervious complacency of this society. Physically, mentally,
spiritually, she is composed entirely of smooth surfaces untouched
by the abrasions of life. She has been "stupefied by a life of un-
alloyed prosperity and propriety." For her, there have been two
kinds of people: those like herself, and those not; and she has lived

entirely "in the shelter of . . . [the] opinions and ideals" of her own kind. Having little contact with other kinds of people, she is not even forced to scorn them. Her "myopic optimism" (p. 156) has allowed her to believe that Alan's escapades had been sufficiently hushed up (his real guilt results merely in voluntary withdrawal from Harvard, whereas Jeff's circumstantial guilt results in suspension) to satisfy the only public opinion that matters. And though she well understands his present alcoholism with its necessary periodic cures, she can blandly treat it as a problem of physical health. Her slight deafness, which allows her to ignore open quarrels between Alan and Bessie over his drinking and her social freedoms, is a perfect symbol of the means by which she has passed through life without having her Unitarian faith or her trust in the "invulnerable order" (p. 156) of her social arrangements materially discomposed.

Within this protective context, Alan and Bessie practice a social and moral irresponsibility which Howells reveals with such great skill and emotional force that the comparative view jumps all the way to Fitzgerald's *Gatsby* to find suitable parallels. Alan has led a life of "dissolute idleness" (p. 278), devoting himself to his club, to horses, and to drinking. His sister and friends believe that he has great intelligence and "could be anything" (p. 161) he chooses; there is a "distinction" in "even the sinister something" in his appearance, a "style in the signs of [his] dissipation" (p. 153) which compels Jeff's envy. In his drunkenness at elegant social affairs, he either retains enough poise or is so quietly taken care of that no notice need be taken of his condition. Bessie, as has been shown, has similar qualities: her intelligence and wit have apparently driven off eligible men, she cares nothing for the normal feminine diversions of music or art, she is driven to seek release for her tensions in such "excitements" as her flirting with Jeff, just as Alan turns compulsively to the decanter.

Like the society of which they are representative, they have charm and gaiety and grace. But such qualities are hardly adequate in themselves to give definition to their lives, to establish relationships within an acceptable framework of mutual moral and social responsibility. Daisy and Tom Buchanan retreated behind their money whenever they were faced with responsibility. In much the same way, Bessie and Alan retreat to the impregnable fortress of their social status whenever their peccadilloes demand payment. This position furnishes ready-made attitudes which place responsibility squarely on ill-bred pretenders to equality like Jeff. Drunk, Alan can avail himself of Jeff's services in getting home while calling him "a damn jay" (p. 176). Sober, he can rest comfortably in the belief that it was the "gentleman" Westover who performed the service and be protected from the truth by Bessie (p. 156). She can play with Jeff and judge herself "not despicable" because "the audacity of her behavior with the jay" (p. 175) is not flirting, but can despise the result enough to bring about Jeff's horsewhipping. Nor does Alan's method of assuming the fraternal responsibility he has long neglected make him compare favorably with the jay. From behind, in a horse and buggy, he attacks Jeff, who is on foot, and simply runs away when Jeff attempts to defend himself. Jeff, on the other hand, meets him face to face, announces his intention to kill, does not even use his boxing skill to counter that of his opponent, and desists before carrying out his threat.

The refusal of total revenge by Jeff introduces additional complications of theme which prove how successfully Howells "broke through into the daylight beyond" (p. vi) in probing the dense mass of material he had accumulated in his story. Nick Carraway learned about the brutal stupidity and carelessness concealed beneath the charm of a Tom and Daisy Buchanan. Howells documented a similar perception of the under-lives of the Lyndes. He made use of it, not in the form of a moral pronouncement, but subtly, as a component of Jeff Durgin's pragmatic assessment of society and his relationship to it. Jeff's action in sparing Alan Lynde "was accomplished through his will, and not by it" (p. 278); it was apparently the instinctive expression of his past moral and social experience: "He glared down into his enemy's face, and suddenly it looked pitifully little and weak, like a girl's face, a child's" (p. 278). In this compressed and richly suggestive image, Howells completes his indictment of the false American dream of social and material success. American society as represented by the Alan Lyndes was not only brutally stupid and careless, it was weak and pitiful, childishly self-destructive.

The associations are even more complex than this, however. The image of the little girl's face meaningfully connects Jeff's subconscious motivation with the lesson Westover had administered to the boy who was terrifying the Whitwell children. The effect of the association is to suggest that the moral and social values of Westover, which have seemed mostly ineffectual, may at last be making themselves felt. Jeff undergoes no profound spiritual transformation. Yet this rejection of final revenge, together with his capacity to wonder at the goodness that motivated men like his brother and Westover, allow the small hope that his amorality is susceptible, in some degree, at least, to conditioning. That fact was perhaps one of the sources of Howells's liking for him. Such strength and vitality, misdirected by the logical inferences forced upon them by society, but potentially educable, are at least preferable to the self-indulgent decadence of the Lyndes.

That potential, however, is at best embryonic. For another explanation of Jeff's action is simply that he turned away in scorn from Alan Lynde's weakness, turned away with the confidence that it offered no impediment to his goals. As a boy, he had reacted to Westover's rebuke for terrifying the Whitwell children by a different exercise of control over them: "He had begun to convoy parties of children up to see Westover at work . . . and to show the painter off to them as a sort of family property. . . . He seemed on perfect terms with . . . [the young Whitwells] now" (p. 31). The beating of Lynde, like his subsequent pelting of Westover and his canvas with apples, is now enough to dissipate his resentment against a force which no longer has any significant power to affect him. His real answer to the Lyndes is the realization of his material ambitions as proprietor of the hotel and of his social ambitions in his marriage.[13] Implicit in his answer is an ironic comment on the quality of the new American dream to which young men aspire.

13. Westover soon perceived that in spite of Jeff's refusal to conform at Harvard, to enter the kind of activities that would neutralize his disadvantages and gain him acceptance, and in spite of his wild misconceptions about the "scandalous" life of fashionable Boston, "Jeff would willingly have been of it; . . . that if he had any strong aspirations they were for society and for social acceptance" (p. 63). Jeff's marriage, then, is clearly not just a love match; it finally negates Mrs. Marven's snub.

To speak of the potentiality of morality in Jeff is to raise the question of Westover's role as a moral positive in *Landlord*. To some extent, Westover's history is also that of a man who has risen. Howells seems to draw on the general outlines of his own past in describing Westover's Wisconsin boyhood, his discovery of his artistic talent, his Italian sojourn to develop it, his return to Boston. The Italian experience provided the basis of two decisions: an acquaintance with Bostonians which convinced Westover that he would like to live among such people; and the opportunity to discover that the conflict of opinion in Milwaukee's view that he was "somebody" and that of New York that he was "nobody" did not really need to be resolved: it was the work that he "was trying to do [that] was the important thing" (p. 204). This attitude, joined with his natural qualities and social graces, allows Westover to be accepted by Boston society, to be in it though he is not of it. In one sense, then, his presumptive marriage to Cynthia will be truly "democratic." As contrasted with Genevieve's arranged foreign alliance and Jeff's valuing of the Vostrands' social position, it will be made without regard for their social difference.

In fact, however, after a visit with Cynthia's father, in which Westover sees that he is "irreparably rustic, that he was and always must be practically a Yankee," a type Westover does "not love or honor," he reacts by thinking Cynthia, too, must grow into such a type "through the lapse from the personal to the ancestral which we all undergo in the process of the years" (p. 306). His proposal comes only after her presence drives away thoughts that the marriage might be "a mistake on the spiritual as well as the worldly side," that it "certainly would not . . . [promote] his career" (p. 306) and might impede it. For her part, Cynthia gives no sign of valuing Westover's social superiority for its own sake, and other factors take away any representative, ideal social significance the match might have. Not only is it true that Westover's social position is not such as to make the marriage an effective comment on false, undemocratic social standards, but, from the other side, Cynthia reduces the social distance between them by being an unusual country girl. Moreover, it is frankly admitted that Westover's ideal of life and marriage is "philistine and bourgeois," and Howells speaks out directly to char-

acterize it as "commonplace and almost sordid" (p. 305). He intends
that it shall be clearly understood that this is an eminently suitable
partnership between two generally admirable people. They are no
longer, however, the average Americans.

Cynthia's father; Jeff Durgin; the Vostrands; the Lyndes; Mrs.
Marven, the patron of Lion's Head who, on a picnic, marked Jeff's
inferior social quality by serving him first so that he could go back to
his horses; Mrs. Bevidge, Boston society matron and organizer of
doubtfully effective charities, who congratulates Bessie Lynde for
having "done missionary work" in entertaining Jeff, the Harvard
jay, at a tea—these are now, quantitatively at least, the average
Americans, confirming the fear expressed by Howells in 1882 that
the "parity" of experience might disappear from American life. Some
counterweight is represented by Westover, Cynthia and her brother
Franky, Mrs. Durgin, and Jackson. However, their special qualities
—their preservation of religious and moral values, their humane
concern for others, or their devotion to family in a more than social
sense—are what now distinguish them from the average. (Jeff,
too, is unusual in his self-confident strength and drive for money and
power, but those are now the goals, the "ideals" of the average
American.) Moreover, even these admirable persons exhibit certain
personal inadequacies which limit the degree to which they may be
expected to influence the general social order.

Westover's qualities, for example, make him, finally, more neu-
tral than forceful. He is characterized by a "simple-hearted ambition" for a "stated existence, a home where he could work constantly
in an air of affection and unselfishly do his part to make his home
happy" (p. 305); by a lack, apparently, of a sense of continuity from
his "emigrant people" whom he left at sixteen (p. 204); by a toler-
ant agnosticism, and by a rather timid approach to the emotional
commitments of life. His example or his influence may have had
a part in causing Jeff to refrain from killing Alan Lynde, but otherwise whatever moral force he represents is ineffectual, not only with
Jeff, but with the Vostrands and the Lyndes.

Cynthia, too, has the defects of her virtue: she tends to be
"cold," she exhibits little interest in matters outside the area of her
personal relations and her immediate family (her intellectual pur-

suits seem more a part of the contest with Jeff than a disinterested love of knowledge or a concern for a socially useful self-improvement), and she is generally more acted upon than active, more in reaction than action. Franky is a decent, hard-working boy whose decision to study for the Episcopal ministry is commendable, though it also seems to have in it an element of social ambition, a desire to rise above the shiftlessness of his father and the necessity for working at the Durgin hotel. Jackson is a genuinely good and unselfish man, but his physical debilitation is a sign of spiritual ineffectiveness: he exercises no influence in the upbringing of Jeff, and his religious feeling expends itself in the tinkering with the planchette and in speculation about life on Mars.

Mrs. Durgin is by far the most compelling of these figures in her pride, courage, strength, independence, and capacity for honest self-appraisal. Again, however, these qualities are narrowly focused on the preservation of her family and the advancement of its fortunes, and her ambitions for Jeff permit her to be less exacting with him than she is with herself. Right up until her mind becomes confused in her final illness, her tendency is to indulge his selfishness, condone his mischief, and excuse his faults. She is initially disappointed at his choice of Cynthia, for she had thought Harvard would provide him not only a legal education but a society wife. She carefully maintains her personal independence and integrity in her dealings with her summer boarders, and she is a moving embodiment of motherly pride in summarily turning out Mrs. Marven for administering a brutal snub to her son after being the recipient of special kindnesses. Mrs. Durgin is herself capable of recognizing the extravagance of this action, its contradiction of her chosen role as an innkeeper, but she is driven by her own kind of vanity and her ignorance of the social conditions into which she is trying to force Jeff. She is a magnificent individual portrait because Howells does equal justice to her shortcomings and her strengths. Both, however, are of a kind to disqualify her from any representative role.

It may be an appropriate final comment on the controlled richness of this novel to note that such characterizations in combination with the general picture of rural life eliminate the possibility of an oversimplified opposition between country and city. It does not celebrate pastoral virtue over urban sophistication. Village insularity exacts a cultural levy: Jackson's manipulation of the planchette establishes the level of metaphysical inquiry; Whitwell's inchoate reflections, the philosophical; various comments on Westover's lack of representational skill, and the successful transformation of Lion's Head Inn into a "tasteless and characterless" (p. 41) mass under Jackson's management and into "runnaysonce" (p. 300) under Jeff's, the aesthetic. If there is a bias in favor of the country, it expresses itself, not through picturing the inherent superiority of the people found there (who include Jeff and Whitwell and, in the past, Mrs. Durgin's father), but through the more uniformly critical picture of the Boston society Howells chose to include in *The Landlord at Lion's Head*.

## Cinderella *Redivivus: Ragged Lady*

The dangers of treating any of Howells's later novels as proof of a decline into banality are illustrated by an examination of *Ragged Lady* (1899). The reasons for its neglect and for the disparagement of such scattered comment as it has received are obvious: it seems to be just another story of the innocent American girl who passes through the worldliness of Europe unscathed to return to America and a decently moral American husband. Read in this way, it does not even have the attractions of such an early essay at internationalism[14] as *The Lady of the Aroostook* (1879): Clementina Claxon does not have the vivacity and intensity of a Lydia Blood; her reactions to European manners and morals are more moderate, or at least less open; her suitors present themselves with almost mechanical regularity without having to overcome gentlemanly scruples about her country bcckground; her story is not enlivened by such deeds of

14. See, for example, the comment of Nathalia Wright, *American Novelists in Italy* (Philadelphia: University of Pennsylvania Press, 1965), pp. 193–194, which is critical of *Ragged Lady* because the heroine's "trip to Italy brings her . . . to maturity, not only without changing her character but without making any considerable impression on her," and because the foreign scene "lacks the power not only of strongly influencing character but even of attracting much attention."

heroism as Staniford's rescue of the drunken Hicks. (The closest approximation is the excitement caused by the fear that a Russian nobleman has committed suicide in remorse for having involved himself without warrant in an affair between Clementina and the Reverend Mr. Gregory.) Lacking, then, a passionate heroine, strong international contrasts, variety of incident, even scanted on the humor Howells customarily supplied in an ironic observer or self-deprecating protagonist, the novel has been found uninteresting or, in the case of one of Howells's most sympathetic commentators, baffling: " 'Ragged Lady' is the one novel of Mr. Howells to the purport of which I am unable to find a satisfactory clue."[15]

Yet one such clue, rejected by this commentator ("Is it Cinderella at the Prince's ball?"[16]), is emphatic and useful. The parallels (as open as a reference to "a pair o' glass slippers"[17]) to the fairy tale are too obvious to be merely accidental, and, even if it were conceivable that Howells would intend to exploit them in any romantic way, their transformation to the uses of this somberly realistic story would quickly dispel any such notion. Clementina (and surely that name is not accidental either) is the "ragged lady," though she is innocently happy in the midst of her poor family and in the intermittent performance of housekeeping duties at the local summer hotel. She is transported from this environment to a life of leisure and travel by becoming the companion of the rich Mrs. Lander, who then reveals herself as a difficult if not wicked stepmother in her irritable whining and demands for attention when she is ill. Clementina is next taken under the social wing of a Mrs. Milray, who becomes wicked stepsister in her subsequent jealousy of Clementina's success in attracting the attention of a variety of swains with whose flattery she would like to compensate for a marriage to an older and unwell husband. Clementina experiences a personal triumph by dancing at a shipboard entertainment.

There is no need to elaborate the particulars further to make it

15. Oscar W. Firkins, *William Dean Howells: A Study* (Cambridge: Harvard University Press, 1924), p. 195.

16. *Ibid.*, p. 196.

17. *Ragged Lady* (New York: Harper and Brothers, 1899), p. 86.

clear that Howells was deliberately and, ironically, echoing the fairy
tale for his own purposes. Nor is there anything mysterious about
those purposes, about the value of the ironic interplay to the realism
he was continuing in *Ragged Lady* to practice. At the same time
that he was enforcing the view that there was the stuff of fairy
tales in common, ordinary American life, if it was properly viewed,
he was also illustrating another element in that familiar attitude.
The magic, the delight, and fascination were not in the transformations of pumpkins into coaches and the lavishing of wealth
and princes upon the heroine, but in the opportunities for *living*—
for emotional and moral experience—which here are "miraculously"
provided but which are available, also, in the "miracle" of the average American life.

Certain expectations are set up in *Ragged Lady* by the conventional elements of the fable: the miraculously perfect ordering of
events so that wickedness is precisely punished and goodness precisely rewarded; the operation of a plan by a supernatural agency
which insures that heroes and heroines, having undergone trials of
worthiness, are properly matched for a blissful ever after. These are
ironically played off against the religious inquiry which actually
constitutes the primary concern of the novel. In this sense, *Ragged
Lady* is complementary to *The Undiscovered Country*. The earlier
novel addressed itself to the question of immortality and concluded
that the business of the living was with the living. In *Ragged Lady*,
the question of religious supernaturalism is present, but the main
narrative concern is with what constitutes a "religious" life, whether
it has supernatural sanctions and either supernatural or earthly rewards or not. It is the absence of a balancing scheme of reward and
punishment, a neat pattern of meaning, in the sufferings which
Clementina undergoes in a real world which has for a time all the
trappings of a fairyland, that confirms the somber realism of this apparently inconsequential fable.

That *Ragged Lady* is something more than a novel of manners
with fabulous overtones is indicated by the variety of religious or
specifically nonreligious viewpoints illustrated by the people with
whom Clementina comes into varying degrees of intimacy. More
importantly, the crucial stages of her development from a happy,

dutiful child to a mature woman who exemplifies a life of responsibility and devotion, a life without pretension and self-seeking, of honest searching for the right, of strength and courage and love, are explicitly set forth in a religious context. Her first declaration of love is received when she is just sixteen, and it comes from the not much older divinity student, Frank Gregory. Even as he makes it, he declares that it must be retracted since he is wholly dedicated to the pursuit of his religious education and has no means of accommodating the additional complications of love and marriage at this time.

This declaration comes immediately after Clementina, in spite of the necessity of concealing her worn shoes by flowing draperies, has been transformed into the "Spirit of Summer" and has ruled princesslike over the annual coaching parade[18] which is part of the summer festivities at the rural Middlemount Hotel. Then, when she mysteriously receives a package containing golden slippers which would enable her to go to the celebration dance, she seems indeed to have come under the protection of a fairy godmother. Suspicion, however, that the slippers are actually the unwelcome gift of the hotel clerk dims the magic and causes Clementina to forego the ball. The fairy tale completely collapses when Gregory now confesses that he had secretly purchased and sent the slippers, and he ends by hurling them into the river. This act merely completes his revelation as an incipient if not yet actual religious fanatic: he has already suffered agonies of conscience at the duplicity of his purchase of the slippers, which Clementina had obviously wanted, and at his subjection of the clerk to unwarranted suspicion, and now he impulsively adds the sin of waste to the other impulsive actions which he feels he should have had the strength to control.

Though Clementina has agreed that she is too young to promise herself to Gregory, she is disappointed when he simply disappears from her life. But a real-life fairy godmother materializes, as a now-widowed Mrs. Lander reappears to put into operation a plan that she and her husband had idly talked about to make Clementina

18. Howells's detailed description of this event (pp. 75–81) skillfully exploits both the realistic values of the local color and the fairy-tale atmosphere of the young girl's experience.

her "adoptive daughter" and companion. The Landers are a lesson in the dangers of sudden transformations: when they had cut themselves off from their simple traditions (Mr. Lander began as a tailor, acquired wealth as a clothing manufacturer) and devoted themselves to a nomadic and aimless existence of following the seasons from resort hotel to resort hotel, they also had cut themselves off from the limited spiritual resources which had given their lives a decency, if not dignity. Now Mrs. Lander carries a letter from her church as "something in the nature of credentials" (p. 110), but whatever the relationship in the past, her connection with the church is now purely nominal. She quickly shows herself as a self-indulgent, petulant, hypochondriacal old woman who exacts full personal service from the Cinderella she has taken from the Claxon hearth. Her generosity has little of the quality of Christian charity: it is initially prompted by her loneliness and is then often to be measured by her desire for gratitude and recognition. Only Clementina's good sense, compassion, and innate dignity enable her to endure the alternating affection and self-pity of this all too human godmother and save the relationship from complete disintegration.

The final effect of Clementina's initiation into social and moral complexities through the financial sponsorship of Mrs. Lander is to bring her to a judgment of the world which takes a religious attitude into account though it is not formulated in those terms. The first such experience is the discovery that Mrs. Milray's demonstrative protestations of affection and kindly social guidance are really based on the desire to patronize Clementina's youth and innocence, to amuse herself while gaining credit and attention. She is ultimately disclosed to Clementina as a vain and shallow woman for whom a wealthy and invalid husband was a social convenience and the source of a divorce settlement which she "employed . . . in the negotiation of a second marriage" (p. 342) with a man younger than herself. Purely social experiences with an international company on shipboard and in Florence at the soirees of Mrs. Milray's sister-in-law are interesting and pleasant but do not awaken in Clementina any desire for a brilliant alliance or for social authority. But her innocence is modified by her acquaintance with "people who had not been so blameless in their morals as they were in their minds and manners" (p. 176), and through such knowledge her innocence becomes aware of "good and evil in things that had all seemed indifferently good to her once" (p. 192). Her assessment, then, is that while "the wo'ld is nice . . . you have to pay for it" (p. 268), and it is not worth the price.

That is a judgment which she reaches because she still thinks she can choose what she does want from the world (p. 269)—she is obviously thinking of marriage with George Hinkle, a humorous American encountered in Florence—and some stern tests in the world of her choice lie ahead. During her travels with Mrs. Lander, she has intermittently heard reports of Gregory, with whom she believes herself in love and to whom she feels herself bound by their youthful passage of romance. One of those reports confirms the intensity and rigidity of religious dedication adumbrated by Gregory's earlier conduct: " 'Every act, every word, every thought of his is regulated by conscience. It is terrible, but it is beautiful' " (p. 180).

Eventually Gregory arrives in Florence to offer himself once more to Clementina, and the terms of his proposal squarely pose the question of the truly religious life. He insists that Clementina must not join herself to his plan to become a missionary simply out of love for him; she must share the religious convictions which support his determination to serve or their life and work "could have no consecration" (p. 225). Though Clementina meanwhile has fallen in love with George Hinkle, she is willing to abide by what she regards as her commitment to Gregory, but not on his terms; she will join him in the missionary life for his sake, but she will not hypocritically pretend to be motivated and convinced by the same religious fervor: " 'If you try to be religious for anything besides religion, it isn't being religious;—and no one else has any right to ask you to be' " (p. 251).

She and Gregory eventually agree that they cannot marry and that they are free from any pledges to each other. Clementina now writes to Hinkle, who is returning to America, to accept his offer of marriage, and the contrasting absence of theological cant or prejudice in this relationship is made specifically clear. Clementina has already told Gregory that, though she believes in God and the Bible, she does not consider herself religious. She and Hinkle discover

that they are alike in belonging to no church, though his family
are Moravians and she has attended the Episcopal services of a minister
who "was one of those men who have, in the breaking down of the
old Puritanical faith, and the dying out of the later Unitarian rationalism, advanced and established the Anglican church . . . by a wise
conformity to the necessities and exactions of the native temperament" (p. 111). Both, of course, are moral: Clementina accepts her
father's view that a sincere desire to do right will also disclose the
means to that end (p. 225), and Hinkle approves what she tells him
of her father's theory of life (p. 250).

The marriage of Clementina and Hinkle on a thoroughly secular
basis of love, mutual respect, and a shared morality would seem
to be a conclusive pronouncement against both the religiosity of a
Gregory and the frank determination of a Miss Milray to make the
"world" in the materialistic and social sense one's "whole life" (p.
269). However, the novel does not end with that marriage but
with the reunion of Gregory and Clementina after both have suffered the slings and arrows of a malign fortune totally unlike that
which befalls the favored figures in the pages of the Grimm brothers. Before Clementina can return to America, Hinkle is involved in
a railway accident, sustaining an injury from which he never really
recovers. They marry, live happily enough with his family in Ohio,
have a daughter, but his health is not restored, and he is killed by a
malarial fever in Florida, where they had gone for a cure. Meanwhile, Gregory marries a widow who joins him in missionary work
in China, and they too suffer. Mrs. Gregory dies in China, and his
health breaks down. Thus the stage is set, six years after Hinkle's
death, for the final scenes in Middlemount reporting the reunion
and future marriage of Clementina and Gregory.

"The question of religion" had continued to concern Clementina
and Hinkle during their marriage, and it was "always related in
their minds to the question of Gregory" whose "narrowness," they
reason, "was of his conscience and not of his heart or mind" (p.
336). Now Gregory is changed by experience. Clementina tells Miss
Milray: " 'He thinks it's all in the *life*.' " In China " 'They couldn't
understand what he believed, but they could what he lived' " (p.
349). He is able now to offer a familiar Howellsian formulation in

being grateful to Clementina for "rating . . . motive above . . . conduct" in her judgment of his past actions (p. 356), and he is willing to disregard her self-assessment that she "neva could be very religious." It is not difficult to do so, of course, because he now recognizes what has been apparent to others all along and is explicitly shaped into thought by one of Clementina's former social mentors: " 'Clementina, I think you are one of the most religious persons I ever knew' " (p. 349).

*Ragged Lady,* thus, is far from a tepid and superficial reworking of the international theme. Though the incidents seem to consist largely of proposals of marriage to the beauteous natural princess (there were also offers from the hotel clerk and an American doctor in Europe), these are merely the terms of Howells's realistic fable. The interest is not in the "mating and marrying" except as that process involves fundamental questions concerning the religious and moral life. Howells's scrupulous detailing of Clementina's social experience has served a contextual purpose, and once the religious question is openly engaged, at about the two-thirds point in the novel, it is apparent that it has been important from the start. What has been presented is a variety of individual determinations of what does or what ought to constitute the "good life." The answer of the novel is that it is not to be found in pure hedonism or in attempting to live by the exactions of an impossibly rigorous conscience, of a theoretical but absolutely rigid theological standard. Though Clementina, out of love and conscience, copes with the harsh circumstances which are forced upon her, she has no desire for martyrdom, and she is not led into marriage with Gregory as the reward for her faithfulness to duty and as a panacea for all ills. She remarks that she would like to be happy and that there would be no sense in the second marriage if she did not hope for this result (p. 349). And though both she and Gregory have grown older and wiser, they have not miraculously resolved all their differences and achieved an identity of thought and faith. As the novel closes, she is insisting that they must start fresh as though they had no mutual past; he is declaring this impossible, arguing that the past cannot be ignored and that they must have the courage to build on it. He claims that he did not love his wife in the way he loves her; she claims her love for Hinkle completely obliterated her feeling for him.

What *Ragged Lady* has provided is not a theological statement, but an example of a "religious" life, a life achieved without the benefit of faith in immortality or a God that directs all our actions and gives significance to our suffering. The suspension of belief on this point, however, is for Clementina no excuse for license: whatever it is that tempts man to wrong, it is not God (p. 188), and the responsibility is therefore the individual's to do right whether the result is personal happiness or personal sorrow. She is a realist's Cinderella whose prince is killed and who does not look to a fairy godmother to make life a tinselled entertainment nor to God to make it an uninterrupted idyl of romantic love and placid contentment.

The recognition of Howells's deliberate use of the Cinderella story also answers, at least partially, one of the few specific charges made against *Ragged Lady*: that it is structurally weak.[19] It is certainly loose, but it need not be seen as formless, particularly if attention is given to the expectations created by the fairy-tale pattern of progress from dire adversity to ideal ever-afterness against which the realism is played off. In this context, the hotel life, the shipboard entertainments, the European salons to which Clementina is introduced are only ephemerally magical, and life with a fairy godmother is also made up of long stretches of nursing and cajoling an ungrateful stepmother. The loose succession of incidents which would be moments of intense excitement in never-never land are, for Clementina Claxon, " 'things I've got used to ova here,' " but whose loss would hardly be devastating (p. 268). And such a realistic report cannot honestly end with neat precision by assigning Clementina and George to a cozy little vine-covered cottage in the midwest. Real life forces compromise, adjustment, and irresolution, and these are what the form of *Ragged Lady* project. Even the opting for marriage with which the novel ends is appropriately shown as an anticlimax rather than final romantic triumph, and the real-

19. See Firkins, *William Dean Howells*, p. 196, and Alexander Cowie, *The Rise of the American Novel* (New York: American Book Co., 1948), pp. 687–688.

istic miracle is that a person of Clementina's innate moral poise and spiritual strength could be nurtured in the apparently arid soil of rural America. The point, then, is not merely that form imitates life. It justifies its ostensibly unstructured lifelikeness by simultaneously revealing the falsity of a coherence and balance achieved by the imposition of miraculous interventions.

# V

## "POOR, REAL LIFE"

### More Contexts

IT has been assumed throughout this discussion of Howells's fiction that the currency of the term *realism* on the literary exchange is sufficiently well established to designate certain known values in all denominations: accuracy of setting, verisimilitude of language, representativeness of person and situation, probability in the treatment of events and their outcome. In preparation for comment on such neglected novels as *The Kentons* (1902) and *Miss Bellard's Inspiration* (1905), however, it is worth insisting on some other fundamental principles in Howells's practice. One of the effects of the attention paid to his economic fiction and selected "tragic" novels like *The Shadow of a Dream* and *The Son of Royal Langbrith*—fiction employing "extraordinary" events or persons—has been to minimize Howells's never-recanted advocacy of the commonplace. What deserves re-emphasis, therefore, is that Howells's choice of material was not dictated by a view of art as merely a transcription of the real. His choice was an expression of faith in the aesthetic and moral effects that could be achieved if *representative* reality were properly dealt with.

For example, the "averageness" of the characters in the broad range of Howells's fiction is certified by their being drawn from the middle range of society, by Howells's deliberate avoidance of the upper and lower limits of American society and American experience. That choice still leaves a diversity of the comfortable and the poor, the sophisticated and the innocent, the good and the bad, the wise and the foolish, the young and the old. What makes the appropriation of the center significant to Howells's realism, however, is his belief that the diversity within cohesiveness found there was not merely the most representative and therefore the truest experience. His judgment was even more specifically moral and aesthetic: that "finer American average" was "the best, and, rightly seen, the most interesting phase of civilized life yet known." The realistic function, then, was not to achieve mere accuracy, but to present the "real" in such a way that it would be "rightly seen" as the "best" and the "most interesting" reality available to the fictionist. Moreover, this was a positive standard proclaimed in opposition to the prevailing and mistaken preference for the unreality "of all sorts of eccentric characters, exaggerated incentives, morbid propensities, pathological conditions, or diseased psychology."[1]

Although Howells was thus prescriptive in his insistence that the business of the realist was with the norms of character and experience, he was always careful not to overstate the novelist's function of insuring that these materials should be "rightly seen." Realism "does not seek to grapple with human problems, but is richly content with portraying human experiences."[2] "Human experiences" meant, for Howells, not events, but the quality of events, and that was determined, not by the circumstances, but by the character of the persons involved. He remembered, in the character of the realistic and unread author Eugenio, that it was his perception that fiction began, not with "an attractive subject," but with the purpose to represent human nature that supplied him with the materials to write about. Once he understood that "'human nature was of a vast equality in the important things, and had its differences only in trifles,'" then the most commonplace of subjects could furnish him

1. *Imaginary Interviews* (New York: Harper and Brothers, 1910), pp. 245, 248.

2. William Dean Howells, *Prefaces to Contemporaries* (1882–1920), edited by George Arms, William M. Gibson, and Frederick C. Marston Jr. (Gainesville: Scholars Facsimiles and Reprints, 1957), p. 56.

"passions, interests, motives, situations, catastrophes, and denouements, and characters eagerly fitting themselves with the most appropriate circumstances."[3]

The view of human nature which Howells provides in an extensive body of fiction is one to which not even all realists subscribe. Essentially, it accepts a duality of man, not a waring duality of active principles of good and evil, but of selflessness and ego, humility and pride, reason and passion, charity and greed. Out of these conflicts grows character, which is increment, not decree. Therefore, the realist's concern with both individuals and situations is for *processes* in contrast to the reader's interest in *results*: "The true story never ends. The close of the book is simply the point at which the author has stopped, and, if he has stopped wisely, the reader takes up the tale and goes on with it in his own mind."[4]

That is why, perhaps, Howells's novels have often failed to satisfy two very different kinds of readers. Those stories that ended simply in marriage or the failure to marry, or which went on beyond the "tragedy" of the death of a major or supporting character to show the flow of life continuing, provoked, for example, Frank Norris's accusations, in "A Plea for Romantic Fiction," that this was the realism of the insignificant governed by churchly respectability. Those that refused to become "problem novels" after the expectations and demands of other critics were accused of being timidly evasive: *The Lady of the Aroostook* avoided dealing with the problem it created, the difficulties of marriage between members of differing social classes, by sending the couple out west; similarly, *An Imperative Duty* evaded the intensified form of the same problem, miscegenation, by declaring that the problem was wholly personal and then transferring the couple to Italy anyway; *A Modern Instance* was puritanical in its treatment of its "subject," divorce; *Dr. Breen's Practice* and *A Woman's Reason* shirked the question of women in a profession or business by marrying the heroines off. Such criticisms were a demand that Howells deal with problems rather than experiences. But Howells, as we have seen, felt that his

3. *Imaginary Interviews*, p. 319.
4. *Ibid.*, p. 288.

highest artistic obligation was to "the representation of character and the study of personality" which, properly done, produced drama enough and referred solutions to the readers by making them examine the bases of their moral convictions and social attitudes.

Howells accepted, in other words, man's fallibility in governing himself and in arranging his relationships with others, and the limitation on his capacity to know his final fate as the boundaries of permissible optimism. His characters are essentially rational beings, and his ideal character would be the individual who could exercise perfect reason joined to love, compassion, self-knowledge, and self-depreciating humor. At the other end of the scale, his optimism rejects innate or total depravity and attributes wickedness to the failure or absence of one or more of these qualities. Evil is a matter of degree, rather than essence. And all degrees of men are caught in mere circumstances—inimical economic and social conditions—which, in his most hopeful moods, Howells could imagine being gradually perfected, but more often could only see being insufficiently modified by the altruism of individuals. Likewise, all degrees of men were caught in the knowledge of mortality and the necessity of assessing the consequence of that fact on their present conduct. Howells's own precarious equilibrium of faith and doubt had the effect, not of releasing him from ethical responsibility, but of focusing his moral attention squarely on the here and now, on the problem of building character through will and reason.

These are some of the reasons for Howells's consistency throughout a long career in insisting on the importance of the commonplace. In one sense, nothing was commonplace: every situation, every relationship, every decision, every action or failure to act had its moral implications. Admittedly, in the very early fiction, this insistence was at least partially rationalization. It stemmed not from this kind of reasoned evaluation of the vital significance of apparently minor events, but from a wish to substitute flashes of personality and bits of scenery for the accretions of experience that lead to character and the interactions of character that produce dispersals of the conventional acceptations. But the measured development and basic consistency of Howells's theory and art are discernible whether the occasions of that art are marryings and matings, foreign travels, summer sojourns, social rises and falls, economic struggles, or religious inquiries. They are all of a piece, all proceed from a common vision which widened and deepened but was not completely reconstituted by the shocks of time and knowledge.

A more direct perspective on the fiction yet to be considered— and one which can remove many of the pejorative connotations of such terminology applied to it as *novels of manners*—is supplied by reference to Howells's "literary passions" of the time. The allusion is not to *My Literary Passions* (1895), but to enthusiasms that were not recorded there. That work is more a listing of Howells's indebtedness to widely variegated sources for clues to the meaning and power of realism than it is a systematic revelation of his own credo. It brings the story up to that point where Howells was ready, out of the knowledge won by such reading as he mentions and his own writing and thinking on the fiction of his own time, to pronounce on the virtues of and differences among the present practitioners of realism. Thus it gives significant attention to such old familiars as George Eliot, Turgenev, James, and Björnson, pays homage again in a separate chapter to the overwhelming eminence and the intellectual and spiritual (though not technical) influence of Tolstoy, and pays brief tribute in the penultimate chapter to Valera, Valdés, Galdós, Verga, Zola, Trollope, and Hardy.

Conspicuously absent from the table of contents are the names of two writers about whom Howells wrote extensively elsewhere in terms that formulate his ideal of realism as succinctly and as clearly as anything he ever wrote. One of these writers, Jane Austen, was actually a "passion" later recorded in praises exceeded only by those offered up to the supreme master, Tolstoy; the other was Ibsen, who exercised a "cold fascination"[5] rather than arousing a passion. Yet the fascination was compelling enough to make Howells read all of Ibsen's plays and declare him "the greatest of the moderns."[6] This

5. *My Literary Passions* (New York: Harper and Brothers, 1895), p. 227.

6. William Dean Howells, *Criticism and Fiction and Other Essays*, edited by Clara Marburg Kirk and Rudolf Kirk (New York: New York University Press, 1959), p. 146.

is strong praise from a man who was not "a great reader of drama" and could quickly list the playwrights who had provided plays that he "greatly relished."[7]

The character of *My Literary Passions* is accounted for by the fact that it was written late, after the major critical battles of the war for realism were fought (especially in the "Editor's Study" from 1886 to 1891). It was more reminiscence than propaganda. Still, the merely incidental comment on Jane Austen and Ibsen is interesting enough to invite speculation. One possibility is simply that the book, written in installments for periodical publication, had no firm organizing plan: "The selection is rather puzzling, but I let myself go, somewhat, and trust to what comes first,"[8] Howells said. Another is that Austen and Ibsen were not associated in his mind with the developing consciousness of realism, with the artistic process of becoming a realist.[9] This would obviously be true of Ibsen, whose plays (*Ghosts, The Pillars of Society,* and *An Enemy of the People*) were published in English in 1889 and commented upon by Howells in the "Study" of May 1889. But a frequent impression is that Jane Austen was a lifelong passion of Howells's, that she was always the divine Jane, and, like Thackeray and Dickens, part of his youthful literary experience.[10] But the printed record shows that Howells did not read *Pride and Prejudice* until 1889[11] and that it was just about that time that he

7. *My Literary Passions,* p. 235.

8. Quoted in Edwin H. Cady, *The Realist at War* (Syracuse: Syracuse University Press, 1958), p. 207.

9. Howells's comments are consistent in their emphasis on the lateness of the passion for Jane Austen: "Jane Austen, whose books, late in life, have been a youthful rapture with me" (*My Literary Passions,* p. 247); "And Jane Austen herself was not an idol of our first or even our second youth" (*Imaginary Interviews,* pp. 28–29).

10. For example, William Gibson comments concerning the relationship between Kitty Ellison and Miles Arbuton in *A Chance Acquaintance* (1873) that "Howells probably found his idea for the clash of such differing temperaments in Jane Austen" (*William Dean Howells* [Minneapolis: University of Minnesota Press, 1967], p. 18).

11. "When I came to read *Pride and Prejudice* for the tenth or fifteenth time at the close of 1917 . . . I found it as fresh as when I read it first in

adopted her work as a critical touchstone of the simple, honest, and natural in the "Editor's Study."

Thereafter came the series in *Harper's Bazar* which was to become *Heroines of Fiction* (1901), three chapters of the first volume being devoted to the novels of Jane Austen, who was now characterized as one of the novelists who "beyond any or all other novelists have fixed the character and behavior of Anglo-Saxon fiction."[12] The reactions to Austen and Ibsen, then, were important to the process of critical assessment by which Howells justified his own work of the past and present and worked to set standards for the American novel in general. They offer valuable clues, therefore, to the principles and methods which governed his work in the period being considered by this study. Again, the inference is not of specific influences on subject matter and technique (though it would not be difficult to suggest parallels between, say, *Pride and Prejudice* and *The Kentons*; and *The Son of Royal Langbrith* can be read as a version of *Ghosts*). The point is that these discussions of the realism found in Austen and Ibsen, written when they were and awarding such praise as Howells accorded to few other writers besides Tolstoy, indirectly comment on his own intentions and practice after the economic novels.

Jane Austen's work did not figure in detailed analysis in the "Editor's Study" for the obvious reason that she was not one of the currently producing realists with whom Howells was then largely concerned. Moreover, she was not a conscious realist, as were those Howells advertised in his columns. But when he examined her novels for the chapters of *Heroines of Fiction*, every encomium that he offered was to a realistic virtue. He might well have been speaking of his own sharpened recognition in saying that "we are still only beginning to realize how fine she was; to perceive after a hundred years that in the form of the imagined fact, in the expression of personality, in the conduct of the nar-

---

1889, after long shying off from it" ("Introduction" to *Pride and Prejudice*, by Jane Austen [1813; reprint edition, New York: Charles Scribner's Sons, the Modern Student's Library, 1918], p. xi).

12. *Heroines of Fiction*, 2 vols. (New York: Harper and Brothers, 1901), I, 38.

rative, and the subordination of incident to character, she is still unapproached in the English branch of Anglo-Saxon fiction." Not only did Jane Austen achieve "supremacy" in these externals; her fiction was equally fine for "its lovely humor, its delicate satire, its good sense, its kindness, its truth to nature."[13]

Since the essays are basically Howells's attempt to validate by comment and quotation these aspects of Jane Austen's realistic excellence, this summation might serve as a reasonable version of Howells's own credo. Neither here nor elsewhere does he indicate any serious reservations, suggest that there are areas of experience whose exclusion from the pages of Jane Austen delimits their realistic value.[14] In fact, it was just a few months later that he made his casual identification of "realistic fiction, or . . . what we used to call the novel of manners."[15] In the essay on *Pride and Prejudice,* written toward the end of his life, the identification became an implicit assumption: "Every page of what is so distinctively a 'novel of manners' testifies to the fidelity and veracity of the author's observation."[16] This is not to argue that the virtues which Howells found in Jane Austen's novels exhaust the possibilities of realism. Howells would recognize and praise the kind of art and truth found in very different pictures of life by such writers as Ibsen and Thomas Hardy, a difference not attributable merely to changed conditions but to radically different visions. What becomes clear from a comparative examination of Howells's statements, however, is that the Austenian realism was closest to his own instinctive preferences and that there is a strong unifying element in his appreciation of the diversity of these writers.

A vital characteristic of the vision of life expressed in an art that made Jane Austen "unquestionably great . . . unmistakably the norm and prophecy of most that is excellent in Anglo-Saxon

13. *Ibid.*
14. Indeed, he says the opposite: "An author is as great for what he leaves out as for what he puts in; and Jane Austen shows her mastery in nothing more than in her avoidance of moving accidents for her most moving effects" (*ibid.,* I, 40).
15. *Literature and Life* (New York: Harper and Brothers, 1902), p. 29.
16. "Introduction" to *Pride and Prejudice,* p. xii.

fiction since her time,"[17] was humor. Howells was so convinced of the importance of humor to greatness that he singled it out as his basis for ranking Jane Austen above Trollope as "the greatest of English novelists"[18] in the only reference to her in *My Literary Passions*. With Tolstoy, he could not quite bring himself to declare humor absolutely essential or to admit that the master lacked it, but he was a little uneasy:

Of a man who can be so great in the treatment of great things, we can ask ourselves only after a certain reflection whether he is as great as some lesser men in some lesser things; and I have a certain diffidence in inquiring whether Tolstoy is a humorist. But I incline to think that he is, though the humor of his facts seeks him rather than he it. One who feels life so keenly cannot help feeling its grotesqueness through its perversions, or help smiling at it, with whatever pang in his heart. I should say that his books rather abounded in characters helplessly comic.[19]

At any rate, the significant point is the conception of humor as extending far beyond the limits of the merely amusing or ludicrous and involving the depths of human experience. Howells sees it in Tolstoy as a way of accommodating the "perversions"; in Jane Austen, he sees it as the instrument of amused rationality, the revealer of the absurdities of human conduct and human relationships; in Ibsen, it is also an instrument of revelation, but of a more profound and deadly condition in the modern world than mere foolishness.

He warns against assuming, however, that Jane Austen was superficial in this aspect of her fiction: "Jane Austen was not the most satirical of English novelists; . . . but she was so entirely the most ironical, that she might be said to have invented (if any one ever invents anything) that attitude." It was this "play of her characteristic irony" which allowed for depth of insight while at the same time controlling the emotional tone of the representation: "This [irony] sounds the depths as well as lights the surfaces

17. *Heroines*, I, 66.
18. *My Literary Passions*, p. 247.
19. *Criticism and Fiction* (1959), p. 53.

of the drama, which it never allows to become utter tragedy, though it involves the effect of the passions which conduce to tragedy."[20] Finally, Howells speaks even more directly to indicate how congenial and right he finds the general portrayal of life in *Pride and Prejudice* and in all of Jane Austen's novels:

We must take leave of the whole company of comedians who have been kept from that bleakness of tragedy which is not very common off the stage, though the dramatists would like us to think differently, and are so often asking us to share their tears for it. There is trouble enough in real life, but it is mostly annulled by the use of common sense and patience even by people who have tried to do themselves mischief. Perhaps something like the oversoul helps the good ending and leaves us quite comfortable if not perfectly contented.[21]

After the unreserve of Howells's praise of the "really unsurpassable degree of perfection" which Jane Austen achieved "by her clear vision of the true relation of art to life,"[22] it is no surprise to find more dispassionate terms being employed to describe Ibsen's realistic qualities. Perhaps the reservation by Howells that best accounts for the qualitative difference—apart from the different literary forms under consideration—stemmed from the general view of life given by Ibsen's plays. It was an assessment of experience so bleak and unrelieved, so characterized by a "scornful despair" and "anarchistic contempt,"[23] that Howells could not embrace it completely and felt compelled to offer extenuation: "If he found . . . [life's] countenance full of terrible and insoluble mysteries, and rendered her likeness so as to impart the most piercing sense of tragedy, it can scarcely be imputed to him for a fault. It is at worst his characteristic, his habit, his business." That demurrer noted, however, Ibsen was admitted with full honors to the royal academy of realists: "It is his prime business and his main business to show things as they are . . ." but that function would not, of

20. "Introduction" to *Pride and Prejudice*, pp. ix, xi.
21. *Ibid.*, p. xxii.
22. *Heroines*, I, 65–66.
23. *My Literary Passions*, p. 227.

course, suffice. "He is above all a moralist," but a moralist of the only kind Howells valued, one who "does not wish to teach so much as he wishes to move."[24]

Howells's analysis of Ibsen's "moving" power, including the statement which has been called "the best single definition of critical realism,"[25] has important implications for the evaluation of his own mature fiction as critical realism, and it is, therefore, worth quoting again in some detail: Ibsen had the "power of dispersing the conventional acceptations by which men live on easy terms with themselves, and obliging them to examine the grounds of their social and moral opinions." Moreover, that examination could not be passed by a mere demonstration of good intentions: Ibsen shows that the "time has come, apparently, when we are to ask ourselves not of the justice of our motives, so much as of the wisdom of our motives. It will no longer suffice that we have had the best motive in this or that; we must have the wisest motive, we must examine the springs of action, the grounds of conviction." Added to all this is a specific endorsement of Ibsen's "dramatic method"—that is, not merely the use of the form of the drama, but the preservation of artistic objectivity. The "morality" of *A Doll's House*, for example, is inherent in the demonstration "that certain actions result in certain tendencies, and that from these tendencies certain things happen. If the actions are selfish, they eventuate in misery; if they are false, they hold the doer in bondage to falsehood from which no truth can avail to free him later."[26]

There was, of course, a vast difference between "the little world of county society"[27] to which Jane Austen looked for her subjects and the field of observation which Ibsen took in. Though she subordinated incident to character, rejecting in good realistic fashion moving accidents and violent events, and he too wrote about "such problems as concern conduct rather than such as concern action," yet

24. *North American Review*, CLXXXIII (July 1906), 14, 7, 5.
25. Everett Carter, *Howells and the Age of Realism* (Philadelphia: J. B. Lippincott Co., 1954), p. 192.
26. *North American Review*, CLXXXIII (July 1906), 3–4, 8.
27. *Heroines*, I, 40.

The problem which a play of Ibsen hinges upon is as wide as the whole
of life, and it seeks a solution in the conscience of the spectator for the
future rather than the present; it is not an isolated case; it does not
demand what he would do, or would have done, in a given event; and
this is what makes the difference between him and the modern English
playwrights. In morals, a puritanic narrowness cramps all our race, which
will not suffer us to get beyond the question of personality; but Ibsen
always transcends this, and makes you feel the import of what has
happened, civically, socially, humanly, universally. In Ghosts, for instance, who is to blame? You feel that nothing but the reconstitution of
society will avail with the wrong and the evil involved.[28]

In their view of human nature, however, there was enough
common, realistic, ground to produce some clear similarities in the
language Howells used to define their differing emphases. Jane
Austen had "the fatal gift of observation" which forced her to see
the absurdities of even her most admirable characters and which
gave her fiction, though it could include "satire" and even "bitter
sarcasm,"[29] its characteristic final tone of humorous irony. Similarly,
Ibsen's

view of human nature is the humorist's; but it amuses him sorrowfully,
and his view of human life is far above the satirist's. It is the realist's
view, the view of the honest man; and in this view he sees that selfishness,
conceit, and falsehood form that sin of hypocrisy on which modern
civilization is founded. It is this which he is always allowing to expose
itself on his scene, and he has no other agency in the affair than to let it.[30]

Forced to choose, Howells would, naturally, admit that Ibsen
was more of a realist than Jane Austen. But he was temperamentally
attuned to the "humorist's" view of human nature which was
part of an ironic rather than a tragic vision. The point can be
supported from his comment on still another writer, a comment
which almost reproduces the language of his personal evaluation
of Ibsen. In My Literary Passions, he called Thomas Hardy "a

28. *Criticism and Fiction* (1959), p. 146.
29. "Introduction" to *Pride and Prejudice*, p. ix.
30. *North American Review*, CLXXXIII (July 1906), 9.

great poet as well as a great humorist" and went on to say that "if he were not a great artist also his humor would be enough to make him dear to me."[31] But when he reviewed *Jude the Obscure,* he again was compelled to qualify his advocacy with a demurrer. Hardy's treatment was honest, but his assumptions were open to question: "One may indeed blame the author for presenting such a conception of life; one may say that it is demoralizing if not immoral; but as to his dealing with his creations in the circumstances which he has imagined, one can only praise him for his truth."[32]

The breadth and depth of the spiritual, moral, and aesthetic attitudes which Howells subsumed under the term *realism,* then, are manifest. In a broad sense, he was a humorist, a writer about the "helplessly comic" condition of man poised before the ultimate mystery of the universe and betraying his own highest potential in the world through his own incapacities and excesses. He was a humorist also in his insistence on man's ability to have a meaningful and responsible part in shaping his earthly destiny and in his willed optimism about the more than individual meaning of that destiny. Such a reading of human experience included an awareness of individual suffering, of overwhelming loss, of the spiritual agony of doubt and guilt and shame. It could express itself, too, in satire and in social comedy. It could become a profoundly critical examination of the specific economic and social conditions which all but extinguished the possibility of a brotherhood of man, "an order of loving kindness" based on reason and justice and selflessness, on the ideal of righteousness rather than personal happiness.

Aesthetically, it attacked any form of distortion in the representation of character and situation which proclaimed itself the norm or indicated that it ought to be. It disavowed any form of moralizing—even if the principles advocated were admirable in themselves—that was an effect of direct sermonizing rather than an artistic experience which forced the readers to a re-examination

31. *My Literary Passions,* p. 249.
32. *Criticism and Fiction* (1959), pp. 151–152.

of the "grounds of their social and moral opinions" with whatever result of change or confirmation. An understanding of the full range of this meaning of realism for Howells makes it possible to judge all his work by the same standard, though it obviously does not make it all of the same quality. At the least, it makes possible the examination of some neglected posteconomic novels as work written out of the same humanitarian and democratic spirit as the earlier work, and out of the same moral vision of the human condition.

## More Matings and Marryings: *Their Silver Wedding Journey,* *The Kentons,* and *Letters Home*

Strictly speaking, *Their Silver Wedding Journey* (1899) is a novel only by courtesy. It is not as truly a novel as the apprentice *A Chance Acquaintance* (1872), which at least achieved a significant if minor expansion from love story and travel account to cultural analysis. *Their Silver Wedding Journey,* on the other hand, although it is naturally more assured in striking off a whole gallery of types and in managing the occasions for their introduction in the course of the Marches' travels in Europe, never really pretends to do more than present the resultant "salad-dressing" for those with a taste for oil and vinegar. The metaphor is Howells's own, as given to the Marches. When Isabel argues that Basil can turn his absence from *Every Other Week* into profit by writing an account of it in which he can " 'mix up travel and fiction; get some love in,' " he replies that such a book would not only be " 'the stalest kind of thing' " but that " 'It wouldn't work. . . . The fiction would kill the travel, the travel would kill the fiction; the love and humor wouldn't mingle any more than oil and vinegar.' " And to her rejoinder, " 'Well, and what is better than a salad?' " he returns an answer which, in spite of Howells's humorous and protective disparagement, is an accurate evaluation of *Their Silver Wedding Journey:* " 'But this would be all salad-dressing, and nothing to put it on.' "[33]

33. *Their Silver Wedding Journey,* 2 vols. (New York: Harper and Brothers, 1899), I, 11. Though it appeared in the same year as *Ragged Lady,*

The two volumes of *Their Silver Wedding Journey* contain almost nine hundred pages of mixed ingredients—the intricacies of travel arrangements by ship, train, and carriage; the pleasures and ennui of sightseeing; the grandeurs and ironies of history; the personalities and involuntary involvements of variegated travelers —but the basic need, something to put them on, is never supplied. There is, of course, a love story—two, in fact, if Kenby's winning of the widow, Mrs. Adding, is so regarded—and there are the usually complaisant Marches to supply the appearance of inter-relationship, but these are devices rather than fictional substance. *Their Silver Wedding Journey*, then, is more nearly an enormous collection of informal essays and loosely attached narrative incidents strung on the thread of the Marches' travels than it is a novel.

In other novels the Marches are vitally engaged in important events (*A Hazard of New Fortunes*), or they perform a serious function of perspective (*The Shadow of a Dream*) or supply coherence and irony to comic action (*An Open-Eyed Conspiracy*). Here they merely provide an occasion for describing motion and incident and character, and dictate the alternating moods of nostalgia or diminishment, practiced sentimentality or disillusionment, with which such matters are viewed. Ostensibly, their fictional responsibility is to promote and interpret the major business: the engagement, separation, and reconciliation of Burnamy, aspiring young writer, and Miss Agatha Triscoe, beautiful daughter of a pseudoaristocratic and semiparasitic father. Even in these matters Howells exercises an occasional omniscience, however, and both the story and the Marches' involvement in it are perfunctory: the story exists for its own sake as mere love interest rather than as an accession to their autumnal experience or as part of the development of an international theme.

The plenitude of travel material—the description of historical monuments and present accommodations, the summary histories of past events and personages, and the sketches of living noble and menial functionaries—first serves such purposes as supplying colorful detail, materials for Basil's light philosophizing, or occasions for

---

*Their Silver Wedding Journey* is discussed at this point because of its kinship with *The Kentons* (New York: Harper and Brothers, 1902).

various "American" reactions among the recent travellers on the *Norumbia*. Then it is simply useful to Howells's old habit of separating people from their belongings.

In this case, however, the separation is not fruitfully exploited for a study of interaction in depth but is used for a succession of bas-reliefs: the midwestern couple from Ohio; the American coquette who is so active in her flirtatiousness that she becomes known to the Marches as "the pivotal girl" (I, 155); the nice young man; the attractive young widow with her sweetly precious son; the decent man "of the humorous, sub-ironical American expression" (I, 50); the newlywed couple, and so on. Such types are either caught in the glancing observation of the Marches or are set to enacting bits of business which exemplify their qualities —as when Major Eltwin, the old Ohioan and loyal patriot, forces himself to apologize for an insult to General Triscoe, the supercilious decrier of the corruptions of the American political and social systems (I, 146). These illustrative particles never cohere into the pointillism of a full-length portrait or into a representative and general American condition. As has already been indicated, some collections of particles—the Burnamy-Agatha Triscoe romance, the more sedate courtship of Mrs. Adding by Kenby, the March journey itself—are aggregated into narrations with sentimentally satisfying resolutions, but their presentation is, as Howells might say, of veteran freshness. Even the Marches are hard put to sustain an interest in their own exercise in nostalgia and eventually bring it to an abrupt and premature ending.

The sense of wasteful expenditure is somewhat mitigated for the student of Howells by the knowledge that the unworked potentialities of much of this abundance were brought to acute realization in *The Kentons* (1902).[34] But one unmined lode which is not reclaimed in the later novel represents a substantial loss.

34. For example, the mere potentiality of duplicity and revenge in Burnamy is a major element in the characterizations of Bittridge and Trannel; the complication in the love affair—General Triscoe's dissatisfaction with Burnamy—becomes a full exploration of the involvement of the whole Kenton family in Ellen's troubles; the sketch of adolescence in Rose Adding becomes the developed picture of Boyne Kenton.

In a full study of Jacob Stoller, Howells might have produced an important fictional documentation of the second generation American: the special problems of prejudice he faced in his desire to become the risen American, the sources of his conception of the ideal rise, and the psychological consequences of both. The history that Howells does sketch and the characterization he projects for Stoller are unsparingly realistic in a generally muted book but are superficially used in the service of provoking a reaction from his employee, Burnamy, which complicates the love affair. It is equally wasteful to expend critical energy on the might-have-been, but the point is useful to the definition of the special quality of *Their Silver Wedding Journey*. It is a finger exercise rather than a performance, it is material for a novel—or several novels—rather than the novel itself.

To say all this, however, is not to indict *Their Silver Wedding Journey* as a failure in perception. But like Basil March, Howells chooses to adopt for the moment the youthful attitude of "the dilettante . . . [the] amateur of the right and the good" (II, 117). That view cannot be perfectly maintained, for it never occurs to a young man that "the world wasn't made to interest . . . or at the best to instruct" (II, 118) him; and Basil has "the grace to be troubled at times" (II, 117) by certain inescapable and unpleasant facts: the Stollers and Triscoes of this world, the physical barriers and separations of caste between the steerage and first-class passengers (I, 90–92), the undeniable reality and power of Tammany (I, 143), and the knowledge of death (I, 99). But these disturbing elements in experience could be granted holiday suspension in the reflection that "In America, life is yet a joke with us, even when it is grotesque and shameful, as it so often is; for we think we can make it all right when we choose" (II, 406). Howells could not, of course, make American life "all right" when he chose, either by his actions or his fictions, but he could, as he was soon to choose, make his fiction responsive to those aspects of it which he here remarked on only casually.

The probability that Jane Austen was a considerable influence during the years following 1899, an influence which was intensified by the preparation of the early chapters of *Heroines of Fiction* (1901), offers a useful approach to *The Kentons* (1902). It helps to explain, for example, Howells's apparent return to a concentrated attention on a problem of mating and marrying after his dissatisfaction with *The Coast of Bohemia*. Such intervening work as *The Landlord at Lion's Head* and *The Story of a Play* were obvious departures from that formula, and others like *The Day of Their Wedding* and *An Open-Eyed Conspiracy* had merely used "romances" as a narrative framework. *The Kentons,* however, has been received and dismissed as "another tired, conventional-unconventional love match"[35] and as the "slight story" of the events leading to the marriage of Ellen Kenton of Tuskingum, Ohio, to the Reverend Hugh Breckon of New York, an experience which Howells "somehow fails to universalize."[36] An earlier critic came closer to Howells's purpose in identifying *The Kentons* as a novel in which, more than in any other he wrote, Howells meant to deal with "the story of a family."[37] This is a perception which needs no support from a comparison with the novels of Jane Austen, but such a comparison is helpful in defining the nature of the realism Howells was practicing in it, and its differences from that, say, of *Ragged Lady,* the nearest preceding novel. The affinities of *The Kentons* are with *Indian Summer* rather than *April Hopes,* and, like *Indian Summer,* it is a beautifully controlled performance which develops a commentary of considerable ironic

35. Cady, *The Realist at War*, p. 263.

36. Alexander Cowie, *The Rise of the American Novel* (New York: American Book Co., 1948), pp. 688–690.

37. Oscar W. Firkins, *William Dean Howells: A Study* (Cambridge: Harvard University Press, 1924), p. 197. To support the evidence of the novel itself, see *Letters,* II, 151. And the argument for an influence from the reading for and writing of *Heroines of Fiction* to *The Kentons* is further supported by this early comment in *Heroines:* "Before 'The Vicar of Wakefield' there had been no English fiction in which the loveliness of family life had made itself felt; before Evelina [in Fanny Burney's *Evelina*] the heart of girlhood had never before been so fully opened in literature" (*Heroines,* I, 14–15). Howells first thought of calling the novel *A Girl's Heart* and interrupted the preparation of the *Heroines* essays to work on it (Cady, *The Realist at War,* p. 263).

complexity on a certain kind of commonly shared human experience.

What a comparison with Jane Austen's work, especially with Howells's favorite, *Pride and Prejudice,* does help to clarify is that the aim of *The Kentons* was still "the truthful treatment of material" which was the hallmark of realism and which made "the divine Jane . . . the most artistic of the English novelists."[38] That "treatment," however, did not have to be a literal transcript of actuality, nor did it have to attempt the impossible task of including *all* reality. The reality to be treated might be "manners," provided "the fidelity and veracity of the author's observation"[39] made the terminology interchangeable, made it possible to speak of "the field of realistic fiction, or . . . what we used to call the novel of manners."[40] Such a treatment involved more than mere accuracy in recording the subtleties of personality and motivation and character, though these were the foundation on which the created work of art based itself. It meant the creation of a believable and consistent imagined world sufficiently connected to the literal world to meet the realistic tests of verisimilitude and probability but organizing its selected facts to express a particular vision of "truth."

No realistic novel, in the common usage of that term, would dare to project its heroine's psychological state through her reactions to a commonly shared though quantitatively varied levity in *three* different men. Nor would it give such brilliance of finish to its whole through a scintillating narrative style,[41] and through

38. *Criticism and Fiction* (1959), p. 38.
39. "Introduction" to *Pride and Prejudice,* p. xiii.
40. *Literature and Life,* p. 29.
41. To cite a couple of examples from an embarrassment of riches: "He [Breckon] rather liked the way Lottie had tried to weigh him in the balance and found him, as it were, of an imponderable levity"; "It had been a matter of notoriety among such of Mr. Breckon's variegated congregation as knew one another that Mrs. Rasmith had set her heart on him, if Julia [her daughter] had not set her cap for him. In that pied flock, where every shade and dapple of doubt, from heterodox Jew to agnostic Christian, foregathered, as it had been said, in the misgiving of a blessed immortality, the devotion of Mrs. Rasmith to the minister had been almost a scandal" (*The Kentons* [1902], pp. 117, 173).

a dialogue which is impossibly entertaining and perceptive even among its average citizens such as Mr. and Mrs. Kenton; impossibly inane among its fools such as Mrs. Rasmith and Mrs. Bittridge; and impossibly and erratically clever and trite among its youthful aspirants to maturity, family status, and social dignity such as Lottie and Boyne Kenton and Boyne's shipboard acquaintance, Mr. Pogis. Such a novel could not make Mr. and Mrs. Kenton quite as helpless before the self-sufficiency of a Lottie, the irrationality of an Ellen, and the mystery of Boyne's adolescence without sacrificing belief in the intelligence of the parents and the devotion of the children to family. *The Kentons*, however, manages these stratagems. If they are technical defects equivalent to the perfection of such fools as Mr. Collins and Lady Catherine de Bourgh and the pertness of Elizabeth Bennet's wit in *Pride and Prejudice*, they do not seriously distort the imaginative truth of Howells's fictional world.[42]

If modern critics have tended to slight *The Kentons* for not being "real" enough, for dealing with just another American love affair in a European setting, Howells's contemporary audience equally failed to understand the kind of reality and truth it represented. For them it was too real, too "commonplace," making them "bray at . . . flowers picked from the fruitful fields of our common life, and turn aside among the thistles with keen appetite for the false and impossible."[43] One of those contemporary readers, however, was exceptional in his perception of the special qualities

42. Though more specific parallels between *Pride and Prejudice* and *The Kentons* might be drawn—for example, between Elizabeth's attraction to Wickham and Ellen's even stronger fascination with Bittridge; between Mrs. Bennet and Mrs. Rasmith; between the similar "business" of providing husbands for marriageable girls—the intent is not to claim this kind of specifically direct influence. It is to suggest that the appearance of *The Kentons* at this point, amid Howells's more deeply serious and socially comprehensive realism, probably derives from Howells's current enthusiasm for Jane Austen and is again an accommodation, not an abandonment, of his realistic principles.

43. William Dean Howells, *Life in Letters of William Dean Howells,* edited by Mildred Howells, 2 vols. (Garden City, New York: Doubleday, Doran and Company, Inc., 1928), II, 161.

of Howells's realism, whether it was of the nature of a social documentary such as *The Minister's Charge* or a distillation of American character and experience like *The Kentons*. As far back as the time of *A Foregone Conclusion* (1875), Henry James had pointed to Howells's power to "embrace a dramatic situation with the true imaginative force" and give "its atmosphere, its meaning, its poetry."[44] When Howells had definitely marked out the American scene as his artistic possession, James had pointed to what was "most remarkable, or most, at least, the peculiar sign, in his effect as a novelist—his unerring sentiment of the American character." Hinting that there were areas of American life that he could wish Howells would attend to more closely, James yet insisted that "no one, surely, has *felt* it so completely as he."[45] And looking back on the occasion of Howells's seventy-fifth birthday, James recurred to his "sense of that unfailing, testifying truth" in Howells's studies of American life and offered an encomium that seems particularly to characterize such a novel as *The Kentons*. What he especially praised was Howells's penetration of the *"real* affair of the American case and character," the "rare lucidity" of his friend's insight into the "comedy, the point, the pathos, the tragedy" of the "home grown humanity" which Howells had deliberately chosen as his "field." Moreover, this capacity to be "inspired and attracted" by the "romance of the real and . . . the charm of the common" was itself a "literary gift" which Howells exercised with a "fine taste" that produced a sympathetic accuracy of observation in a tone "both sharp and sweet."[46]

The relevance of this kind of appreciation to *The Kentons* is confirmed by a letter, specifically about that novel, in which James once more emphasizes his sense of the almost miraculous freshness which Howells managed to impart to his appropriated material, the virtuoso skill with which Howells achieved exactly

---

44. "Howells's 'Foregone Conclusion,' " *The Nation*, III (January 7, 1875), 12.

45. "William Dean Howells," *Harper's Weekly*, XXX (June 19, 1886), 394.

46. "A Letter to Mr. Howells," *North American Review*, CXCV (April 1912), 561.

the appropriate tone: "You have done nothing more true and complete, more thoroughly homogeneous and hanging-together, without the faintest ghost of a false note or weak touch—all as sharply ciphered-up and tapped-out as the 'proof' of a prize scholar's sum on a slate. It is in short miraculously felt and beautifully done."[47]

The problem of the management of tone was especially delicate in *The Kentons,* as James's admiration for Howells's bringing it off suggests. It was a problem of balance, of using as the supporting narrative another story of mating—with its familiar adjuncts of deceptions and heartbreaks, of misunderstandings and reconciliations, of all the potentially romanticistic trappings and complications—without becoming merely tiredly cynical, fatuously earnest, or cheaply satiric. From the early exploration of a similar situation in *A Chance Acquaintance* to the posthumous *The Vacation of the Kelwyns,* Howells had never relinquished his use of affairs of the heart. Even in the early novel, however, he gained authority for his interest in the affair of Kitty Ellison and Miles Arbuton by making them representative cultural types brought into conflict and definition by the personal interest, and by flatly declaring against the snobbish insensitivity of the Bostonian gentleman. The wider concerns in *The Kentons* are noted in his remark that the love affair is not merely the problem of the two young people involved. But the matter of the tone with which these interests should be treated remained open.[48] He did not choose, for example, the wholly relaxed comedy of *Indian Summer.* Nor was it to his purpose to choose a somber tone in deliberate contrast to what were apparently the materials of a graceful, witty, and comic love-idyl, as he had done in *April Hopes.* What he wanted—and what

47. Henry James, *The Letters of Henry James,* edited by Percy Lubbock, 2 vols. (London: Macmillan and Company, Limited, 1920), I, 406.

48. "Without contending in behalf either of his Ohioans, with their little angularities and large virtues, or of his experienced worldlings, with no angularities at all and their virtues more considerably mixed with manners, Howells interprets both with the lucid intelligence of an angel smiling at a beloved community of men" (Carl Van Doren, *The American Novel, 1789–1939* [New York: The Macmillan Company, 1945], p. 134).

he so effectively achieved that Carl Van Doren could call *The Kentons* a "flawless" novel, telling a story which "is clear yet full, continuous yet unhurried, balanced yet as natural as the flow of water or the movement of clouds across a blue sky"[49]—was a tone modulated between pathos and comedy, accommodating the mid-depths and mid-heights of both, and sounding always the true pitch of a seasoned and sympathetically perceptive observer of the human comedy.

The high achievement of *The Kentons* is, however, more than a matter of tone: if it is "flawless," there must be a harmony among all its elements. Put to the test of serious analysis, the novel reveals an unobtrusive and flexible structure, skillfully designed to meet demands far more complex than those occasioned by the development of the affair between the love-injured girl from Tuskingum—Ellen Kenton—and the sophisticated and light-hearted young Unitarian minister, Hugh Breckon. There are, in fact, three major overlapping spheres of thematic concern. At the center is the love story, which is chiefly useful, not for its detailing of the emotional progress of Ellen and Breckon toward each other—as with most of Howells's love stories, this one is more or less clearly ordained from their first meeting—but for its exploration of the mystery of Ellen's attraction to the blackguard Bittridge, and of Breckon's "slipperiness," whose source is his humorous deflation of himself and others, both of these temperamental anomalies making for obstacles in the path of true love. A second focus is on the parental generation which, in spite of a determined effort to give understanding, sympathetic support, and rational and humane ethical principles to its children, can do little more than suffer helplessly while those children effect their destinies by experiencing and rejecting Europe (Lottie), or by somehow attracting and winning a good man after almost throwing herself away on a bad one (Ellen), or by simply suffering through adolescence (Boyne). Boyne is the other major interest of the novel, and Howells's portrait of the painfully mixed experience of adolescence, its moral certainties and its touching gropings for love and

49. *Ibid.*

assurance, its shrewd insights and its absurd, wish-filled fantasies, announced in not altogether consistent alternations of bass and treble, is an underrated piece of realism.

The inclusive structure which Howells used to support this rich diversity—which, as usual, is further enriched by subsidiary but vivid characters and incidents: Bittridge's bleached-blonde mother at tea with the Kentons; the foolish and wise worldlings, Mrs. and Miss Rasmith, at their champagne supper on shipboard; Mr. Pogis, Boyne's English counterpart, at unequal contest with the flirtatious Lottie—is merely straightforward chronology. From a beginning in Tuskingum, where Ellen becomes involved with Bittridge, the novel follows the Kentons to New York in their attempt to help Ellen throw off the effects of that involvement, details their extended escape by ship to Europe, and records the plighting of the troth which makes the escape complete and final. Within this loose and apparently merely episodic design, however, can be discerned a three-part division which is responsive to the thematic concerns of the novel without attempting to impose a neat correspondence.

The three units are not hermetic compartments, each developing one of the major thematic interests. They are narrative progressions in which the focusing lens clarifies by concentration one element of a picture while dimming but not completely obscuring the rest of the framed segment of life. Thus, roughly the first third of the novel (Chapters I–VIII), while accomplishing all the necessary expository business, projects Ellen's helplessly perverse fascination with Bittridge, mainly through the suffering of her parents and their troubled speculations concerning their proper course of action. This section ends as Ellen, ill with shock at Bittridge's enforced liberties, is carried on shipboard for the journey to Europe. Now it is largely Breckon's viewpoint that conveys such matters as his own developing fondness for Ellen, his problem of conscience concerning his continuation in the ministry, Boyne's infatuation with Miss Rasmith, and the transparent attempts of Mrs. Rasmith to mate Breckon with her daughter. This longest section is the solid center of the novel (Chapters IX–XIX) and prepares for the climax, in which Boyne's escapade is the dominant action. He is tricked into attempting to act out one of his fantasies by approaching the Queen of Holland, and in the resulting contretemps of his arrest and release, Breckon and Ellen are brought into such close sympathy that the minister immediately declares himself to her father.

In the Reverend Mr. Hugh Breckon, Howells created a winning exemplification of certain aspects of his own temperament and character. Breckon is sincere, helpful, and forbearing, but he is no mere do-gooder. He has a sense of humor which most often functions to keep him keenly aware of his own and others' human limitations and frailties. The question which his journey is designed to give him leisure and perspective to answer is whether he should continue in the ministry. It has arisen because his congregation has divided in its opinion of whether he is old enough and, more especially, grave enough to be a suitable spiritual leader. That he must often have evoked such doubts in at least certain elements of his congregation is clear when he very early in the voyage manages to offend Lottie Kenton, who is not morally severe, with a joking definition of his faith by differentiation: " 'It's said that the Universalists think God is too good to damn them, and the Unitarians think they are too good to be damned' " (p. 104). Lottie is eventually led by such responses to her probings to pronounce him "slippery" (p. 108) and "trivial" (p. 111).

He initially fares little better with Ellen, who, by contrast with Lottie, is intellectual and reflective. When he pretends that an injury suffered in her behalf is so painful as to require her assistance at meals and then discloses the joke, she is offended. He is led to self-condemnation for allowing "his levity to get the better of his sympathy, and his love of teasing to overpower that love of helping which seemed to him his chief right and reason for being a minister" (p. 131). Even his attempt at a serious statement of his personal problem of conscience cannot escape the objectivity which will not ignore human limitation and which leads to wry deprecation:

"I'm at the head of a society . . . ethical or sociological, or altruistic, whatever you choose to call it, which hasn't any definite object of worship, and yet meets every Sunday for a sort of worship; and I have to be in the pulpit. . . . If I were a Calvinist I might hold fast by faith, and fight it out with that; or if I were a Catholic I could cast myself upon the strength of the Church, and triumph in spite of temperament. . . . But . . . being merely the leader of a sort of forlorn hope in the Divine Goodness, perhaps I have no right to be so cheerful" (pp. 194–196).

In the world of *The Kentons*, this religious-ethical problem serves to explain Breckon's presence on shipboard, to characterize him, and to establish the rightness of Mrs. Kenton's judgment that he is "one of the kindest and nicest" gentlemen she ever saw, and the judge's that, though Breckon likes joking and laughing, "he isn't a light person" (p. 191). The analysis need not be pursued further. In fact, the novel does not reveal the process by which Breckon arrives at the announcement to Judge Kenton, when his hesitant broaching of his desire to ask for Ellen's hand is misunderstood as a reopening of the religious question: " 'Oh! . . . *That!* I've quite made up my mind to go back' " (p. 291). The affairs of the world which Howells does detail with his customary fullness and lucidity are the vicissitudes which ultimately lead to Breckon's offer of himself to Ellen, his being informed of Ellen's past relationship with Bittridge, and, with Ellen as his wife, his restoration to his ministry in New York; the willful and flirtatious independence of Lottie before she, too, is settled in comfortable married domesticity in close proximity to her family in Tuskingum; and Boyne's painfully comic transition from adolescence into young manhood, from "heroical romance" (p. 311) to Blackstone.

The persons who actually suffer most in these various comic crises of individualism are Mr. and Mrs. Kenton, and their return to his regimental history and the nightly checker games in which she cheats is an earned reward. In the comic vision of this novel, these several outcomes are all earned rewards, though that fact need not be insisted upon. This is a world in which a certain amount of real trouble and pain must be endured as courageously and wisely as possible; a world which includes not just such good, decent folk as the Kentons, but despicable people such as Bittridge, reprehensible egotists such as the medical student, Trannel, simpering fools such as Mrs. Bittridge, and sophisticated fools such as Mrs. Rasmith. But it is a world in which "moral quality tells everywhere," in which "to be a clever blackguard is not so well as to be simply clever" (p. 316). Therefore, since Breckon and the Kentons obviously possess the telling moral qualities from the start, interest in their circumstantial fates can be superseded by interest in their individuality and in their comico-serious relationships.

In the final third of the novel, Howells gives further evidence of his skill in achieving, within the general chronological pattern, both a thematic unity and a structural symmetry without resorting to mechanically balanced effects. Boyne, with his imagination fired by his reading in heroical romances and his sense of his potentialities supported by what he understands to be his grown-up relationship with Miss Rasmith, finds himself increasingly in the grip of a romantic passion for the young Queen of Holland. In his emotional confusion, he turns to Ellen for enlightenment and sympathy, confessing that he feels himself to be in the grip of something like a "possession" (p. 254). Ellen's recent experience with Bittridge conditions her natural desire to minister to Boyne's needs with delicacy, if not with full understanding of the particulars of his dilemma. She had felt like a drunkard who knew the cause of her disease but was helpless to act to cure it; had felt that she "had no character at all" (p. 34) and could only despise herself. She therefore solemnly accepts as a secret trust the miniature of the queen which Boyne has purchased, recognizing, though she could not formulate the fact, that Boyne is at that precarious stage at which he is "a mass of helpless sweetness," that he "sometimes took himself for an iceberg when he was merely an ice-cream of heroic mould" (p. 224).

But the more subtle and more important parallel between Boyne's present and Ellen's recent past is in Boyne's relationship with Trannel, one of the young men whom Lottie attracts as by a law of nature. Trannel has a "malign intelligence" (p. 241), which easily penetrates to the secrets of Boyne's fantasy world, and a malicious nature which makes him delight in encouraging Boyne's most outrageous visions of derring-do. But Trannel has his complexities:[50] he has "a fleering wit" (p. 266) which delights in the sarcastic, the sacreligious, the patronizing; but he *is* a wit, and in an instant he can turn charming and "everything that could be wished in a companion for a day's pleasure" (p. 269).

Boyne is not alone in being gratified and victimized by Trannel's erratic displays of temperament, but, as Ellen was, with Bittridge, he is made especially vulnerable by his innocence and the strength of his emotional commitment. He is divided in his feelings toward Trannel by "fascination" and "dread" (p. 241), can recognize Trannel's wit while being uneasily aware "that it doesn't make you like him any better" (p. 256). He is powerless, however, when Trannel chooses to be friendly and confidential. He is thus reduced, after initial scorn, to "silent rapture" (p. 275) by Trannel's purportedly autobiographical tale of his selfless renunciation of the princess of Saxon-Wolfenhütten, though it is obviously based on a novel with which Boyne is well acquainted. The ultimate exercise of this hypnotic power occurs when Trannel takes advantage of the spell he has wrought to convince Boyne that the Queen of Holland is actually beckoning him to approach her carriage. As soon as the resulting confusion is resolved, Trannel is banished from the Kentons' presence and from the novel.

For those readers willing to give some credence to Howells's claim, through his imaginary Eugenio, that he "was always breaking new ground" and never more so "than when he seemed to be ploughing the same old furrows in the same old fields," *The Kentons* is a case in point. Eugenio complained that when an "author has broken ground in the direction of a new type of

50. It is another sign of Howells's mastery of his materials and the novel's perfection of tone that Breckon draws a lesson from his reading of Trannel's character which is undoubtedly a factor in his decision to continue in the ministry and in bringing him to a declaration to Ellen. He unwillingly becomes aware of a likeness between himself and Trannel. His dislike is increased by the notion that "Trannel seemed himself in a sort of excess, or what he would be if he were logically ultimated" (p. 267). His shrinking from this "realization of their likeness, with an abhorrence that rendered him rigid" (p. 269), may surely be seen, though Howells felt no need to detail the process, as the negative side of the positive resolve to become a better, more seriously committed man and minister.

heroine," the reviewer almost invariably recognizes "one of those enchanting girls whom the author in question has endeared to generations of readers." Howells must surely have thought that in depicting the mysterious alchemy by which an Ellen Kenton was magnetized by the crude assurance of a Bittridge and a Boyne Kenton by the openly condescending camaraderie of a Trannel, he was at least revealing "the infinite variety of character which lay hid in each and every human type."[51] Still true to his conception that "stories" were merely the means by which the author acquainted the reader with what he thought about persons and situations, he "thought" about a variety of them in *The Kentons*: about family life and the difficulties of communication between generations; about conditions which affect experience in Tuskingum, Ohio, as compared with those in New York or Europe; about the compromises and solaces of age, the ecstasy and anguish of adolescence; about religious belief and ethical conduct.[52] If these reflections are delivered lightly and are productive of no moral revolutions and social reconstitutions, neither they nor the artistic form in which they are embodied need be dismissed as simply trivial. Within Howells's own "play of . . . characteristic irony . . . [which] sounds the depths as well as lights the surfaces of the drama,"[53] there are ample rewards for a sensibility responsive to something other than sweeping generalizations and great pronouncements.

*Letters Home* (1903), perhaps an extension of the shift of mood after the realistic labors of *The Landlord at Lion's Head* and *Ragged Lady*, is, at any rate, Howells's single experiment

51. *Imaginary Interviews*, pp. 298–299.

52. He did not "think" about the specifically sexual attraction of Bittridge for Ellen, though he make it clear that she responds to his approaching her on the grounds of her physical attractiveness rather than her locally respected intellectual capacities. There is no suggestion of a sexual component in Boyne's feeling for Trannel, a transference of his response to Miss Rasmith. The nature of Ellen's confusion, however, is clarified by the implicit contrast with Lottie's sexual self-confidence.

53. "Introduction" to *Pride and Prejudice* (1918), p. xi.

with the epistolary novel, and his choice of that form is perhaps explanatory of the surprising comic tone he takes with materials he had elsewhere treated with profound seriousness. He well knew that the epistolary form was "the most averse to the apparent unconsciousness so fascinating in a heroine."[54] He dealt with that problem by making the central character an aspiring writer, Wallace Ardith of Wottoma, Iowa, and by limiting the letters of the girl with whom Ardith becomes romantically involved, America Ralson, to five. He was equally aware that many other conventions of the realistic novel would also have to be adapted or suspended.[55] The principal critical interest in *Letters Home*, therefore, is in assessing the significance of the variation in tone between it and the earlier novels from which it apparently draws many of its character types and elements of its subject matter, *A Hazard of New Fortunes* and *The World of Chance*.

The parallels to *Hazard* are striking: Mr. Ralson, head of the Cheese and Churn Trust, is a recent multimillionaire who comes to New York to finance his daughter's social assault on the Four Hundred. Like Dryfoos, his concerns are the making of money and the use of it to provide for his own comfort and his daughter's social status and happiness. Like Mrs. Dryfoos, however, Mrs. Ralson, New England-born and country-bred, has no interest in the life of the city and lives on memories of life in Wottoma and hopes for the success of her daughter, America. Like Christine Dryfoos, America Ralson is a passionate beauty whose real interest is not in social status but in the excitement of the variety of enter-

---

54. *Heroines of Fiction*, I, 3.

55. Howells may have been stimulated to try his hand at this form by an edition of Richardson's novels by William Lyon Phelps, which was his subject in the "Editor's Easy Chair," *Harper's Monthly*, CV (August 1902), 479–483. He speculated "that in the hands of a more consummate artist than Richardson it might achieve unconsciousness," but admitted it had not yet "achieved even such make-believe unconsciousness as rewarded the artist in . . . *Henry Esmond* and *David Copperfield*" (p. 482). On one point, Howells specifically tried to improve the method. He complained that the characters of the letter writers were not distinguished by identifying language, that all the characters talked the same (p. 483). In *Letters Home*, the distinctions are clear and realistically appropriate.

taining occasions and young men which she looks to society to supply. The secretarial functions of Mrs. Mandel are supplied to the Ralsons by Miss Frances Dennam, a New England conscience transplanted for nurture to Lake Ridge, New York, before the need for economic independence brought her to New York.

Wallace Ardith, former journalist and potential fictionist, more closely resembles P. B. S. Ray of *The World of Chance* than he does any character from *Hazard*. Like Ray, he is thoroughly captivated by the "novelty" of New York, which is "simply inexhaustible," and by the "drama of its tremendous being."[56] However, his literary pursuits simply fade into the background as he becomes involved with his fellow Wottomans, the Ralsons, and falls into reciprocated love with America. A complication producing the major story-line occurs as Ardith, who out of compassion has taken lodging with still other Wottomans, the Baysleys, unwittingly creates the impression that he loves the daughter, Essie. Mr. Baysley is employed by the Cheese and Churn Trust and is finding life in the city financially difficult. When Ardith extends his kindness to nursing the Baysleys in their successive bouts with the grippe and to taking Essie to dinner, he becomes more committed than he had intended or wished. He responds to her gratitude with some kisses and caresses and finds himeslf morally committed to one girl while he has declared his love to another.

This is the kind of situation which by the Howellsian law of the "economy of pain" can eventually be solved by common sense in favor of America's claims on Ardith. It is not solved, however, until Ralson, like Dryfoos before him, tries to provide for his daughter by buying Ardith from the Baysleys with a check and a job back in Timber Creek, Iowa. In still another echo, Ardith falls into casual acquaintance with a proper Bostonian, Otis Binning, whom he then frequently encounters at various social events and at the Ralsons'. Binning is not as brilliantly witty as Kane of *The World of Chance*. His kinship is evidenced, nevertheless, in his ability to turn a clever phrase in reporting with amused detachment on the differences between New York and Boston and on

56. *Letters Home* (New York: Harper and Brothers, 1903), p. 60.

as many of the complications in the affairs in Baysley and Ralson households as he is able to penetrate.

A parallel to the economic novels conspicuous by its absence, however, is a point of view which would supply a social and a moral criticism of Ralson and the conditions he represents, rather than a merely aesthetic response. That lack points to the impasse Howells had reached with respect to the problem of fictionally reporting the social and economic inequities which contradicted and vitiated the ideals of a supposedly democratic country. He was content, in a comic novel like this, to let those implications play beneath the surface and simply use the multifarious conditions of city life for atmospheric effects. (In fully serious novels such as the earlier *The Landlord at Lion's Head* and the later *The Son of Royal Langbrith,* such inequities were allowed to be significantly felt, but they were not allowed to become the controlling matter, as they were in *Hazard* and other novels.) Though psychological in Howells's terminology,[57] *Letters Home* is not so much a study in individual depths as it is an assertion of what might be called an optimistic psychology of American life. Howells chose to be offhand about cheese trusts and the financial and moral straits of their employees, about the commercial aspects of literature, about a latter-day Puritan's struggle to reconcile her experience of the pleasures and conveniences of wealth with her ethical and social principles because *Letters Home* is an act of faith. It is an exercise in the comic mode after the initial shocks of disillusionment and deeper understanding had been absorbed in such novels as *A Hazard of New Fortunes* and *The Quality of Mercy.* Its implicit assumption, allowing Howells to use the "histories" of the principal letter writers to establish individually typical points of view adding up to "America," was that which he explicitly assigned a few years later to Aristides Homos as an explanation of "the illogicality of American life":

The personal equation modifies it, and renders it far less dreadful than you would reasonably expect. That is, the potentialities of goodness implanted in the human heart by the Creator forbid the plutocratic man

57. See G. F. Cronkhite, "Howells Turns to the Inner Life," *New England Quarterly,* XXX (December 1957), 484.

to be what the plutocratic scheme of life implies. He is often merciful, kindly, and generous . . . in spite of conditions absolutely egotistical.[58]

The emphasis in *Letters Home*, therefore, is on the way in which the "personal equation" affects individual relations rather than the system: the Four Hundred remain inviolate, and the Cheese and Churn Trust goes on with Ralson at its head and Baysley as one of its functionaries. Howells did not rebound to a foolish and blind optimism. But he was willing to show once more that people were not entirely governed by conditions in their public and private lives, that they did not always take advantage of the opportunities provided by the system to be cruel, or egotistical, or indifferent, that they need not be rigidly fixed beyond the possibility of growth and change by their training and environment. Thus, to cite just a few examples, from one point of view, Ralson is merely "repulsive in his savage sincerity" (p. 91); from another, though he is "wicked" as the head of the Trust, he "is good in his way" (p. 116). Ardith is alternately a mass of egotism in his roles as assimilator of literary material and jilted lover, but he is a kind and responsible human being outside these roles. America might have been another Christine Dryfoos, all passion and vindictiveness, "alluring in *her* savage sincerity" (p. 91) but predatory; she is finally more kitten than wildcat. Frances Dennam is at first a kind of personified conscience delivering rigorous judgments on morally fallible mortals; she ends by embracing and defending the whole Ralson clan and Ardith as well.

Howells was aware that the comic spirit could be indulged in this way only at a certain cost in dramatized complexity and emotional power. It is perhaps the primary function of the point of view provided by the discerning Otis Binning—since he is never fully enough possessed of all the facts to be identified as the authorial voice—to offer *statements* of both the limitations and the complexities and thus gain for Howells a degree of extenuation. It is Binning who provides a continuing discourse on the general cultural changes which his present experience of New York in-

58. William Dean Howells, *The Altrurian Romances*, introduction and notes by Clara and Rudolf Kirk (Bloomington, Indiana: Indiana University Press, 1968), p. 290.

sistently forces upon his awareness. It is he who offers a reminder of a possibly ugly undercurrent in the romantically satisfactory outcome of Ardith's accession to a place in the Ralson family. He suggests that Ralson's dismissive classification of him as an "intellectual . . . a kind of mental and moral woman, to whom a real man, a business man, could have nothing to say after the primary politenesses" does not extend to Ardith "because Mr. Ardith is still young enough to be finally saved from intellectuality, and subsequently dedicated to commerciality" (p. 125). His later reflection on this situation is even more ominous:

I have no doubt but in his heart he despises the fineness of the pretty boy, and hopes to coarsen him to his own uses. The worst of it is that the fineness of Ardith will render him the easier victim; money compels even the poetic fancy, and he will misimagine this common millionaire into something rare and strange, and of rightful authority over such as himself (pp. 297–298).

Finally, Binning justifies the interest he has taken in these people in terms which make it clear that Howells intended them to be generally accepted. To his equally Bostonian sister-in-law, Binning writes:

I have sometimes had my misgivings that this affair was not worthy of your interest, but you have convinced me that it was worthy of mine. These people whom it seems to have concerned less intimately, who are as it were the material out of which our romance has fashioned itself, have certainly their limitations. . . . If they were not so intensely real to themselves, they might seem to me characters in a rather crude American story.[59] In fact, are not they just that? They are certainly American and certainly crude; and now that they are passing beyond my social contact, I feel as safe from them, and from the necessity of explaining them, as if they were shut in a book I had finished reading. . . . If I could find the author I should like to make him my compliment on having managed so skilfully that he left some passages to my conjecture (pp. 298–299).

59. It was on April 26, 1903, in the year *Letters Home* was published that Howells wrote to C. E. Norton: "I am not sorry for having wrought in common, crude material so much; that is the right American stuff" (*Letters*, II, 173).

# VI

## PSYCHOLOGICAL VARIATIONS

The "Long Breath" of the Past: *The Son of Royal Langbrith*

IF the deliberate limitations of *Letters Home* were the price that had to be paid for a final gathering of Howells's creative forces, the general success of his remaining novels was to prove that it was a small price indeed. With the qualified exception of *Fennel and Rue* (1908), all of the novels of Howells's last years continued to show a capacity for fresh observation and insight, and *The Son of Royal Langbrith* (1904), must be considered with Howells's best work in this or any period of his career.

Howells was dissatisfied with the title,[1] perhaps because the title character, James Langbrith, does not dominate the narrative interest as does Jeff Durgin in *Landlord*. Until late in the novel, Langbrith, through his ignorance of the truth of his father's past, is the unwitting agency of emotional anguish and moral uncertainty in his mother and the man who wishes to marry her, Dr. Justin Anther, with the effect of focusing the drama on their efforts to work out their destinies. The problem of James's dealing with the knowledge of his father's wicked past is reserved for the final por-

---

1. "Bibliographical," *The Son of Royal Langbrith,* introduction and notes by David Burrows (Bloomington: Indiana University Press, 1969), p. 3.

tion of the novel, where it is handled economically and where the effects of the disclosure, not merely on him, but on others with whom he has been intimately involved, are assessed. *The Son of Royal Langbrith,* then, does not have the breadth of *Landlord:* it does not involve itself with questions of social mobility and social decadence, it does not document the effects of religious atrophy on the moral life of a whole society.

There are, however, compensations of fullness and complexity in individual characterizations and in the intensity generated by the exploration of the manifold ramifications of a problem of individual responsibility to "truth." Dr. Anther is unquestionably the most masculine hero Howells ever drew, the most appealing combination of strength and compassion, spiritual depth and humane tolerance, self-confidence and humility. Amelia Langbrith, on the other hand, is the weakest of Howells's sympathetically presented women, and James Langbrith comes as close to being a prig as is possible without becoming a caricature or object of hostile satire. The control which Howells exercised over these and other characterizations in the advancement of his purpose to dissect the question "whether it was better or worse for other men that a man's evils should remain unknown when no specific purpose could be served by their discovery" (p. 3) is one more evidence that he did not abandon art with economics.

*The Son of Royal Langbrith* is technically skillful in devising a simple but flexible form to encompass the range of effects whose causes are in the past which did not die with Royal Langbrith. Langbrith, honored by the community as a successful industrialist and public benefactor and by his son as an ideal father and man, was actually a thoroughgoing scoundrel. The problem of what to do with this conflict between appearance and reality, what to do with the knowledge of truth, becomes actual rather than merely theoretical when Anther proposes to Mrs. Langbrith. She has never had the courage to destroy her son's image of his father and of the past by revealing the truth to him, and her marriage without that revelation will be for him a sacrilege. The novel develops from this situation in almost strict chronological progression, and it necessarily has to develop a double account of those acting with the knowledge of the truth of Royal Langbrith's character and those acting on complete misconceptions. Howells turns the technical solution to thematic advantage, alternating units of narrative, dealing now with the story of Anther's frustrated attempts to find a satisfactory way to marriage with Mrs. Langbrith, and now with the story of James Langbrith's idolatry of his father and eventual discovery of his true nature.

The two opening chapters serve as a prologue to state the interrelated problem. Anther proposes and is refused, because Mrs. Langbrith does not have the courage to destroy her son's "reverence for his father's memory" (p. 9). Their conversation reveals the fact, though not the specific terms, of Langbrith's evil in the past, and reveals Amelia's weakness in passively allowing her son's imaginative egotism to embroider a legend of the father, in being unable to find the strength to tell him the truth. Nor can she find even the courage to allow Anther, in his capacity of a long-time family friend and prospective step-father, to assume the task.

The issue proposed, Howells turns to his portrayal of James Langbrith (Chapters III–XI), who in conceit and ignorance comes home on vacation from Harvard to the New England mill town of Saxmills to be a "tyrant" (p. 66) to his mother, with his social sophistication and his desire to assume a "seignorial supremacy" (p. 151) in the village life. When he culminates his visit with an entertainment which is a compromise between a Boston dinner and a Saxmills tea, at which he broaches to the leading citizens of the town his idea for a memorial tablet for his father, the ironic terms of conflict are established. Anther, whom James rather patronizes as the devoted friend and admirer of his father, receives the idea with unexpected coolness, and his mother is vague. Still another complicating irony is introduced by James's proposal to Hope Hawberk, daughter of his father's former partner. Part of the truth which has been kept from James is the fact that his father blackmailed Hawberk from the business by threatening disclosure of an actually innocent relationship with a woman to the "almost maniacally neurotic" (p. 87) Mrs. Hawberk. Howells is at the top of his bent in preserving a measure of sympathy for

James while revealing the full measure of egotism in his ancestor worship and the callowness of his assumption of intellectual and social superiority. He is open in presenting young Langbrith as a "disagreeable fool" but also insists that he is "not finally an ignoble fool" (p. 151). He is a fool in Howells's view primarily because he is young, because he is absolutely certain of his ability to know and to judge men and events, because he looks at life as an open book of black and white drawings. He is capable, however, of correction, of accepting with some grace and humor the deflation of his swollen notions of his wisdom and importance, and it is the chief function of his college friend Falk, and, to a lesser extent, of Hope, to provide the lancings.

James having returned to Harvard, Anther moves to center stage in the next section (Chapters XII–XVII). He renews his proposal to Amelia, but when she counters with the suggestion that he simply make his home with her and James and then asks him to encourage her son's plans for the memorial celebration, Anther departs in anger. But he is as strong as she is weak, and he can neither remain angry nor rest content with their present relationship. In desperation, he discusses the problem with Judge Garley and in so doing reveals the specific extent of Langbrith's iniquity. The present and long-standing addiction of Hawberk to opium was directly caused by his being forced from the business while Langbrith appropriated his inventions which were the basis of its success. (It is later revealed that the library which James proudly regards as the symbol of his father's public benefactions was actually a cynical gesture, paid for out of the first year's profits from Hawberk's inventions.) Langbrith's personal life was equally vicious: he had made a mistress of the very woman he had used to threaten Hawberk, and he returned from drunken debaucheries with her and others in Boston to administer physical beatings to his wife. The problem with which Anther wrestles is how to adjust his personal claims to happiness to his moral responsibility to the woman he loves and to the community at large. He agrees with Garley that no good purpose can be served by destroying the public image of Langbrith. There remains, then, "the personal view" (p. 91): his right to marry Amelia, or, rather, their right to each other. But James, ignorant of the truth, would regard the marriage as a shocking betrayal of his father's memory; and to tell him the truth would be an even more shocking and painful destruction of the father image.

In the central unit of the novel (Chapters XVIII–XXVII), which is appropriately the longest, the ironies proliferate as James puts his plans for the celebration into active motion. Anther is forced into a public role of tacit approval by the assumptions of the townspeople concerning his role as family friend. Privately, however, he first tries to stop the dedication and then acts to satisfy his conscience toward the minister, Enderby, whom James has asked, along with Garley, to deliver an address. He goes first to Langbrith's brother, John, in charge of the mills since Royal's death, and asks him to tell James the truth. In John Langbrith, as much as in the sheer depravity of Royal, Howells embodied his criticism of captains of industry wholly given over to materialistic aims, scornfully ignorant of and unconcerned with all matters irrelevant to the conduct of their business. John's only reply to Anther's moral plea is, " 'I can't go outside my job' " (p. 147).

Still refusing to act solely for his own sake, Anther nevertheless feels compelled to reveal to Enderby that the situation is " 'an atrocious invasion . . . of [his] office' " (p. 160). Enderby, however, offers a definition of truth that might well serve as a gloss to Howells's exploration in this novel: it is " 'that absolute entirety of fact which includes not only every circumstance, but also every extenuation in motive and temperament' " (p. 158). The infinite complexity of this kind of truth places it beyond the reach of certain human knowledge and judgment, and Enderby can only say that he will choose a course which seems to offer the greatest hope of virtue. Anther himself has been following a similar course, but he is not even allowed his resolve to stay away from the ceremony, for Amelia specifically asks him to attend for her sake. This crisis toward which the action of the novel has been inexorably moving now precipitates additional ironies.

Hope Hawberk is so moved by James's kindness to her father in welcoming him to the speaker's platform where his opium delirium has led him that she joyously agrees to marriage. For James, this is the ultimate drop of bliss in a perfect day: he had been overjoyed by Anther's public appearance on the platform, had accepted Enderby's address confined to the general ethical significance of the dedication as perfectly attuned to his father's impersonal reserve. Out of his sense of well-being, he conceives the plan of asking Anther to occupy his father's office. Full of his own beneficence, he surprises Anther and his mother in an embrace expressing her decision to marry without telling him the truth. A bitter quarrel ensues in which his impassioned defense of his father rings mockingly. He goes to Hope for comfort, explaining, in ironic counterpoint to Anther's presence at the ceremony just ended, that he will not attend the marriage, for that would be a lie, would make him seem to condone it. She persuades him to grant at least that he understands that his mother feels that she is doing the right thing and that he will be present at her marriage. But it is too late; Amelia's small reserves of nervous courage have been exhausted, and she tells him that she will not marry.

With James alienated from his mother and off to Paris for study, the novel moves into a new phase (Chapters XXVIII–XXXIV), in which Anther is once more dominant and in which new pressures from the fermenting evil of Langbrith's concealed history are felt. Amelia hovers on the brink, not merely of spiritual and mental apathy, but of evil itself in the hint that Anther's treatment of Hawberk's addiction should be affected by the fact that a cure would probably mean revelation. Hawberk does improve sufficiently to recover his memory, but, like the others who have struggled with their knowledge of Langbrith, concludes that neither he nor Hope can profit from disclosure at this time. Yet events arrange themselves to bring about that disclosure. John Langbrith suddenly decides that he must have a vacation and, in a complete contradiction of attitude, demands that James return home to run the business. This demand James can refuse, but the death of Hope's father constitutes an appeal to which he must respond immediately. He meets his uncle on the train to Saxmills, and harsh words between them lead him to a contemptuous comparison of the gentlemanliness of his father to the boorishness of his uncle. It is his smug complacency, then, which, appropriately enough, triggers the revelation, and it comes in the most painful way possible, couched in the brutally vindictive language of an outraged man.

But the primary strength of this section of *The Son of Royal Langbrith* is Howells's quiet, yet deeply moving, account of the final resolution of the affair between Anther and Amelia. Whatever else happened to Howells in growing old, he retained the indispensable artistic gift for a sort of objective analysis which does not deny past emotions in favor of new ones, but assigns precise value to both. Certainly this gift is to be seen and felt in his delicate handling of the always potentially comic or bathetic relationship of middle-aged lovers, and especially his handling of it in constant interrelationship with conventional young romantics.

The problem he set for himself here was a sensitive and fully honest depiction of the effects of age and the strain of the relationship itself on both Anther and Amelia. The most that she is capable of are occasional moments of intensity when emotion and will combine in almost hysterical expressions of willingness to give herself in marriage to Anther. More and more Anther comes to understand that such moments are as characteristic of her weakness as her usual desire to temporize. The effect of the knowledge is not to blunt his love for her, but to deepen it with compassion and to purify it of selfishness. For example, after James has left home in bitterness, Amelia tells Anther that her feeling toward her son has changed. Typically, she has no real understanding of herself, but explains that since childhood she has reacted thus to being forced to act in a way for which the reason has not been made clear. She is not vindictive, but the intensity of her love for the offending person is immediately diminished. Anther will not take advantage of the moment. He remarks, " 'You're one of those who need to get their strength back when they have been tried' " (p. 229), and he suggests that her feeling toward James may change again. At another of her offers to marry him, he reflects "that he saw in her the little maximum of her force, which perhaps spent itself in the words and would have left nothing for the deed. The deed must be altogether his." His refusal is his highest tribute to her: "'Because we can be more to each other if we remain as we are'" (pp. 230–231).

On the other hand, there are no self-conscious heroics in Anther's refusal. He understands that his own period of intensity of feeling has passed and that the tenderness he feels for Amelia comes not only from having abandoned the hope but "almost the wish, of making her his wife." For Howells, Anther's finely attuned self-awareness and firm self-control equal character:

One hints at cognitions which refuse anything more positive than intimation, and which can have no proof in the admissions of those who deal conventionally with their own consciences. It was because Anther was not one of those that he was a nature of exceptional type, and because he could accept the logic of his self-knowledge that he was a character of rare strength (pp. 227–228).

And Howells's realizing sense of the full truth of his dramatic situations led him to a further remark. He anticipates Yeats's moving comment on the necessary death of the passion of youth to make the knowledge of age: "Bodily decrepitude is wisdom: young/ We loved each other and were ignorant."[2] In the days before his death by typhoid fever, which occurs before James is able to reach home, Anther speaks to Enderby of the affair "as if it were a great while ago." There is both strength and pathos in the honesty of his self-appraisal:

From being the man in later middle life who had wished to form the happiness of a woman long dear to him, he had suddenly lapsed into an elderly man to whom it was appreciable that he could not have made her happy, but only more miserable, if he had pressed her to obey the prompting of her own affection for him (p. 267).

The fact of Anther's death is made known simultaneously to the reader and to James Langbrith, as the novel moves into its

2. "After Long Silence," in *The Collected Poems of W. B. Yeats* (New York: The Macmillan Company, 1952), p. 260.

denouement (Chapters XXXV–XXXVII). Its effect on James is to increase the determination brought on by the revelation about his father to make atonement through renunciation and self-sacrifice. Thus these last chapters are a fitting coda to the ironic counterpoint of the novel, for they quickly recapitulate the moral action. Like others before him, James must now decide what to do with the knowledge, and typically he fails to see the complexity of the problem in resolving to publish the truth broadcast, make financial restitution to Hope, and release her from their engagement. He is persuaded by Hope and Enderby that the more reasonable action and the "heavier penance" (p. 265) is to give up the moral relief such a public confession offers and bear the burden of truth in silence.

The novel is brought to an end, not with a tying up of loose ends, but with a final report on them. James and Hope marry, James takes over the mills, they have a child. John Langbrith, released for his long-delayed trip around the world, is approached in Paris by Langbrith's former mistress and mother of his illegitimate daughter, for whom James now establishes an allowance. Mrs. Langbrith, having too late made public declaration that she would marry Anther, whom she devotedly nursed during his fatal illness, makes her home with her son and daughter-in-law. Her relapse into passivity is such that interested observers like Mrs. Enderby are vexed at being unable to determine whether its source is "tender reverence" for her past with Anther and present enjoyment of "the happiness of her son in his wife" (p. 271) or mere resigned drifting with the currents of life. Howells had no intention of supplying a more definite answer for this or any other question raised. He was in perfect agreement with at least the first half of the reflection he assigned to Dr. Enderby: "It was one of those experiences . . . that intimate a less perfect adjustment of the moral elements in this life than we may hope for in the life hereafter" (pp. 233–234). Whatever the hereafter might hold, Howells had clearly indicated the imperfection of earthly arrangements; at the same time, however, he had shown the human capacity to deal with that imperfection through reason, through love, through humility—and through hopefulness, if not faith—so that imperfection need not be permitted to become moral chaos, and personal unhappiness "a ruin spreading wide and sinking deep" (p. 4).

By building its intensities on the overriding issue of Royal Langbrith's depravity and making its basic concern with all the characters, except minor functionaries, their witting or unwitting involvement in its effects, *The Son of Royal Langbrith* sacrifices comprehensiveness for penetration. One of the greatest gains from the concentration on an apparently simple but in fact ambiguous moral question was that the attempts of the involved individuals to come to terms with it provided a thoroughly believable instance of complicity and a natural dialectic for its presentation. In an unforced and unschematic way, the problem is submitted for analysis and judgment to a variety of viewpoints—the scientific, the legal, the philosophical-theological, the idealistic, and others—with the effect of producing, not a committee report or consensus which reduces the problem to fully manageable terms, or of suggesting that it is the diversity of the human element that makes the problem insoluble, but of showing that the inherent nature of the problem puts it beyond the reach of perfect human adjustment.

What saves *The Son of Royal Langbrith* from a schematic awkwardness and unrealistic rigidity in its presentation of the variety of interpretations of the moral problem is that they are shown as conditioned perspectives, a product of character as well as function, and not merely doctrinaire reactions. The role of doctor or judge or theologian introduces a characteristic cast of thought into the consideration, but that is not necessarily the sole determinant of the result. Howells provided even for those characters such as Judge Garley, who could not be represented in complex depth, sufficient individualizing to prevent their being empty types completely defined by the profession or social position in which they perform. This is obviously truest, because of his central importance to the story, of Dr. Anther, whose qualities of imaginative compassion and unselfish love combined with his common sense and trained habit of scientific or rational diagnosis in his search for a prescription for action. Having progressed by his own best instincts and reason from a relatively simplistic viewpoint to an attitude which could encompass love for Mrs. Langbrith's weakness, sympathy for James's disagreeable but not ignoble folly, and silence concerning Langbrith's evil, he has come back to a "scientific" judgment of Royal Langbrith: "He seemed to have exhausted the hoarded abhorrences with which he had hitherto visited the sinner's memory, and to regard his evil life as a morbid condition with which the psychological side of pathology had to do rather than morals" (p. 267).

Judge Garley is more nearly susceptible of complete definition as a "legal mind" (p. 168) and by his sense of responsibility to "public duty" (p. 149). He is quick to pronounce that, as far as the community is concerned, the best course of action is "to leave the late Royal Langbrith's memory alone." When Anther insists, however, that such a judgment does nothing to satisfy "the personal view" (p. 91), the judge, after promising "with bland placidity" to "think it over" can arrive only at a view based on the "evidential" aspects of the situation. He argues against the disclosure because the case could not be proved. " 'You would stand unaided and alone, and the outraged sentiment of the community would be against you. . . . Your exposure of the boy's father would be attributed to the worst motives, in the absence of any, and the tide of pity for him would bear you down' " (pp. 148–149). The inadequacy of strict legalism is suggested in the fact that Garley turns to it as a refuge rather than a solution, that he is more concerned with the forms of truth and justice than with their spirit. He is rather easily able to convince himself of his public duty to deliver the requested address at the library ceremony, and though Anther does not "condemn" him, he is ruefully aware of the falseness of the impression Garley makes and of "how false he had been in making it" by giving to his speech "a surface as impenetrable as it was shallow" (p. 170).

Dr. Enderby, the representative of the religious viewpoint, also speaks at the ceremony—Anther had not informed him of the truth until it was too late for him to dissociate himself even if he would —and draws some inferences "concerning the ethical significance of the business they were about" (p. 171). He is a dedicated man, for whom there is no separation between the precepts of his calling and the actions of his life, and Anther sincerely tells him he "did the best that any man could, in the circumstances" (p. 173). He represents, in fact, what might better be called a philosophical-religious point of view; it is his wife who, out of a conscience inherited from Calvinistic forefathers and a pleasure in the intellectual intricacies of the process, attempts to find a strict theological or scriptural interpretation of the meaning of Langbrith's wickedness and the suffering it caused. But the logic of her reasoning would produce an "earthly justice [that] would include the innocent alone" (p. 276), and Dr. Enderby is realistic enough to reason from the premise that he has "never seen any instance of justice in the world" (p. 159), and humane enough to pronounce for mercy.

There are still other sharply defined viewpoints, though not specifically associated with a professional attitude. There is the fundamentalist hostility to the Langbriths of Mrs. Smithfield, Hope's grandmother, which is also associated with vindictiveness and unreasoning hatred in contrast to Enderby's counsel of mercy. There is the pure selfishness of John Langbrith, which first insists on disassociation and then expresses itself in dyspeptic anger and injured vanity. There is the practical unselfishness of Hope's father,[3] which he has won to through his own suffering and causing of suffering. There is the egotism of James Langbrith, expressing itself in idealistic romanticism, both in his original misconceptions and then in his plans for reparation, until it is finally brought under the control of reason and compassion for others. Most important, there is the instructive reaction of the appropriately named Hope: hers is the sane, "normal" hopefulness of life itself, the acceptance of the experience of simply being alive and capable of enjoying the beauty of the season, the laughter and nonsense of youthful companionship, the anticipations of the future. This is an attitude partly temperamental and partly willed in the face of the horrors of her father's opium addiction and the sourness of her grandmother's pessimistic re-

---

3. The name Hawberk (hauberk) is perhaps suggestive of Howells's conception of the character. Hope's father is a kind of tragi-comic chivalric figure, a potential doer of great deeds (Hope believes him a "genius" [p. 256]) who armors himself against reality with opium and expends his gifts in purely imaginary accomplishments for the ladies under his protection. There is a kind of gallantry in his eventually successful fight against addiction and nobility in his lack of vindictiveness against Royal Langbrith.

ligiosity, so it is not merely a cheap and shallow evasion of reality. Therefore her response to James's pessimistic avowal that his mother is betraying both his father and himself in proposing to marry Anther is that he is acting as though he were "insane" (p. 195), and that "it's the best thing that could happen" (p. 194). When the truth about his father is known to him, as he indulges in equally excessive vows of reparation, including the release of Hope from their engagement, she claims that the injury to her father gives her the authority of control, and it is she who proposes that Dr. Enderby be consulted. He, naturally, confirms that they should marry and keep silence "until such time as the Infinite Mercy, which is the Infinite Justice, shall choose to free you of it" (p. 265).

Such a spectrum of representative but individualized attempts to understand and neutralize the corruption sown by Royal Langbrith not only results in a dynamic illustration of the workings of complicity, but is a kind of classic instance of Howells's refusal of tragedy. His remark that it "finally seemed too easy" to develop the patent potentialities for tragedy in *The Son of Royal Langbrith,* that he preferred to sacrifice the "greater theatre" for the "greater drama" (p. 4) is again, however, an insistence on artistic principle and realistic integrity. Howells fairly represented the contending forces before choosing a limited optimism in a denouement which showed the specifically virulent effects of the past evil having been absorbed.[4] Some participants in the trouble have died, but their deaths are not directly attributed to the trouble which has disturbed their private lives: Hawberk contracts pneumonia; Anther, typhoid fever; and Mrs. Smithfield presumably dies of old age and choler. There is continuation and accommodation in the daughter born to Hope and

---

4. See "Bibliographical," p. 4: "It appears to me that the father's secret came to the son in a natural way and a right way, and that it ceased with him and his in a just and reasonable sort." Howells consistently held to the view that the effects of evil can be absorbed and dissipated. He had also made this point in 1895 in the story "The Circle in the Water." In the "Editor's Easy Chair," *Harper's Monthly,* CIX (July 1904), 309, he said: "It used to be gloomily imagined that consequences were cumulative, especially evil consequences. . . . But it seems more probable that the first effect is the greatest, and that all the later effects diminish until they cease."

James and in the potential singing career, supported by James, of his father's illegitimate daughter.

These are not merely the nostrums of a quack realist: they are legitimate possibilities. The characters have struggled in their various ways with conflicts between personal sorrow and duty, passion and reason, appearance and reality, idealism and practicality, and some have been led to the ultimate conflict between doubt and faith. If the scales have been tipped toward faith—in an Enderby, a Hope, a James, and most movingly in an Anther—that result has not really been determined by a belief in the kind of complicity that Enderby formulates in the proposition that the pain the evildoer inflicts serves as " 'the sort of vicarious atonement which has always been in the world' " (p. 277). Such a vision of cosmic order is available to faith and is appropriate to Enderby, but it is not shown as the fruit of Anther's experience or the lesson of the healing marriage. This is merely to say that the novel is not prescriptive.

There are, however, demonstrated grounds for refusing the other extreme, the tragic view, the marriage of vital "hope" and chastened idealism being the most obvious but not the most important. Anther's experience is more profound and of more general significance. He has been tried by a malignity which seems to be specifically directed against all his possibilities for deserved happiness, and his qualities as a man enable him to survive without succumbing to hatred of God or man. In fact, before his personal problems have approached resolution, when "he ought logically to have been contrasting his hopeless life" with the renewal of hope for Hawberk in his release from his opium addiction, Anther instead feels "something of the peace that passes understanding in his heart" (p. 218). This is the moment of climax for Anther, the moment—as immediately subsequent events show—when he has surrendered his pursuit of personal happiness, purged his love for Amelia Langbrith of any selfishness and thus "found himself at peace with desires and purposes that had long afflicted him with unrest" (p. 226).

This kind of goodness—which is positive and active and not unique, since Hope and James have given promise of being able to achieve it, if necessary—is the affirmation of the novel, its realism rather than its tragedy. Though the connection is not explicitly made, dramatic appropriateness and generalizing import are gained for Anther's deep spiritual experience by having it follow on another version of complicity which the doctor had heard Enderby develop at the dedication of the memorial tablet. The words were full of irony for Anther, who was unwillingly on the speakers' platform, who had himself informed Enderby of Royal Langbrith's true character, but who had heard them and offered such approval of them to Enderby as he could summon from his bitterness. The lesson which Enderby had drawn, though its full meaning was hidden from the audience, concerned the independent power of good as well as evil:

It was not only the evil that men do which lived after them, but the good also lived, laying upon the future a more powerful obligation to virtue than any bond to vice that evil could impose. God had apparently willed that the good should continually and eternally show itself, and the evil should hide itself, for evil, brought into the light of day, corrupted, and good, whenever manifest, purified and restored and strengthened all men for good. Such, in fact, was the potency of a good deed that, if done from the most selfish motive, it took no color from the motive. It returned through its beneficent effect upon the world to the God of goodness (pp. 171–172).

Such a theory, whether the theological terms are granted or not, is given credence by the example of Anther's life.

The realistic excellence of *The Son of Royal Langbrith* makes appropriate a final retrospective comment on tragedy in Howells's fiction.[5] Here were the materials, as Howells was clearly aware, for a confrontation of the forces of good and evil and an intensely

5. The novel also supplies a further gloss to the earlier discussion of the value of humor as a control over otherwise intolerable events or circumstances. Howells said of the heroine's last state of affairs and attitude in the novel: "Hope herself took the humorous view of her grandmother's opposition [to her marriage], as she had taken the humorous view of her father's long tragedy, not because it was not real and terrible, but because temperamentally she had no other way of bearing it, because in that way she could transmute it into something fantastic, and smile at what otherwise must have broken her heart" (p. 268).

personal tragedy of human strength and human weakness frustrated by conditions not of their own making. These were—depending, to be sure, on one's definition—far more susceptible of a tragic interpretation than any that Howells had ever used before: Bartley Hubbard is selfish, and Marcia is undisciplined, but they are not evil; if there is evil in *A Hazard of New Fortunes,* it is in an economic system of man's own making and, theoretically at least, susceptible to man's correction; if there is a malign Fate in *The Shadow of a Dream,* it cannot be successfully distinguished from man's own capacity for error through passion and pride and irrationality. *The Son of Royal Langbrith,* then, would seem convincing proof that Howells had always meant what he said in denying both the general "truthfulness" and the artistic validity of tragedy. If this novel is the test, then *realism* is surely a term of high praise, and one that Howells would gladly continue to accept in his remarkably fruitful sixty-seventh year.

## Love and Marriage: *Miss Bellard's Inspiration*

It is not surprising that *Miss Bellard's Inspiration* (1905), immediately following *The Son of Royal Langbrith,* should be a less ambitious performance. But that proximity has, perhaps, unduly affected its reputation. Moreover, in dealing with what seems a particularly inane instance of mating and marrying, it has invited cursory dismissal as evidence of the fading creativity which turned Howells back to old and tired themes. Actually, if Howells's age is to be taken into account, this novel exhibits a remarkable modernity —and that not merely because it portrays a "new woman." Psychological undercurrents that were merely latent in *April Hopes* and *The Shadow of a Dream* surface here in the cruel and sordid circumstances of an incompatible marriage against which the light and familiar story of courtship is played off. Lloyd Morris, in fact, has claimed that when Howells "in his later work . . . returned to love as a central theme with some frequency," he "brought to it an insight and perception of complexity that he had never before displayed." His reference includes not only *Miss Bellard's Inspiration,* but the following *Fennel and Rue* (1908) and the short fiction of this period.

Morris argues that Howells "recorded those darker aspects of love—its possessiveness, its cruelty, its ambivalence—which analytical psychology was later to explore."[6]

The firm structural technique which Howells devised to carry the ambivalences also suggests control rather than exhaustion. In spite of the title, which refers to the solution of the question of whether Lillias Bellard will marry Edmund Craybourne, the core of the novel both thematically and structurally is the account of the present marriage and eventual separation of Arthur and Clarice Mevison. The stories are linked in counterpoint by being largely enacted at the summer home of the Crombies, who serve as reflectors and mediators through being made privy, in varying degrees of willingness and knowledge, to the developing events. Mrs. Crombie is Lillias's aunt; Mr. Crombie is Arthur Mevison's former colleague at Réné's *atelier* in Paris. Lillias comes to the Crombies for a socially proper milieu in which to conduct the resolving stages of her courtship with Craybourne, whose calling card actually precedes her arrival. The Mevisons come by direct invitation when they are discovered staying at the hotel across the river, where Craybourne has rather reluctantly made their acquaintance after overhearing a vicious marital quarrel from their next-door room.

The Crombies might be described as cousins to Isabel and Basil March, though they seem completely freed from the economic chance-world and can function as free intelligences in analyzing and judging the complications of love and marriage which are thrust upon them. But this freedom is limited by their temperaments, their past experience, and their present emotional states, compounded of irritation at the disruption of their planned seclusion, admitted ties of kinship and old friendship, and half-admitted vicarious excitement in sharing in the contrasting dramas enacted under their social auspices.

Hester is one of those Howells women who superficially seem all irrationality and contradiction but whose actions finally reveal a

6. Lloyd Morris, "Conscience in the Parlor: William Dean Howells," in *Howells: A Century of Criticism,* edited by Kenneth E. Eble (Dallas: Southern Methodist University Press, 1962), p. 227. This article originally appeared in *American Scholar,* XVII (Autumn 1949), 407–416.

shrewd consistency and practical insight. Archibald seems to take his chief pleasure in appreciating his wife's mental machinations and in assimilating their essential meaning while commenting with dry wit on their apparent extravagance and contradictoriness. He, too, however, has his realistic reserves, which determine when he will simply retreat from the process of his wife's circumlocutions and when he will make his own commitments to the relationships which have invaded his home. They make for Lillias "the happiest married couple she had ever seen, the most united and harmonious,"[7] and in a less absolute sense that is their function for Howells: they are a recognizably imperfect norm, achieved by adjustment, accommodation, and love, against which the romantic extremes, terrible and comic, of the other two couples can be measured. Technically, the omniscient point of view is used throughout the novel, but only in two "love scenes" (Chapters X and XII) between Lillias and Edmund and in a grotesque accusatory confrontation of Lillias by Mrs. Mevison (Chapter X) are both the Crombies excused from providing the filtering consciousness by which the reader's perceptions are directed, if not controlled.

What is new to Howells's practice here, at least as a technical variation, is the handling of the double story. He had often used the Marches, as in *The Shadow of a Dream* and *An Open-Eyed Conspiracy,* to achieve artistic distancing and to establish the controlling tone; in *The Son of Royal Langbrith* he had alternated the Dr. Anther–James Langbrith stories from the omniscient point of view. Here the Crombies serve the additional function of thematic unification, of bringing the stories of marriage and courtship into illuminating interrelationship. It is the Mevison affair, however, that dominates and supports the claims for Howells's continuing vitality. It is introduced by Craybourne as soon as he and Lillias have been brought on stage and explained; it becomes the referential element in the Crombies' daily decisions and in Lillias's thinking about her own future until the Mevisons leave; and it is a factor—Mrs. Mevi-

---

7. *Miss Bellard's Inspiration* (New York: Harper and Brothers, 1905), p. 32.

son establishes residence out west of Craybourne's hotel in the accomplishment of a divorce—in Lillias's surrender of mere reason in favor of "inspiration" in deciding to marry Craybourne.

Thus the fourteen chapters of this spare but deceptively rich novel are organized in a neatly ordered progression: Introduction (Chapters I–IV): exposition of character and situation, with Lillias appearing on scene in Chapter II and Craybourne in Chapter IV; Narrative Body (Chapters V–XII): the Mevisons introduced by hearsay in Craybourne's account of the overheard quarrel (Chapter V), successive appearance of Arthur and then Clarice (Chapters VI, VII), Lillias's overhearing of another Mevison quarrel, which by deliberate repetition intensifies her merely theoretical reaction to Craybourne's report and prepares for Mrs. Mevison's insane accusations (Chapter X), and dramatic climax, in which the reconciled Mevisons leave the Crombie house and Lillias rejects Craybourne (Chapter XII); Conclusion (Chapters XIII–XIV): Lillias's departure for her role as a New Woman, a professor of oratory (Chapter XIII), Crombie's advice to Craybourne to follow her, and notification that marriage for the young couple and divorce for the Mevisons will be the ultimate outcome (Chapter XIV).

There is also something old and something new in the materials with which Howells worked. Old, of course, is the courtship: Howells's new woman[8] is new only in her circumstances, which give her economic independence from marriage; but in her torturous reasoning—that she and Edmund are too much in love to be happily married, that they must be warned by the example of the

---

8. If Howells owed anything in this conception to Ibsen, the borrowing was thoroughly Americanized and completely assimilated to Howells's own temperament and artistic purposes. The speculation about this element and the treatment of divorce seems relevant, however, for Ibsen was very much in Howells's thoughts at about this time. He assigns to a dinner-table discussion in "His Apparition" (1902) some ideas about the performance of *Ghosts* very similar to those expressed in an essay in *Harper's Weekly*, April 27, 1895. See *Criticism and Fiction and Other Essays*, by William Dean Howells, edited by Clara Marburg Kirk and Rudolf Kirk (New York: New York University Press, 1959), p. 145.

Mevisons—she is blood relation to Helen Harkness of *A Woman's Reason* (1883), whose "divine logic of the heart"[9] was equally incomprehensible to all but other women.

New is the dissection of the love-hate relationship which binds Arthur and Clarice Mevison in helpless suffering and shame: they practice a grotesque social masquerade, punctuated by her cruelties in pinching her lamed husband or attempting to upset his chair. These incidents are terrible in their triviality, for they are an attempt to mask the profound alienation and sick abberation which they vent. Bartley and Marcia Hubbard had torn at each other out of the lawless passion of their natures, and the disintegration of their marriage had been patiently and powerfully delineated. The Mevison misalliance is more one-sided, and, in some senses, more ugly and frightening: Mrs. Mevison is a more self-aware and intelligent woman than Marcia, a spiritual succubus as well as a jealous and undisciplined wife. And the very economy of the presentation of this latter-day modern instance, the sympathetic but almost matter-of-fact way in which Crombie receives his friend's confession of its horrors, is a measure of the social change between 1882 and 1905, and, implicitly, a condemnation of it.

The sense of dark ambiguities beneath the facade of the Mevison marriage is easily accessible to Mrs. Crombie's perceptions when she invites them to transfer from the hotel. Mevison tries to avoid inflicting their uncertain intensities on his old friend, but his wife, in a charade of meek willfulness, "a warble of the sweetest caressingness" (p. 105), insists on accepting the Crombies' hospitality. Mrs. Crombie reports to her husband that " 'she's either the most consummate actress, or the fondest wife, or the most perfect little fiend that I ever did see' " (p. 108). The truth of Crombie's suggestion that she might be all three is quickly demonstrated during the Mevison visit. In Mevison's formulation of his own case, his wife loves him so intensely that she demands "every atom, every instant" (p. 126) of him. She has forced him to give up painting, not because she was jealous of the nude models, but of all "other"

9. *A Woman's Reason* (Boston: James R. Osgood and Company, 1883), p. 213.

relationships, including especially the painting itself, which gave him a "life" apart.

In explaining all this, Mevison seems to justify Mrs. Crombie's instant liking for him by the largeness of his understanding and his humility before the perfervid possessiveness of his wife's love:

"Still . . . I was not the only sufferer. Slavery was always worse for the owner than the slave. I know it hurt her worse than it hurt me. . . . It caused her pain and shame and sorrow twice as much as it caused me. She knew that she spoiled my life, and that whether I was aware of it or not, at the bottom of my soul I longed to be rid of her. . . . The conviction grew upon her, and goaded her, till she had to accuse me of it. I knew the truth first from her; though I denied it at first a thousand times, I had to own it at last. That made things intolerable. What she could bear, so long as I denied it, she could not bear when I owned it. . . . She sees as well as I do that we must part; but it is her helpless fate to torment me more and more into what if we could we would both avoid" (pp. 127–128).

But the quality of Mevison's abnegation is quickly rendered anomalous by his being persuaded, in despite of this analysis, by a night visit from his wife not merely to remain with her, but to feel as if they "were beginning all over again" and "going forward on ground where there will be no room for the old—anxieties." Crombie perceives that this is spoken from "some profound insecurity" (p. 171), and it prepares for the final possible irony that Mrs. Mevison may be the initiator of the divorce proceedings: she takes up residence in Craybourne's hotel for that purpose and charges "extreme cruelty and gross neglect of duty" (p. 222) against her husband.

The strong sexual component in the alternating love-hate relationship, the on-and-off marriage—hinted in the physical expressions of caresses and outright physical attack, Mrs. Mevison's deliberate awakening of her husband from his first sound sleep in weeks, and in the reconciliation achieved by another nocturnal visit to her husband's bedroom—is nakedly revealed in the surrealistic confrontation between Lillias and Mrs. Mevison. First she attacks wildly, claiming that the engagement to Craybourne, "that wretched cockney," is mere protective coloration for Lillias's flirtatiousness, that Lillias has been "making a set" (p. 144) at Mevison and plotting their separation. She shifts to a mixture of abject pleading and attack, then to a frank confession of pleasure in shocking the "goody-goody pretences" (p. 145) of the girl, and finally to the accusation that her husband is the aggressor toward Lillias and could be returned to her by being discouraged. If Mevison remains ignorant of this maundering irrationality, he is perfectly aware, as he has confessed to Crombie, of the extreme vulgarity of his whole situation. However, he does not have the will—or, perhaps, the wish—really to break from it. He is more sinned against than sinning, but he is no paragon of suffering virtue sacrificed to preserve the semblance of ideal marriage.

However, in the total scheme of the novel, the Mevison marriage remains merely *a* rather than *the* modern instance of matrimony. It is therefore presented not in the world-weary accents of the cynic, or the satiric tones of a reformer, or with the bitter laughter of a disillusioned humanist. The tone is controlled both by the fact of the very different marriages, actual and incipient, of the Crombies and the young lovers, and by the screening of the report on the Mevisons through the perceptions of the "adjusted" oldsters. It is part of Howells's skillful use of this method that the revelation of the full extremity of Mrs. Mevison's obsession in her scene with Lillias is not known directly by the Crombies. They presumably cannot quite imagine this excessiveness of passion, and are, therefore, not infallible commentators or mere *raisoneurs*. But they are normal, intelligent, sympathetic, moral, and experienced, and therefore capable of mediating for the reader between the comic absurdities of the essentially sound courtship and the destructive absurdities of the fated married lovers.

This mediation, however, would hardly be needed were the contrast between the two couples as clear-cut and uncomplicated as such a formulation implies. Actually, there is an interpenetration of meaning from one story to the other. When Mrs. Crombie remarks, after her call on the Mevisons at the hotel, that their passionate misery should be a good "object-lesson" for Lillias and Craybourne, that they should learn from it "to go slow in their demands upon each other" (p. 111), she can hardly anticipate that her niece's reaction will be to reject the marriage itself, but her warning against "romantic" or any kind of compulsive selfishness is a valid one. Howells's deliberate exaggeration of the comedy of courtship—a comic intention that goes unrecognized in the interpretation of Lillias's final "inspiration" as "the most absurd piece of motivation in all Howells"[10]—is a gloss on the inherent extravagance in the sexual and psychological warfare of the Mevisons: a purely romantic, unrealistic surrender to emotion, however merely comic or absurd it may seem, has within it a potential for destruction or harmful imbalance that is anything but amusing. It is no accident that the novel closes with the Crombies unconsciously voicing the double-interpretation. Archibald "coarsely" suggests that Lillias has at last evidenced "horse-sense" in putting aside reason for inspiration (actually, of course, the terminology is reversed). Though Hester is brought to "tears of entire satisfaction" by the prospect of the marriage, her final insight is unwittingly ominous of future trouble, if not disaster, in the Mevison pattern: " 'She can make him go to England and live now, if she wants to. He will do anything for her' " (p. 224).

## The War of the Sexes: Fennel and Rue

Fennel and Rue (1908) is of a piece with Miss Bellard's Inspiration in dealing under the guise of a slight romantic story with hidden psychological stresses and neurotic intensities. Though patently not tragedy, nor even a story of disappointed love in any conventional sense, as might be suggested by the allusion of the title, this brief novel is certainly dark in its depiction of the feminine "wiles and lures"[11] and the masculine tergiversations which are the components of courtship and even "love."

The initial circumstances of the story were taken directly from Howells's own experience: an author is petitioned by a girl who claims to be dying to disclose to her the outcome of his current serial, and investigation reveals a hoax. In the novel, after the author,

10. Alexander Cowie, The Rise of the American Novel (New York: American Book Co., 1948), p. 689.

11. Fennel and Rue (New York: Harper and Brothers, 1908), p. 64.

Verrian, has answered the letter in terms which claim dispassionate moral justice but actually reveal wounded vanity, this introductory situation is held in abeyance. Meanwhile, Verrian becomes unknowingly acquainted, as a post-Christmas guest at Mrs. Westangle's, with the letter writer, Miss Shirley, who has been engaged by the hostess as a professional "mistress of the revels" (p. 39). Out of sympathy for Miss Shirley's precarious health and her need for a striking success at Mrs. Westangle's to provide openings for further employment, Verrian plays a crucial part in cajoling the other guests into enjoying her entertainments: a male attack on a snow fort defended by the ladies, a skating tea, and a game of "Seeing Ghosts." In the process of being helpful and denying it to such inquisitive fellow guests as the feline Miss Macroyd and the bluff real estate man, Bushwick, Verrian becomes more emotionally involved than he realizes or admits to himself.

Events now arrange themselves to bring Miss Shirley to confess her identity as the letter writer, and they go their apparently separate and socially different ways. However, one more chance meeting occurs at the theater, and during the subsequent conversation Miss Shirley reveals to Verrian her engagement to Bushwick. On Verrian's advice, she tells Bushwick in Verrian's presence of the past relationship: her false letter, Verrian's stiff letter of censure for the hoax, her suffering which contributed to her illness and her emotional breakdown at Mrs. Westangle's. Bushwick, in a lover's condemnation of Verrian's moral stuffiness and cruelty, refuses further to acknowledge Verrian's presence or existence and escorts his fiancée out of Verrian's sight and world.

There is even more plot than this summary suggests. For example, Verrian's mother seriously tries to promote an interest leading to marriage with Miss Andrews, a fellow participant with Verrian in "Seeing Ghosts." It was she who caused Miss Shirley to faint in confusion and guilt through her posing of a theoretical problem which paralleled that caused by the duplicitous letter. It is, however, the book's weakness that this sort of profusion of separate incident (necessitating twenty-one brief chapters) does not produce a plot strong enough to bear the weight of serious interpretation placed upon it. This is true even in the face of Howells's conscious disclaimer of concern for plot, which took the form of a paraphrase of his own critical dictum. He based Miss Shirley's appeal to Verrian on the fact that "It was not for the plot she cared; she had read too many stories to care for the plot; it was the problem involved" (p. 3). But in this case he actually attaches more significance to his "problem" than he is able to convince us of. The potentialities of the novel as a probing dissection of the "gossamer tenuity" (p. 64) of the spider web woven by "nice" but predatory young ladies to trap a male, or as an interesting study of the double consciousness of the literary mind, which examines its own impressions as material for fiction even as the experiences produce them, are not fully realized.

The primary difficulty is that the kind of importance that Verrian attributes to the trick that is played on him,[12] in combination with his later social anxieties at the anomalousness of Miss Shirley's status in Mrs. Westangle's arrangements and in his own relationship to her, make him more a prig and a snob than a suitably sensitive and perceptive literary and moral intelligence. There is something of Miles Coverdale about Verrian in his fear of emotional commitment, his incessant analysis of his own motives and his assumption of moral superiority with regard to the motives of others, his willingness to accept life simply as material for his fiction, and his loss of love through these withdrawals from vital involvement. And the reference to Hawthorne as a valid suggestion of Howells's intent is supported by the characterization of Verrian's fiction: "The quality of his work . . . was quietly artistic and psychological. . . . He

12. Howells was never very successful in basing his fiction directly on his own experience. An earlier instance had produced the inferior *A Fearful Responsibility* (see William Dean Howells, *Life in Letters of William Dean Howells*, edited by Mildred Howells, 2 vols. [Garden City, New York: Doubleday Doran and Co., Inc., 1928], I, 74–75, and Everett Carter, *Howells and the Age of Realism* [Philadelphia: J. B. Lippincott Co., 1954], pp. 107–108), and "The Eidolons of Brooks Alford" and "The Memory That Worked Overtime" in *Between the Dark and the Daylight* were also doubtfully successful uses of such material (see Edwin H. Cady, *The Realist at War* [Syracuse: Syracuse University Press, 1958], p. 243).

belonged to the good school which is of no fashion and of every time, far both from actuality and unreality" (p. 27).[13]

But in spite of such attempts to indicate Verrian's worth as a writer and to project "all that was sweet and kind and gentle" (pp. 15–16) in his nature, his "counter qualities" (p. 16) dominate the impression he conveys. When his vanity was wounded by the hoax, "he coldly and carefully studied what deadlier hurt he might inflict" (p. 13). When Miss Macroyd "piggishly" (p. 111) commandeered the Westangle victoria at the Southfield station, leaving him to offer Miss Shirley transportation in the carryall he had managed to secure, he at first felt rather amused and inclined to treat this forced intimacy as "rather a favor" (p. 37); but having learned of Miss Shirley's commercial mission to Seasands and been rebuked by her for not transferring to the returned victoria, he "sulked" (p. 41). His reaction to receiving a smuggled note thanking him for his help in making the snow-fight a success is defensively vain: it can only mean that rather than pursuing the business of being mistress of the revels she is trying to involve him in "the one great business" of a woman's life (p. 63). He is "furious" (p. 66) at being mistaken for an actor. Finally, when Miss Shirley announces her engagement to Bushwick, he attaches great ethical significance to their "secret" concerning her part in the hoax and insists that " 'You mustn't share such a secret with any one but your husband. When you tell him it will cease to be *my* secret' " (p. 127). In the light of this evidence, his refusal to court Miss Andrews, who is, according to his mother, "innocence itself" and "the woman I would be willing my son

13. Cf. *My Literary Passions* (New York: Harper and Brothers, 1895), pp. 186–187: "They [Hawthorne's novels] were so far from time and place that, although most of them related to our country and epoch, I could not imagine anything approximate from them. . . . But none of Hawthorne's fables are without a profound and distant reach into the recesses of nature and of being." Oscar W. Firkins was reminded of *The Blithedale Romance* by *The Shadow of a Dream* (*William Dean Howells: A Study* [Cambridge: Harvard University Press, 1924], p. 135), and it might be suggested that there are more obvious parallels between Seasands and Blithedale, the use of seances, and perhaps even between Bushwick and Westervelt as western materialists.

should marry" (p. 118),[14] rather than producing deep sympathy for Verrian's unwillingness to be the cause of the same kind of unhappiness he is suffering, confirms the notion of his passive selfishness.

If Verrian's characterization is made murky by what seem unintentional obscurities or emphases rather than fruitful ambiguities and complexities, the sinuosities of Miss Shirley are rendered debatable by being reported only in the dubious testimony of Verrian and his mother. Mrs. Verrian immediately judges her as "not single-minded" (p. 8) on the evidence of her letter. After the revelation of the hoax, Mrs. Verrian speculates that the original objective might have been to open a correspondence, to introduce "excitement, adventure" (p. 25) into a dull village life.

Verrian's first reaction to the still unidentified Miss Shirley is that her "confidences . . . had perhaps been too voluntary," that she might be "accused of provoking him to imagine" (p. 43) many things about her. She pretends to believe that Verrian is an actor, only to confess the pretense in an incident which causes him to taste "a delicious pleasure in the womanish feat by which she overcame her womanishness" but in which he is unable to discern her motive (p. 76). He continues to feel a fascination in her which "seemed to emanate from her frail prettiness no less than from . . . [her] fearful daring" (p. 83). When the whole story of Miss Shirley's confession of her identity is reported by Verrian to his mother, she immediately enters into a comparison with Miss Andrews, whose motive for confession would have been truth for its own sake rather than *her* own sake. Mrs. Verrian goes on to suggest that the confession was actually one more stratagem that would "clinch" (p. 114) Verrian's interest. Similarly, when Verrian is brought to self-castigation and praise for Miss Shirley's courage in revealing the past to Bushwick, his mother suggests that the action might better be described as deceptive "bravado" (p. 129), based on

14. Another element in this curious novel which is sure to suggest itself to certain modern readers is the Oedipal character of the relationship between Verrian and his mother.

the certainty that Bushwick would not reject her but that, if he should, Verrian would be hooked.

What finally seems clearest from this novel—which is reminiscent of such early work as *A Chance Acquaintance* or, perhaps, *Private Theatricals* in its subject matter and very unlike them in tone—is that, if it is a failure, it is a failure in new directions and not just an exhaustion of spirit. Still very much in evidence, for example, is the familiar Howellsian ease in limning the social parvenu, Mrs. Westangle, and in commenting on the emptiness of the social life into which she is gaining entrance by being "chic" under the tutelage of Miss Shirley. But Howells avails himself of such still fertile resources only to the extent he deems necessary—as in the acidic miniature of Miss Macroyd—to supply a vehicle to carry his somber consideration of an affair characterized by fennel and rue. Notably absent in Verrian is the wit which frequently redeems the moral earnestness of Howells's heroes, and in Miss Shirley the vivacity and élan of his good and wicked girls alike (Kitty Ellison, Mrs. Farrell).

These deliberate exclusions—and the decision to make Verrian with all his ambivalences the narrative intelligence—argue for a purpose other than an exhausted return to the materials of past success. They argue for an attempt at new depth, new complexity, new insights into the sexual war and its social battlefield, new awareness of the dangers for the writer in confining his "ethics and aesthetics, his ideal of conduct and of art" (p. 13) to his fiction and failing in his vanity to commit them in action to the tests of experience. At the age of seventy-one, Howells did not produce a fully realized work of art in *Fennel and Rue*, but the nature and quality of its objectives deserve notation.

## Religion and Life: *The Leatherwood God*

If *The Leatherwood God* (1916) is unique in Howells's fiction as both a western and a historical novel, it is as a psychological novel very much a related part of the pattern of his total output. In fact, it is in the latter terms—which have themselves been challenged, however—that it best sustains critical analysis as a coherent fictional exercise. As a western it is mostly atmospheric. As a historical novel —except for its admitted use of "historical outline"[15] for the story of the self-proclaimed God—it is vague. As a study of individual problems imagined as growing from certain actual events, however, it is perceptive and entirely consistent with the views of human nature and with the rational ethic that Howells had been developing and expressing in his fiction for almost half a century.

The western setting of the novel "in the valley of Leatherwood Creek" in Ohio is sharply particularized, and its inhabitants, who had only lately "ceased to be pioneers" (p. 3), are unmistakably western in dress and speech. Abel Reverdy's admiration of Squire Braile's two-room cabin, plastered outside and whitewashed within, puncheon floored, lofted over both rooms, and graced with both clock and a "chimbly-piece with . . . [a] plaster of Paris Samuel prayin' in it" (p. 13), is reminiscent of Huck Finn's pleasure in the even greater elegance of the Grangerford home. The difference, however, is more significant. Twain made his more extensive description of the Grangerfords' "culture" (including the matchless poetry of Emmeline) serve, finally, as part of his revelation of the thin veneer of civilization which overlay the barbarity and indulgence in raw sentimentality which governed the Grangerford-Shepherdson feud; the description became a functional part of a complex representation of a whole society and Huck's maturing experience. Howells uses his description for a humorous characterization of a shiftless backwoodsman, through his attempt to be ingratiating, and to establish one measure of comfortable prosperity in this isolated Ohio community.

Also provided is a more general notion of the greater wealth of Peter Hingston, first citizen of Leatherwood, and of the hard-won decency and respectability of the David Gillespie home and that of his sister and her husband, Nancy and Laban Billings. These and other details—for example, the description of the largest log edifice in the community, called the Temple, where Joseph Dylks is both worshipped and reviled; the distinctive features of speech, such as

15. "Publisher's Note," *The Leatherwood God* (New York: The Century Company, 1916).

Reverdy's ruing the way Matthew Braile can "take the shine off a religious experience" and describing his reaction to the sudden cessation of one of Dylks's meetings as making him "feel all-overish" (p. 15); the sketching of "the Hounds, disturbers of camp-meetings and baptisms, and notorious mockers" (p. 117) and the fuller characterization of their leader and incipient politician, Jim Redfield; and the cumulative representation of the social, economic, and religious arrangements and interrelationships in the Leatherwood community—all of these make the happenings distinctively of a western place and of an earlier time. But they do not coalesce into a proof of the "westernness" as a *determinant* of the essential drama. They are the special characteristics which identify people and scene; they do not explain the action. This is not merely to recognize that Howells has universalized the action, especially through the parallels to the passion of Christ. It is to say that the scepticism of a Matthew Braile, the scruples of David Gillespie and Nancy Billings, and the religious charlatanism of a Joseph Dylks could easily be transplanted in a way that the socially implanted "conscience" of a Huck Finn, the plight of a Nigger Jim, the unconscious moral hypocrisy of an Aunt Sally Phelps could not.

Essentially the same point can be made about the historicity of *The Leatherwood God*. Years after the events, Braile offers an explanation of Dylks's success in attracting a fanatic following by promising that " 'They who put their faith in me shall never taste death, but shall be translated into the New Jerusalem' " (p. 75). Braile speculates that " 'life is hard in a new country, and anybody that promises salvation on easy terms has got a strong hold at the very start' " (p. 232). He immediately broadens the observation, however, to a comment on the general desire for reassurance of immortality which he knows through himself: " 'We want to be good, and we want to be safe even if we are not good; and the first fellow that comes along and tells us to have faith in him, and he'll make it all right, why we have faith in him, that's all' " (p. 232).

To the question of why Dylks was not successful in establishing "his superstition in universal acceptance" (p. 232), Braile speculates that " 'the scale was too small. . . . The backwoods, as Leatherwood

was then, was not the right starting point for a world-wide imposture'" (p. 233). This view is countered by the argument that
Leatherwood, Ohio, was no narrower a stage than Manchester, New
York, where four years later Joseph Smith founded Mormonism,
and in turn is countered: "'Joe Smith only claimed to be a prophet,
and Dylks claimed to be a god'" (p. 236). In the introductory chapter to the narrative, Howells had emphasized the special conditions
which made the people of Leatherwood ripe for religious manipulation: "In their remoteness from the political centers of the young
republic, they seldom spoke of the civic questions stirring the towns
of the East; the commercial and industrial problems which vex
modern society were unknown to them. Religion was their chief
interest" (p. 4). And they have even been touched by a kind of
ecumenical spirit which presumably makes Dylks's incoherent evan-
gelism easier to accept: they were of "Presbyterian, Methodist,
Lutheran, and Moravian ancestry . . . but the general prosperity
had so far relaxed the stringency of their several creeds that their
distinctive public rite had come to express a mutual toleration"
(p. 4) which enables them to worship in common on some occasions at the Temple.

In effect, then, Dylks is explained as a historical accident rather
than as the product of a historical movement or broadly significant
historical circumstances. When he arrived in Leatherwood, it was "a
center of influence, spiritual as well as material, after a manner
unknown to later conditions" (p. 3), conditions which apparently
changed a considerable time before Squire Braile reviews them with
T. J. Mandeville of Cambridge, Massachusetts, "in the first of the
fifties" (p. 229). The claims of *The Leatherwood God* to history,
thus, are based on its use of a real set of events and a general
accuracy in describing the setting of those events in place and time.
Even if Howells were not already on record concerning mere historicity as a literary value—"It is not much to say of a work of
literary art that it will survive as a record of the times it treats"[16]—the

16. "Emile Zola," *North American Review,* CLXXV (November 1902),
591.

expectation (strengthened by a knowledge of his many past performances) would be that the novel's primary concerns would be found elsewhere.

The nature of this "elsewhere" Howells defined in saying that "the moral and meaning of *The Leatherwood God*" was to be found "in its commonsense psychology,"[17] and in specifically naming Nancy Billings as "the chief figure of the drama."[18] H. L. Mencken, in his attack on "The Dean," correctly saw that the novel had to offer itself as psychological but was infuriated that it did not fulfill his notions of how that should be accomplished:

The central character, one Dylks, is a backwoods evangelist who acquires a belief in his own buncombe, and ends by announcing that he is God. The job before the author was obviously that of tracing the psychological steps whereby this mountebank proceeds to that conclusion. That fact, indeed, is recognized in the canned review, which says that the book is "a study of American religious psychology." . . . Howells does not *show* how Dylks came to believe himself God; he merely *says* that he did so. . . . Nor do we get anything approaching a revealing look into the heads of the other converts—the saleratus-sodden, hell-crazy, half-witted Methodists and Baptists of a remote Ohio settlement.[19]

The distortions in this attack result from seeing Dylks as the central character and from assuming the novel's purpose to be a study of *American* religious psychology. The religious question is certainly an important one, as it had been in many of Howells's preceding novels; the specific concern, however, is not with a broad historical process, but with some individual tests of religious and ethical conscience as confronted by a spreading infection. Howells makes no attempt to suggest that Dylks is anything but a local phenomenon, never represents his "buncombe" as a challenge to *American* religion or as possible only in an American setting. And

17. William McMurray, *The Literary Realism of William Dean Howells* (Carbondale and Edwardsville: Southern Illinois Unviersity Press, 1967), p. 121.

18. *Letters*, II, 356.

19. H. L. Mencken, " 'The Dean,' " in *The War of the Critics over William Dean Howells*, edited by Edwin H. Cady and David L. Frazier (Evanston, Illinois: Row, Peterson and Company, 1962), p. 129.

Dylks, of course, as Howells himself indicated, is not the central character: he is the bearer of the disease. His effect on the Gillespies is to produce family discords, religious doubts and religious fanaticism, individual moral suffering and equivocation; and from those matters, Howells's novel takes its shape and meaning.

The relationship of Dylks to both the broader and narrower circumstances is established by the early revelation that he is Nancy's husband, presumed dead following his desertion of her some dozen years earlier at the birth of their child, Joey. Nancy has since married Laban Billings and borne him a daughter. The threat which Dylks is thus able to hold over her to insure her silence in the community to which she has moved is that of legal bigamy and the scandal of its disclosure. Nancy alone might have been strong enough not to be silenced by such a threat, but its force is increased by its extension to the head of her family, her older brother, David Gillespie. He is quick to pronounce that Nancy and Laban must not live together another instant as man and wife, but he is not as quick to accept his own duty to reveal the imposture of Dylks to the community or even to his own daughter, Jane: "'I'm not certain what to do, about her, and about the neighbors. This is a cross to me, too, Nancy. I have lived a proud life here; there has never been talk about me or mine'" (p. 48). When the offer of a job for Laban in a nearby communty provides an excuse for his separation from his family, David is glad to accept this moral subterfuge and remain silent, even when his daughter becomes one of Dylks's most convinced followers. Because of this failure of religious and moral courage, David suffers a series of alienations: from his daughter, from his sister, from the community, and from his God.

Though Nancy is stronger, her dilemma is also more complex. One formulation of that dilemma is that she is caught in the dualism of experience represented by the dark religious power of Dylks (which is also sexual, as Nancy herself implicitly recognizes in commenting on her marriage and on Jane's fascination with him [pp. 84–85]), and the light of Matthew Braile's rationalism.[20] It is per-

20. See McMurray, *The Literary Realism of William Dean Howells*, pp. 118–121.

haps a little closer to Howells's precise formulation, however, to say that she is simply caught in the age-old crisis of faith, the desire to trust in the traditional concept of "an all-wise and all-powerful" (p. 109) and "good" (p. 110) God as preached to her from the pulpit, and the desire to "rationalize" that God, make such actions as His sending Dylks to mislead the community and threaten her deserved happiness with Laban understandable to her notions of judtice and individual desert.

She had of course committed herself to one side in marrying Dylks in the first place, but she has long since understood that he "was a power of darkness" who "stole away . . . [her] sense" (p. 85), and that experience in no way endangered her fundamental faith. Though it is true that she is still "wedded" to both Dylks and Laban, and that Dylks lives on with her in the person of Joey, that is a legalistic construction of the relationship. Any commitment she has to the actual Dylks can be fulfilled, as she illustrates, by the performance of Christian charity in giving him food and drink, humbling herself to kneel before him in dressing his torn scalp, and in asking Joey to be kind to him and finally identifying him to the boy as his real father.[21] Otherwise she can dismiss him out of "an impulse of indifference rather than consideration" (p. 168) to the care of Squire Braile.

Thus Braile becomes an appropriate symbol of the limitations—indeed, the evasiveness—of a strictly legalistic judgment of Dylks's imposture and the unsatisfactoriness of rationalistic abstractions as an immediate guide for Nancy. Braile is himself perfectly well aware that "justice is one thing and law is another" (p. 153), but he uses that law to insure that Dylks can " 'bring down the New Jerusalem

---

21. Another way of dealing with Dylks is represented by Jim Redfield, who has to be restrained from greater physical assault but who tears the hair from Dylks's head. It is this action which frees Jane from Dylks's spell. It is revealing that its effect is to direct her emotions toward Redfield, but it does nothing to reunite her with her father, to whom she had issued the dare to defy Dylks's proclamation that it would be death to harm his person. When she resentfully says to her father, " 'We've both got the same God, now,' " he starts to retort in kind, "but the abhorrent look of his daughter stayed his words" (p. 140).

Over-the-Mountain, or anywhere else he pleases, so he don't bring it down on Leatherwood' " (p. 193), a solution which is on a moral level with David Gillespie's decision to keep his silence. Braile's elucidation of a God such as he believes in effectively removes Him from a real part in the decisions which Nancy must make. Such a God lets man " 'play the fool or play the devil as he's a mind to' " (p. 111), and sin is defined as " 'going against what you knew was right at the time being' " (p. 109).

Nancy's actions eventually support this ethical formulation, but they have gained the authority, not of her reasoning, but her suffering. She has lived, not reasoned, to her conclusions; and she has paid a price in both a difficult compassion and a loss of supportive family solidarity. When David remarks that he does not "blame" her for sending for Laban immediately after the news of Dylks's death, she replies, " 'I wouldn't care if you did, David' " (p. 224). Compressed into this brief comment is the history of their changed relationship and a measure of the unbridged alienation between his moral cowardice and her tested faith. More indirectly, but still as a product of her trying to use experience with Dylks as a warning against Jane's "brutality" (p. 209) in dealing with her patient suitor, Hughey Blake, and her successive responses to the "power" (p. 207) of Dylks and Jim Redfield, Nancy herself suffers rejection. Jane's final words to her in the novel are, " 'Aunt Nancy, I hate you' " (p. 210).

It is perfectly in keeping with the realism with which the psychological drama centered on Nancy is detailed that we learn that its final outcome had the usual quota of imperfections: though Joey marries the Hingston girl and takes over the operation of the Hingston milling business, Nancy and Laban and their daughter live only for a short time before they are almost simultaneoulsy mowed down by an epidemic fever. Jane and Jim Redfield live in something apparently less than idyllic harmony: " 'He's got along with her, and she's got along with the children—plenty of them' " (p. 235). Moreover, the fiasco of Dylks's last leading of his little Flock, which resulted in his own drowning, does not bring his pernicious influence to an end. His legend and the miracles associated with him are reconstructed and refurbished over the years so that some "died in the faith; and the living that were young in it in the late eighteen-twenties are old in it now in the first of the fifties" (p. 229).

Mencken, then, was right in noting that only the externals of Dylks's story were dramatized, but he was wrong in the significance he attached to that fact. Dylks was valuable to Howells as a disturbing force, rather than as a complex individuality—the explanation of how he came to conceive of himself as God could indeed be confined to two pages, as Mencken points out[22]—because the subject of the novel was not the nature of religious fraud, but the practice of a religious or good life. The difficulty of actively and consciously practicing such a life is the problem that Dylks's appearance forces into focus, and the novel pictures a wide range of the generally practiced and evasive answers.

There is the merely passive goodness of a Hughey Blake or the loving goodness of a Laban Billings, both of which must be supported by a stronger will. Or there is the kindliness and public charity of a Peter Hingston, based on a placid satisfaction with material prosperity and a self-contentment which is easily corrupted into egotism. There is the "fierce godliness" (p. 55) of a Richard Enraghty, actually an intellectual and spiritual pride which is even more easily corrupted into visions of personal glory. There is the rigid dogmatism of a David Gillespie which almost immediately collapses into doubt and despair when subjected to personal testing by the power of Dylks over both his daughter and his sister. There is the rationality of a Matthew Braile which tries to solve the community problem posed by Dylks by sending him elsewhere and which can content itself with abstractions because of his detachment from experience (Dylks poses no threat to his own intelligence or his wife's firm gospel faith, and their only child died at an early age). There is the religiosity of a Jane Gillespie, which is actually an expression of her passionate and sensual nature. And there is the unbaptized self-reliance of a Jim Redfield who works his rich bottomland, studies the law with Braile, wins Jane Gillespie, and presumably ends in the state legislature.

Dylks's *story* is, necessarily, told in the novel, and it is told in a

22. *The War of the Critics*, p. 129.

"series of picturesque, dramatic, and violent scenes"[23] unequalled in Howells's other fiction. It is deliberately told, moreover, in such a way as to accentuate its travestying of the Crucifixion. There is no denying that Howells was concerned to project his own scorn for the religious hysteria which swept the whole community of Leatherwood, Ohio, and his awareness of the universal implications of this latest parodic re-enactment of the Christian tragedy. Equally, there is no mistaking that this scene is backwoods Ohio, just as his other novels are unmistakably set in New England or Venice or New York City and populated by Yankees, by Bostonians, by sophisticated expatriates and even more worldly Europeans. But the *drama*, as Howells pointed out, was indeed Nancy's, and, in that sense, personal and timeless.

23. Cady, *The Realist at War*, p. 267.

# VII

## CODA

Idyllic Ironies: *The Vacation of the Kelwyns*

Iᴛ is fitting that *The Vacation of the Kelwyns* (1920) should be the final novel to be considered in this study, though it was written earlier than *The Leatherwood God*. The novel gives the impression of a skilled performance by a depleted artist who yet masterfully turned this condition to an advantage by invoking a nostalgic mood to justify familiar scenes and themes: farm boarding houses, Shakers, a conventional-unconventional love match, mild class conflicts giving rise to annoying rather than profound ethical questions, comparisons of city and country manners. The double sanction Howells apparently claimed for these materials which he had worked so often in the past was indicated by the subtitle, "An Idyl of the Middle Eighteen-Seventies." This was to claim as operative the conventional dispensations of a pastoral world which is out of time and space and to invite nostalgia for a specifically innocent historical time after the Civil War. These are essentially the terms in which *The Vacation of the Kelwyns* has been discussed,[1] when it has been

1. See Richard Chase, *The American Novel and Its Tradition* (New York: Doubleday and Company, Inc., a Doubleday Anchor Original, 1957), pp. 177–184, and William McMurray, *The Literary Realism of William Dean Howells* (Carbondale and Edwardsville: Southern Illinois University Press, 1967), pp. 122–130. Chase's discussion is brilliantly provocative, but his

discussed at all, and they are a true but only partial description of the elements dramatically at work within it.

*The Vacation of the Kelwyns* is given surprising vitality and comic point, rather than just sentimental charm, by the play of irony among these elements. Such a proposal is really self-evident, for the "idyl" is limited to the love story: the tale of the Kelwyns and their attempts to cope with the couple who are supposed to serve as their tenant farmers and domestic aides is hardly one of the peaceful, simple, natural rural life. As for the historical time of the mid-seventies, that was indeed a simpler era, but largely because its ominous undercurrents had not yet surfaced into crises demanding recognition and attention. But the undercurrents—of mere social change in the permissible relations between a young lady and a young man, and more seriously of economic dislocations and religious decay—were already sufficiently present to distinguish the present time of the novel from the immediate postwar period which "was nearer the Golden Age than any the race has yet known" but which "was even then rounding away . . . into the past which can hardly be recalled in any future of the world."[2]

The apparent simplicities of the novel, then, are functional: the evocations of pastoral serenity and historical certainty are attractive and even momentarily convincing as contrasted with the complexities of the present. They are also, however, purely imaginary: the real rural life, the novel indicates, was never "pastoral," and the Golden Age can never have a present existence. The wry point of *The Vacation of the Kelwyns* is that no absolutely uncorrupted and undisturbed Eden is imaginable even in the elegiac or the pastoral mood. (That this point is made ironically rather than

---

essentially patronizing attitude toward Howells is indicated at its very start where he suggests that *The Vacation of the Kelwyns* might be considered Howells's best novel. Chase sees the novel as embodying "symbolic reconciliations and harmonies" (p. 183) whose too easy achievement and too sweeping portent for America's future are characteristic of the "real laziness" of Howells's mind, an example of the "great refusals" (p. 177) which reduced even his best work to mere "social comedy" (p. 184).

2. *The Vacation of the Kelwyns* (New York: Harper and Brothers, 1920), p. 159.

by direct statement or obvious dramatic incident, that the under-current of sadness and wistfulness is not made stronger are the deliberate limitations of the novel and the appropriate basis for its designation as social comedy.) What is dramatized by the summer sojourn of the Kelwyns in the imperfect paradise of southern New Hampshire is the limited gain that may result from the attempt: a sharpened perspective on what ought to be the ideals of character and motive, of conditions and relationships, in both Arcadia and Athens and a strengthened determination to strive for their approximation.

Some such meaning must attach to the detailed account of the domestic (and even social) relations that obtain between the city Kelwyns and the country Kites if *The Vacation of the Kelwyns* is to be regarded as anything more than the most trivial comedy of manners, transplanted from drawing room to farm kitchen. This central plot develops when Kelwyn, postgraduate lecturer in the department of Historical Sociology at Harvard, brings his wife and two children to a summer home in New Hampshire, rented from the Shakers of a nearby community and supplied by them with a tenant family, the Kites, who will also cook the meals, keep the house, saddle the horse, and generally look to the comfort of the renters. Disillusionment with this apparently mutually advantageous arrangement is immediate, as the first meal prepared by Mrs. Kite proves a disaster of speckled milk, tea strong as lye, odoriferous self-rising bread, and rancid butter. From this unpromising beginning, the workability of the arrangement declines, rather than improves. A series of stratagems to instruct the Kites—by patient suggestion, by direct example, by threat of dispossession, and by still other means of enlightenment and persuasion—in a better performance of their duties (and in a stricter sense of their social quality as the hired) all end in despairing failure. Kelwyn resolves the moral problem of his responsibility to deal with their personal short-comings and legal derelictions by moving his own family and leaving the Kites in possession of the contested domain.

Howells exhibits his usual arts in using much of the novel to depict the helpless gentility and real good will of the Kelwyns as they encounter the stubborn ignorance and sullen pride of Mr. Kite and the well-intentioned ineffectuality of the wife he esteems perfect in all her domestic performances. But no magic regenerations can be effected in this earthly realm. Moreover, that is not quite the point, either: Kelwyn's own boyhood included self-rising bread, and the "ideals" (p. 28) which Mrs. Kite cannot now satisfy are acquired rather than innate. The Kelwyns' ideas of pastoral perfection depend on certain strategic exclusions of reality and certain importations of suburbia to the forest of Arden. The implicit and inescapable moral comment that is developed, then, beneath the entertaining super-ficialities of the domestic confrontation is not merely that the pastoral world or the nostalgic past cannot be revisited, but that they never existed. The Kites are the true inhabitants of Arcady (they, in fact, enjoy a certain social superiority over such neighbors as the drunken Tad Allson and his slattern wife); the Kelwyns are the interlopers, who want merely to indulge themselves in a sense of its simplicities and naturalness without surrendering their sophistications; they want to act the roles of shepherd and shepherdess, but clearly do not want their disguises to be so successful as to hide their real identities.

But all this is just one aspect of Howells's ironic manipulation of the conventions of the idyl. As usual, he also develops a love story, in this case between Mrs. Kelwyn's visiting cousin, Parthenope Brook, and Elihu Emerance, who in his present course of "experi-menting through life" (p. 132) appears at the Shaker community looking for work and, through Howellsian arrangements, becomes a boarder with the Kelwyns. Parthenope, orphaned daughter of a sculptor and a painter, has been educated intellectually in an art school and socially in Boston. She has been "formed" on novels which "inculcated a varying doctrine of eager conscience, romantic-ized actuality, painful devotion, and bullied adoration, with auroral gleams of religious sentimentality" (p. 56).

Emerance, in contrast, was brought up on a farm, has been a teacher, and has ideas about many possible careers, most of them not quite respectable in Parthenope's eyes and clearly deficient in nobility and eccentric in purpose. In one sense the process of accommodation between them which leads to a mutual declaration of love is made possible—or at least the process is made easier—by the somewhat relaxed social conditions of the Kelwyns' summer chaperonage.

Again, however, that is merely Howells's obvious use of the pastoral circumstances. What gives an undercurrent of pathos to Howells's projection of this love idyl as a bit of life from a Golden Age is that, even in the fondly remembered seventies, it was barely possible: it was more the dream than the reality even then.

Parthenope and Emerance could experience something like the perfect unconsciousness and communion of an ideal world because they come together, not really in a Golden Age, but in a moment of time and with special qualifications: "Emerance's traditions were probably not those which would have made him feel it strange that he should be wandering about the lonely country with a young girl" (p. 158). The "something of a wilding quality" which Parthenope has inherited from her artistic parents has not been quelled in the "much more regulated" world of her aunt because her aunt "lived rather out of her world" (pp. 158–159). Thus they "could not feel their relation to the conventional, the social fact," and they could for a moment "in their intense personalization," without realizing it, be "elemental . . . akin to earth and air, and of one blood with the grass and the trees, with the same ichor in their veins" (p. 159). In the mood in which he imagined this intense harmony of individual with individual and both with nature, Howells could indeed think of it as a product of an (evanescent) millennium:

If [Parthenope] had known it . . . she was standing on the verge of that America which is now so remote in everything but time, and was even then rounding away with such girlhood as hers into the past which can hardly be recalled in any future of the world. It was sweet and dear; with its mixture of the simple and the gentle, it was nearer the Golden Age than any the race has yet known (p. 159).

Such moods, however, could not be sustained long enough to impart their tone to the entire novel. The remembered time may have approximated the Golden Age, but even Howells's nostalgia was forced to admit a more complex reality than a walk in the woods as the characteristic condition. When Emerance, in his country simplicity, offered to cook and prepare a meal for the Kelwyns at which he then joined them, they ought to "have been remanded in common to the Golden Age, or at least to the Homeric epoch" where the Kelwyns could have found this social iconoclasm "poetic, primitive, delightful" (pp. 89–90). Instead, they were all merely uncomfortably conscious of the social realities of even the eighteen-seventies. The purity of this instance of pastoral experience is qualified precisely to the degree that it fails to achieve the condition of "an escape from society and the complexities of one's own being."[3]

Yet the direct relationship between Parthenope and Emerance does seem at first to be treated in terms of their own "understanding of the pastoral situation tacit between them" (p. 151). There is little suspense in their first unspoken and then openly confessed love, but there is a good deal of pleasure to be had from Howells's management of their mutual accommodation from opposing theories of life during the "simple idyl of the passing days" (p. 151) in the country. In such a setting, under such benign conditions, and with the diversions provided by a dancing bear, fortune tellers, and organ grinders, they can live in a self-created world which cannot be penetrated by reality. A pedlar's tale of adversity causes Parthenope to reflect on " 'How hard life seems when you come face to face with it!' " But the reflection on reality is not real to them: "They tried to be sad, but they could not. Perhaps life as they saw it reflected in each other's eyes was not hard; the trouble they borrowed did not really harass them" (p. 153).

The consciousness of this young couple is only of each other, and that presumably has the effect of modifying the dogmatism of each. Parthenope's experience, as Richard Chase has phrased it, "is the familiar educative one by which pride is relaxed, prejudice dispelled, and ignorance enlightened as to the limited utility of the Ideal. It is a lesson, too, in the necessity of deriving the Ideal from the reality of circumstance, a lesson in the conditioning of the will by the actualities of one's life."[4] But this is only half the story. Emerance's determined experimentalism has been in its own way as single-minded as Parthenope's dedication to the ideal, and he does not remain completely unaffected by their relationship. His jack-of-all-trading is revealed as a kind of lower-class dilettantism, the ob-

3. Chase, *The American Novel and Its Tradition*, p. 184.
4. *Ibid.*, p. 180.

verse of Parthenope's theoretical idealism, and, in its way, equally "unreal." He is brought to an awareness of the necessity of becoming, as he himself says, something more than "a dreamer and experimenter, a mere empiricist." He cannot continue to "live in the ideal" (p. 236), as Parthenope lovingly claims he does; he must make a choice of possibilities and accept the limitations of that choice. And that is one way of saying that he must live in the real.

To conclude, moreover, that this is the forthright, uncomplicated "meaning" which Howells attaches to his story is to overstate the case. To take no note of the inherent ambiguities in even the limited pastoral situation and to propose, in spite of the clear signs that Howells gives of his awareness that the idyllic condition does not obtain throughout the land (a point which will be developed in a moment), that "all will be well" is to oversimplify the novel and Howells's vision. This is the meaning Chase finds in the marriage of Parthenope and Emerance, "a marriage of principle and impulse." Certainly, considering the total context of Howells's work, the most that can be said is that all is well within the conditions the novel has portrayed, and these are clearly special and carefully defined. If Howells is indeed saying that "American life is characterized by this kind of split, that when it occurs in exacerbated form, dessication and aimlessness ensue, and that ever new modes of reconciliation must be found," he is not necessarily offering a precise formula of reconciliation and a wholly optimistic bulletin on the future of America. It may be argued that this novel "is justly called an 'idyl' " not "because all the emphasis is on the need for the fresh surge of impulse, the creative, genial welling-up of emotion, the relaxation of willed principle (of which he thinks there will never be a lack)"[5] but because the emphasis is ideally distributed, because the novel ostensibly presents an ideal fusion of the conflicting approaches to experience.

Yet the Kelwyns, who are not without their genialities and impulses, simply abandon the attempt at reconciliation, and it is Emerance who points out that the Kites are not deserving of pity (p. 221). His own relaxation of principle extends only to the re-

5. *Ibid.*, p. 182.

jection of the doctrines of Puritanism which, however, "was true in life, and it's as true now as ever" (p. 227). Moreover, his only objection to Parthenope's formulation of her conception of the ideal by which a man should live is that she is apparently rejecting his wish to live up to it as her husband (pp. 239–240). Finally, on this point, it should be re-emphasized that the fact that this is Howells's love story accounts for a good deal. It is really only the lovers themselves who think they have achieved a completely new and perfect harmony which will remake the world. There are a variety of factors in the novel which emphasize, not merely the idealized quality imparted to their particular story, but the deliberate softening of contextual considerations of present and future to preserve the enclosing idyllic mood. The intimations of the real world are there to be felt, to enhance the desirability of a completely closed kingdom of imagined or selectively remembered goodness, naturalness, and simplicity in the Edenic country, and to make clear its impossibility.

For example, if a projection of the actualities of the union of Parthenope and Emerance is to be made, the novel itself provides an ironic paradigm: the marriage of the Kelwyns. The parallel is not exact, naturally, but what may reasonably be supposed to have been the eager youthful accommodations as well as the youthful certainties of civic usefulness, public virtue, and private rapture have been subdued in the Kelwyns to a more mundane working relationship. His country origins and economic dependence on a scholarly career have been joined to her social superiority and enough of her money to enable them to live upon a "scale of refined frugality" (p. 1); she has "a conscience that . . . [gives] those she loved very little peace," and he has "a good deal of ancestral Yankee humor . . . which . . . [comes] out in the stress put upon him by his wife's requisitions in hypothetical cases of principle and practice" (p. 2). The result is not so much a merger as a "compact" in which "both the parties . . . are seldom in the same mind or mood," and one of the disadvantages of what at times is a "useful variance" is that "they are often as hurtful as helpful to each other. They cannot always agree about a question, though they see both sides of it. If one is cheerful, they keep a sort of balance, though the other is gloomy, even though they do not unite in a final gayety" (p. 39). A projection by analogy of the "mixed" marriage of Parthenope and Emerance might suggest that its portent is not so much of ideal harmony and reconciliation as of accommodated reality.

The idyllic tone is preserved, however, because this projection is not explicitly made. In the same way, the idyl is preserved against the threatening encroachments of knowledge from the wider world. The obvious signs of material and spiritual decay in the rural scene remain merely an element in the intellectual exchanges forming part of the courtship of the lovers; the rumors of tramps abroad in the land and the actual appearance of a "gigantic negro, with a sullen, bestial face" (p. 154) and a little sailorlike Frenchman (p. 153) can be treated respectively as "a horror" (p. 154) and as picturesque. These signals of industrial unrest throughout the land can be remanded to another order of existence. The view which ignores the problems that the Shakers are at least trying to deal with and makes them merely objects of curiosity in the performance of their worship, which easily dismisses their "attack on the earthly order" as "bigoted and conceited" and permits much amusement in Kelwyn "at the notion of his august science stopping to inquire into such a lowly experiment as that of those rustic communists" (p. 8) is mere venial complacency and not irresponsible arrogance in this muted world. What Howells is emphasizing, however, in these glimpses of a harsh and troubled reality is not that these problems will all disappear in a radiance of the good allegorized in the union of Parthenope and Emerance, but what he has already stated in his subtitle: that this is an *idyl* set far enough back in time to take on a nostalgic glow of possibility if one wishes to surrender to it. These reminders of the unresolved complexities of the real world both enhance the pleasure of the imagined simplicity and protect its creator from the charges of absurdity or cruel and willful blindness.

That Howells was in this way exercising deliberate control over his chosen materials can be given one more illustration, appropriately from the final pages of the novel, where he takes a last look at the lovers and their patrons. The first of these scenes is of a kind too often taken as Howells's portrait of young love, a portrait which is not sufficiently distanced to protect the author himself from sentimentality. Actually, Howells uses that sentimentality both to play with and to give dimension to the theme that has been accused of reducing itself to a simple "all will be well." When Parthenope asks if she may link arms with Emerance, he replies that he will permit the "experiment"; when he defines their present happiness in terms of the Kelwyns' refusal to exercise their authority to dispossess the Kites instead of referring it to their plighted troth, she conquers her dismay with "sublime resolution." Among other things made humorously clear is the fact that she is still "idealizing" and he is still "empiricizing," and they too have probably "started in life together" (p. 256) toward a compact rather than a fused identity.

The split in American life which Mr. Chase has characterized has been at best bridged, and that only at a point of private experience. On the public question, the Kelwyns have the last word, again in deceptively mild and witty language. Kelwyn, still reflecting on the specific matter of the Kites and feeling that situation adequately dealt with, yet adumbrates the larger question posed in the relationship and by such intrusions as the tramps. He remarks to his wife that what he feels remiss in is the " 'private portion of the public debt which we all somehow owe to the incapable, the inadequate, the—the—shiftless.' " She counters that such attitudes incorporated into his sociological lectures will cost him his influence among the students and the academic community, and he replies: " 'Then I won't do it. If I can't exert my influence without losing it I won't exert it' " (p. 257). It is a perfectly keyed, wittily phrased statement of the paradox at the heart of Howells's idyl. The pastoral too closely examined is merely crude or decayed rusticity; the past stripped of its nostalgia is merely an earlier present. Like Kelwyn, who had first "laughed sadly" and then, pleased by his paradox, "cheerfully" (p. 257), Howells chose in the interests of his idyl to offer no large solutions but to adopt the optative mood.

## Final Contextual Comment

That the last of Howells's novels to be published should have returned to the mid-seventies, almost to the time when he wrote his first, is critically convenient: for, rather than being a surrender to nostalgia and an admission of creative exhaustion, *The Vacation of the Kelwyns* is a controlled exhibition of how memories and well-worked situations may be made to reveal psychological subtleties and yield instructive social and moral ironies. Written when Howells was well into his seventies, it supplies a retroactive justification for recalling from almost total neglect such earlier novels as *The Day of Their Wedding, An Open-Eyed Conspiracy,* and *Ragged Lady.*

It is also possible, as usual, to consult Howells himself for further evidence of the continuity, integrity, and self-consciousness of all his work, from beginning to last. There could not, for example, have been many months, if any, between his work on *The Children of the Summer* (posthumously, *The Vacation of the Kelwyns,*[6] and the writing of the "Editor's Easy Chair" in which he insisted that simplicity in art was not unconsciousness:

The most elementary things cannot be set down without the connivance of the author's consciousness that he is doing it with the hope of its effect on the reader. . . . A tale . . . is told for the sake of him who hears it . . . and the conditions of its existence are three: the fable-stuff filling all spaces like an intellectual ether, the author who gives specific form to a portion of this ether, and the public which appreciates it. The very most primordial beginning of it is the consciousness in the author, and consciousness is the end of that sort of simplicity which is . . . praised for . . . [its] supposed unconsciousness.[7]

If there was surrender in Howells's last years—in *The Leatherwood God* and *The Vacation of the Kelwyns*—it lay in the giving over of the intensities of the present for the more easily penetrable and manageable past. But his faith in the commonplaces of democratic American life as the right stuff for American writers was in no way diminished (was, in fact, a strong element in the nostalgic turn). As late as November of 1908, he conducted in the "Easy Chair" a debate between an old novelist and a young novelist on a subject which he had argued all his life with Henry James: the fictional advantages of the "greater density" of European life. The argument

6. See Edwin H. Cady, *The Realist at War* (Syracuse: Syracuse University Press, 1958), p. 255.

7. *Harper's Monthly,* CXXIII (June 1911), 150.

of the old novelist was a statement of artistic faith that Howells had professed in a lifetime of distinguished and varied fiction:

Grapple fearlessly with the empty native ambient. You have already recognized that it is very sparsely peopled; that its interests are elemental and its motives few. But if you will begin to deal with them you will find them of a size commensurate with the environment. If you penetrate their interiors you will discover whole new worlds of spirituality, of personality.[8]

Howells was not unaware of charges of repetitiousness brought against him, and it was just about this time, too, that he permitted himself to long for an ideal reader, one "who had liked him from the beginning and was intimately versed in all his work." Such a reader would perceive the "ever-renascent art" in what seemed merely familiar to others and would be aware "that the increasing purpose of the author in the treatment of the well-known types had been to reveal the infinite variety of character which lay hid in each and every human type."[9] It is, indeed, easy to rattle off certain types who people Howells's fiction—doctors, lawyers, ministers, journalists, writers—but it is equally easy to cite names from each category which indicate the broad range of Howells's portrayals, though the limited citations do not do justice to "the infinite variety" which his imagination could conjure.

The doctors range from the crude Mulbridge (*Dr. Breen's Practice*) to the socially sophisticated and morally sensitive Olney to the deeply humane Anther; the lawyers, from the prissy Atherton (*A Modern Instance*) to the mercurially brilliant Putney to the rationalistic Braile; the ministers, from Mr. Waters, who, like Emerson, gave up the pale negations of Unitarianism for divine goodness (*Indian Summer*), to Sewell, formulator of the doctrine of complicity (*The Minister's Charge*), to the fanatical Peck to the humorously nonfanatical Breckon; the journalists, from the socially responsible Ricker (*A Modern Instance*) and Colville (*Indian Summer*) to the cynical or morally insensitive or malign practitioners

8. *Harper's Monthly*, CXVII (October 1908), 798.
9. *Imaginary Interviews* (New York: Harper and Brothers, 1910), p. 299.

of yellow journalism like Bartley Hubbard (*A Modern Instance*), Pinney (*The Quality of Mercy*), and Bittridge; the writers, from Brice Maxwell, with his conscious ideals for realistic and socially useful art, to P. B. S. Ray with his personal dreams of fame and fortune, to Mr. Twelvemough with his rationalizations for romantic fiction (*A Traveler from Altruria*), to Verrian with his concern for psychological reality which is vitiated by neurotic self-concern. To these "types" could be added artists, businessmen, country squires, society matrons, religieuses, innocent American girls and their more experienced and selfish cousins, domineering wives—to extend the list would be to belabor the obvious.

Moreover, certain of Howells's fiction supplies contrasting support for his suggestion that if his characterizations were "not new, they were newer" and "being more fully ascertained they were truer."[10] When Howells wanted to take advantage of a broad type— a stock character—he could do so with wit and skill. In a group of stories dealing with psychic phenomena,[11] he introduced a recurring set of characters who serve chiefly to establish a framing device for the telling of the tales. They include Wanhope (a psychologist, whose name may be indicative of the degree of faith Howells placed in that calling), Minver (a painter), Acton (a writer), and Rulledge (a clubman). There is a good deal of humorous give and take among these characters, controlled by the "typical" bias of each, with Rulledge's amiable dullness and romanticism the special foil to Minver's sophistication and wit. Wanhope is "characterized" by his tendency to seize on every comment as an opportunity for psychological speculation, without regard for the interruption to the story he is telling. Acton's presence often occasions humorous and satiric comments on the uses to which fiction would put the events or relationships of the recounted experiences. This kind of typicality could be openly exploited precisely because it was not central to Howells's purposes and could be made to function as an expression of his own uncommitted attitude toward the psychic material. On

10. *Ibid.*

11. See *Questionable Shapes* (New York: Harper and Brothers, 1903) and *Between the Dark and the Daylight* (New York: Harper and Brothers, 1907).

the other hand, the great body of his fiction, dealing with mundane realities, includes, as the list indicates, a sizable gallery of recognizably true and subtly differentiated individuals.

Yet, there remains the charge that the situations in which he involved his characters were repeated from novel to novel and were, to begin with, unimportant and uninteresting. Aside from the fact that such complaints usually ignore Howells's announced theory of the novel—his unconcern for mere plot, his disdain for the "moving accident" as a technique of character revelation, his contempt for the falsely passional, for "effectism"—they often seem to be made by refusing the evidence of the fiction itself. It has, at any rate, been one of the purposes of this systematic examination of the novels between 1889 and 1920 to suggest differences and qualities, to grant Howells his hope for a reader "alert to detect those fine differences of situation which distinguish a later from an earlier predicament."[12] It has been proposed, for example, that *The Story of a Play* need not be dismissed as just one more treatment of the conventional-unconventional formula, *The Day of Their Wedding* as a thrifty but simplistic exploitation of the Shaker materials Howells had started gathering in the seventies, *Ragged Lady* as an uneasy amalgam of elements previously used in international novels (such as *The Lady of the Aroostook*), travel books (such as *Tuscan Cities*, and treatments of the New England conscience (such as *Dr. Breen's Practice*). Moreover, it is not as important that the particular terms of the analyses offered of these and other novels should be given blanket acceptance as that the serious artistry and varied forms of Howells's realism be admitted.

The more that his total work is approached from that sense of possibility, the more it will be discovered that Howells at least had an attitude, a theory, which governed his productions and which long ago replied to many of the objections raised against him. Those who cannot penetrate beneath the "mating and marrying" he used simply as a vehicle might note an "Easy Chair" in which he made a persona remark, " 'A man—or even a woman—falls in love and marries, once for all, and has done with it, and because of the dramatic quality

12. *Imaginary Interviews*, p. 299.

of the experience, our imagination is kindled and we see the fact out of proportion."[13] Those who decry the absence of tragedy may at least be instructed in the quality of his optimism from one of his reviews of a long-forgotten novel: "It is one of the consoling suggestions of the book that there is no such thing as utter tragedy. Ruin itself is structural, and out of the wreck of all happiness the fabric of hope arises."[14] His own suffering made him write that death "tears apart every fiber of your being when it comes to your beloved." Yet, like men in all times, he bore it and found that in "the very ecstasy of . . . anguish, there was somehow peace, there was refuge, there was escape."[15] That he felt compelled to make his fiction reflect this view is a measure of the "honesty" he believed to be a necessity of realism; that he did not feel compelled to make every novel yield this meaning needs no defense. If the modern temper cannot abide a writer able to avoid existential torment and despair at the evil loose in the world, it is yet well to know that Howells had his reasons:

The novelist who fails to grasp the difference between wrong and evil
fails of the means of rendering life truly. He does not see that though
people continually do wrong, and do the same wrong over and over again,
and though each wrong is necessarily irreparable, and no breach of the
law can be mended, yet without ill-will, without malignant intent, without
hate, there is no reason for the despair to which he leaves his reader.[16]

The sheer quantity of Howells's output made some variation in quality inevitable and obvious. What deserves more attention, however, is that any attempt to establish a canon of Howells's best work spans his career from early to late. Edwin Cady's list, for example, starts with A Modern Instance (1882), includes The Landlord at Lion's Head (1897) and The Son of Royal Langbrith (1904), and ends with The Leatherwood God (1916).[17] A reasonable argument

13. "Editor's Easy Chair," Harper's Monthly, CXXII (April 1911), 797.
14. "Editor's Easy Chair," Harper's Monthly, CXXI (August 1910), 475.
15. "Editor's Easy Chair," Harper's Monthly, CXXX (February 1915), 475.
16. "Editor's Easy Chair," Harper's Monthly, CV (November 1902), 967.
17. Cady, The Realist at War, p. 269.

could be made for *The Undiscovered Country* (1880), at one end, and *The Vacation of the Kelwyns* (1920), at the other. This would make for a time span of something like forty years out of the fifty Howells spent in the writing of fiction, which is more significant than the individual selections within it. And even more significant is the evidence offered that Howells worked conscientiously—that is, literally according to his conscience, scrupulously, honestly—on all of his work.

The ideals of realistic fiction which Howells zealously supported in his editorial and public roles were not merely applied at his convenience to his own work. Naturally, some "motives" produced weightier, more complex novels than others, but all the work came from the same intelligence and the same sense of responsibility. It came, too, from the knowledge that honest work gives moral satisfaction and spiritual health. His industry in practicing his craft was both a need and a reward, as, he noted on another occasion, it should be for all men: "To be past the fear of want, that is an essential condition of happiness; but to be beyond the chance of work, which is the right and the duty of all, is the supreme misery, the very image of perdition."[18]

So Howells worked almost to the end to express in his fiction the value of a "lenient, generous, and liberal life." He was a man whose understanding of human nature made him, in a broad sense, a humorist; whose experience with and reflection on the conditions in which human beings must function made him a meliorist; whose observations of human behavior made him a sceptical rationalist; and whose personal and vicarious experience of suffering and death and catastrophe as well as joy and love and success made him a hopeful agnostic. These attitudes expressed themselves in a fiction which was analytical rather than prescriptive, and which rejected the methods and assumptions of satire, romanticism, and tragedy as the controlling principles in the representation of man's condition and fate. In short, this Howells was a realist.

18. "Editor's Easy Chair," *Harper's Monthly*, CIV (February 1902), 504.

# INDEX